A Teme Valley Walk

93 miles, from Worcester to the source of
the river

with a link to Newtown

by
David Milton

Meridian Books

Published 2002 by Meridian Books

© David Milton 2002

ISBN 1-869922-45-X

A catalogue record for this book is available from the British Library

Meridian Books
40 Hadzor Road, Oldbury, West Midlands B68 9LA

Printed in Great Britain by MFP Design & Print, Manchester

Contents

must visit –
Any bank
holiday

'Wonder as you wander through the valley of the River Teme'

Go West is delighted that David Milton has decided to launch his Teme Valley Walk in association with the Teme Valley project. Go West supports rural regeneration by helping community groups to share their history and heritage (natural and built). We hope that visitors will enjoy discovering some of the remarkable stories of this fascinating border area and be tempted to return again and again. It is an area where life is tranquil and unhurried, where local food is fresh and wholesome and the people extend a friendly welcome.

The Teme Valley Project, launched in July 2002, will focus much of this activity in and around ancient church buildings. Many have made special arrangements for visitors and walkers are welcome. Rest awhile on a churchyard seat and enjoy the view. If the church is open, go inside, read the stories in the stonework and use the information provided to explore the church, churchyard and the local area. For more detailed information visit the project web site: www.temevalley.org.uk.

Dedicated to all those who walk alone.
And we fit in your landscape as the sixth to the five senses
But the pastures close as the cowboy knows
And the world's cut up by fences...
(Ralph McTell, *The Gypsy*)

Introduction

I first had the idea of designing a walk along the River Teme some time before I began work on what eventually became my first book, *The Elan Valley Way*, in 1998. I abandoned the project at that time because I was not completely happy with the route beyond Knighton and wanted to spend time researching alternatives in that area.

The project languished while I worked on *The Elan Valley Way* and my second book, *The Riversides Way*, but my interest in it was revived when I accompanied my publisher, Peter Groves (Meridian Books), on a short circular walk he had designed along the Severn and Teme to the south of Worcester. Accordingly I spent some time experimenting with alternative routes between Knighton and Newtown and by August 2000 had a definitive route along the river mapped out.

I spent the next three months walking, recording and writing up this route – completing it by the end of November – in a period of concentrated activity.

The Teme is not a river one can easily walk alongside. Rights of Way along it are limited – in part due to the fact that the river was never more than locally important as a navigation and so was not provided with towpaths as were, say, the Severn and Thames.

For the purposes of my route I have attempted to remain as close to the river as is possible but have not been afraid to take to the hills along its course where footpaths, public transport or accommodation needs dictate. This policy is probably most noticeable at the end of Stage 2 where the route briefly climbs out of the Teme catchment area to reach Great Witley – to avail itself of the access to a regular bus service and accommodation there.

As with my previous two books I have avoided using 'A' and 'B' class roads whenever possible.

The Teme is a very special river for me and one which has had happy associations throughout my life. I was born and brought up in Worcester and so became familiar with its banks at a very early age. It flows just to the west of Worcestershire's Abberley Hills, the scene of many of my early walking experiences, over forty years ago now. It also, and perhaps most importantly for me, passes through that border area of England and Wales which is known as the Welsh Marches, where I do much of my walking these days.

I hope anyone attempting the walk derives as much pleasure out of the route, and the river itself, as it has provided me with over the years!

Many of the people who were involved in the writing of my previous two books have again helped with the new walk. As always, many new friends were made as a result of the project. Among these, in particular, I must thank Brian Draper who has been only too pleased to share his vast knowledge of the Teme, and its settlements – gained over many years – with me.

Alan Jones again accompanied me on most of the walking – putting his, now legendary, gate-opening and Welsh pronunciation/translation skills to good effect – while the Morrow brothers looked after the test walking of the route for the third walk/book running.

The weather smiled on my efforts. Apart from the first couple of miles out of Knighton, one stormy October morning, I managed to stay quite dry throughout. I walked three stages, from Tenbury Wells to Knighton, just days before the onset of the serious floods of late October/early November 2000 and experienced nothing more serious than a squally shower or two. A week later most of the early part of Stage 1 and parts of Stages 3 and 4 of the walk were under several feet of water, with the area making the national news headlines for days on end!

I have chosen to describe a walk from east to west, up the river, for two main reasons. First, by walking in this direction the sun is usually behind one, and not in the eyes. Second, I felt it was that much more 'romantic', so to speak, to walk to the source of the river – lending almost a feeling of 'exploration' to the latter stages of the walk!

The stage endings have been dictated by the availability of Public Transport and accommodation. Thankfully this has resulted in a walk of eight stages of fairly even length – the longest is 13½ miles and the shortest 10.

Rather than end the walk at the river's source – and effectively in the middle of nowhere as regards transport and accommodation – I have included a link to Newtown, bringing the total distance of the route to 93 miles.

There are separate sections covering Public Transport and Accommodation elsewhere in the book. As regards Public Transport I have tried to give as accurate a picture as possible of the situation which existed at the time of publication but the information should always be confirmed before setting out. Rural Public Transport in Britain is sadly under funded and often poorly integrated. Changes to routes and timetables often happen at short notice. To help the prospective traveller I have given a list of 'useful' telephone numbers as regards sources of information and timetables.

Similarly, in an area of variable and changing accommodation availability, I have provided the numbers of the relevant Tourist Information offices. Where I am aware of only one or two establishments offering accommodation at the location I have also given details of these – not to be regarded, in any way, as a personal recommendation on my part.

The walk is suitable for undertaking at any time of the year and should cause no problems for the fairly fit, experienced walker. Being a riverside walk, in places, after periods of prolonged rainfall the possibility of flooding must be considered. The walker is advised to contact the Environmental Agency's national flood advisory telephone service – 0845 988 1188 – before setting out on the walk in these circumstances. In particular the start of Stage 1, along Severn and Teme between Worcester and Powick, is always liable to experience bad flooding. The scenes at the confluence of the two rivers during the serious floods of November 2000 will long remain in the memory!

All paths on the route were passable as of April 2002 – when I carried out a full re-walk of the route – with three very minor exceptions on Stage 6, where I have described the alternatives open to the walker. As far as I can ascertain all of the route is either over Public Rights of Way or areas of Open Access. Please remember to follow the Country Code and respect the land and its people – and hopefully you will be welcomed in return.

Finally – the usual 'health warning' – in a publication of this nature the odd mistake is bound to occur and also changes which affect its accuracy may arise. I apologise in advance for the former; the latter we all must live with. I hope any problem the reader/walker might encounter does not spoil the enjoyment of the walk.

Enjoy your walking, and may your god always walk alongside you!

David Milton, Sheldon, Birmingham.   August 2002.

Mileages

	00	Elgar Statue, WORCESTER
03	03	Powick Bridge
03	06	Bransford Bridge
02	08	Leigh
05	13	KNIGHTWICK (end of Stage 1)
03	16	Berrow Green
02	18	Ham Bridge
01.5	19.5	Shelsley Beauchamp
03.5	23	GREAT WITLEY (end of Stage 2)
03	26	Stanford Bridge
05.5	31.5	Eastham
02.75	34.25	Rochford
02.25	36.5	TENBURY WELLS (end of Stage 3)
04.25	40.75	Little Hereford Bridge
02.75	43.5	Ashford Carbonel
03	46.5	LUDLOW (end of Stage 4)
03	49.5	Bromfield
02.25	51.75	Bringewood Forge Bridge
02.75	54.5	Burrington
03.5	58	LEINTWARDINE (end of Stage 5)
03.5	61.5	Bucknell
04.5	66	Stowe Church
02	68	KNIGHTON (end of Stage 6)
05.5	73.5	Llanfair Waterdine
04.5	78	Bettws-y-Crwyn
03	81	FELINDRE (end of Stage 7)
06.75	87.75	Source of River Teme
05.25	93	NEWTOWN (end of Stage 8)

Ordnance Survey Maps covering the walk

1:50000 (Landranger).

136 Newtown, Llanidloes
137 Ludlow
138 Kidderminster & Wyre Forest
150 Worcester & the Malverns

1:25000 (Explorer).

201 Knighton & Presteigne
203 Ludlow
204 Worcester & Droitwich Spa
214 Llanidloes & Newtown

The River Teme

'Teme is Severn's wild sweet daughter, a wayward child'

Francis Brett Young

The River Teme (Afon Tefeidiad, in Welsh) rises in the Kerry Hills of Powys – in an old disused quarry on the slopes of Bryn Coch, a northern extension of Cilfaesty Hill – and flows generally east or south to join the River Severn just below Worcester, a total length of just over 75 miles.

One of the most beautiful and fast-flowing rivers in the country, it remains quite secretive for much of its length. Riverside rights of way are limited and even where paths do exist the walker may have some difficulty in seeing the river itself, so plentiful are the trees and luxuriant the vegetation along its banks.

'Teme' is an early Celtic river name – possibly meaning 'the dark one' – and the river has, in turn, lent that name to the town of Tenbury Wells ('Tamedeberie' in Domesday Book and later 'Temettebury', meaning 'the stronghold on the Teme'), a settlement it nowadays all too often threatens with severe flooding. The noise of its fast flowing waters and rapids helped name Ludlow ('Ludelaue', meaning 'the mound/hill beside loud waters') and neighbouring Ludford.

The Teme flows through a landscape steeped in history and shaped by human conflict, industry and endeavour – the Welsh Marches – before reaching the rich farmlands of Herefordshire and Worcestershire, with their hop-yards and cider apple orchards.

From its source deep in Welsh sheep country and adjacent to the prehistoric Kerry Ridgeway – the oldest route in Wales – it flows past the former woollen mill town of Felindre and below the grassy hill fortification at Knucklas, with its Arthurian legends. It passes Knighton – set astride the eighth century boundary fortification of Offa's Dyke – the surrounding hilltops crossed by ancient drovers roads.

Passing into England, it skirts the wooded Coxall Knoll – the hill fort at its summit a possible site of the last stand of the ancient British leader Caractacus against the invading Roman legions – and the village of Brampton Bryan – its castle the scene of an English Civil War siege, in 1643, when the Parliamentarian Lady Brilliana Harley famously, and successfully, defied Royalist forces for forty-six days.

It next reaches Leintwardine, where the Romans built riverside baths and where a retired English hero of the American War of Independence – General Sir Banestre Tarleton – caught salmon to send to his friend, the Prince of Wales.

Plunging through Downton Gorge and past Bromfield it approaches Ludlow – former seat of the Council of the Marches and effectively the capital of that region, and of the neighbouring English counties, in Tudor times – skirting the town beneath the walls of its imposing castle, a former stronghold of the powerful, medieval Mortimer dynasty of Marcher Earls.

At Tenbury it flows past a low mound which, legend tells us, is the grave of Caractacus but which could just as easily be the site of the town's castle or even a ford marker. Continuing downstream it passes Shelsley Walsh – where the Court House has Gunpowder Plot connections – and below another hill fort, on Woodbury Hill – reoccupied in 1405 during a week-long stand-off between a combined Welsh and French force, under Owain Glyn Dŵr, and the English army of Henry IV: a high point of Glyn Dŵr's rising and one which saw him penetrate England as far as Worcester and the Severn.

Soon the river reaches Whitbourne, where a seventeenth century Bishop of Hereford – Francis Godwin – worked on 'The Man in the Moon', the world's first science fiction novel. Just downstream, at Knightwick, it makes its last major alteration in course before approaching, and finally joining, the River Severn just to the south of Worcester – where it flows through meadows which saw both the first skirmish and last, decisive, bloody battle of the English Civil War.

More than even the Severn, perhaps, the Teme can justifiably claim to be the river whose landscape and scenery influenced the musical development of the young Edward Elgar, England's most famous and successful classical composer.

Born at Broadheath, just outside Worcester, in 1857, Elgar's earliest views and impressions would certainly have been of the outlook across the Teme valley, towards Malvern and its hills. No doubt he walked and bicycled alongside or over the river and something of it has surely found expression in his music.

Although not immediately apparent today, the banks of the Teme were once home to industry. The remains of many mills can still be seen at Ludlow while just upstream, at Bringewood Forge, ironmaking was well established by 1600 – reaching its peak in the early eighteenth century when no less than fourteen mills on the river hereabouts represented the greatest concentration of water power in England at that time.

Today the only mill on the river capable of operation is the old grain mill at Ashford Carbonel, which dates from 1819.

Just upstream of the Teme's confluence with the Severn, at Powick, the old power station was – when opened in 1894 – the first commercial scale hydro-electric power station in the world.

The Teme passes close to a number of highly individual buildings, each of which has its own tale to tell. There is Downton Castle and its estate, for example – where Richard Payne Knight brought his Picturesque landscaping beliefs to bear on the surroundings and where Thomas Farnolls Pritchard built a likeness of his more famous Iron Bridge in stone.

Leigh has the largest medieval cruck built tithe barn in England, Tenbury Wells a fantastic 'Chinese Gothic' prefabricated spa building; while near Great Witley the Teme valley is overlooked by the Abberley Clock Tower – an imposing Victorian 'folly' with a story to match!

Never important as a major river navigation, the Teme was, in theory, only navigable for the first mile or so upstream of its confluence with the Severn – to a wharf situated alongside Powick Old Bridge. In practice, and with the co-operation of the mill-owners on the river, vessels could reach much further upstream. The bells for Shelsley Beauchamp church were transported from Gloucester by water, up the Severn and Teme, in 1790. The quarry at Southstone Rock, near Shelsley Walsh, possibly also made use of river transport as early as the twelfth century, when the church at Eastham, further upstream, was constructed of travertine blocks quarried there.

On the higher reaches of the river the craft more likely to have been seen, however, was the ubiquitous coracle – still made and used at Leintwardine today.

The river was never more than of largely local use as a navigation and it was not provided with towpaths, as was the busy Severn. This is one reason why riverside footpaths are so few on the ground today.

From its source in Iyrchyn Quarry, on the slopes of Bryn Coch, the infant River Teme runs south for about a mile, rounding Cilfaesty Hill and collecting small tributary streams from steep sided moorland valleys. It then enters its own upper valley – known as Cwm Gwyn, 'the White Valley', because of the early mists which occur hereabouts – and heads south-east.

At Felindre it receives the waters of the sizeable Killowent (Cill Owen) Brook while just upstream of Llanfair Waterdine is the confluence with Crochen Brook. It passes Knucklas and soon reaches Knighton, all the time gaining the waters of more side streams. Beyond Knighton it heads east, passing Brampton Bryan where the high weir – just downstream of Parson's Pole Bridge, to the north of the village – marks the limit of the salmon run upriver.

Still flowing east it reaches Leintwardine where its largest tributary to date, the River Clun, joins. The original course of the Teme beyond this point is open to debate but what is known is that at the end of the last Ice Age the river became trapped by ice and debris and formed a large lake in what is now the Vale of Wigmore (a side stream here still bears the name 'Wigmore Lake'). This eventually overflowed to the north-east, the river cutting a new channel for itself through what is now Downton Gorge.

The meandering section of the present river between Leintwardine and Downton – where it flows first south-east and then north-east – is known as Leintwardine Fishery. There are several abandoned meanders and ox-bow lakes hereabouts – known as Nacklestone Ox-bows.

Between Leintwardine and Steventon, just south of Ludlow, the winding nature of the Teme means that it crossed on three separate occasions by the more direct pipeline route of the Elan Valley Aqueduct, en route from mid-Wales to Birmingham – at Graham's Cottage Bridge, Downton Bridge and Steventon Bridge.

Beyond Downton Gorge the river passes Downton Castle and Bringewood to reach Bromfield where the River Onny joins. It then turns south-east towards Ludlow, the confluence with the River Corve just upstream of the town. Beyond Ludlow, and neighbouring Ludford, it turns south, with the settlements of Ashford Carbonel and Ashford Bowdler on either side of an old ford across it.

Downstream of Ashford Carbonel the river bends eastwards, past Little Hereford church and Burford – where Ledwyche Brook joins it – to reach Tenbury Wells, and the confluence with Kyre Brook. Still flowing east it passes Rochford and receives the waters of the River Rea. To the north here is the confusingly named settlement of Knighton on Teme – unlike its namesake, upstream on the Welsh border, definitely NOT situated ON the river but above and well away from it.

Meandering generally eastwards the Teme passes Eastham, Lindridge and Eardiston before heading south-east to Stanford Bridge – where the old concrete bridge was, at its opening in 1905, the longest single span of concrete in the world.

It next passes the Shelsleys – Kings, Walsh and Beauchamp – and reaches Ham Bridge. Downstream of this it heads south past Whitbourne and Knightwick, via a series of large meanders, and then cuts between the steep slopes of Osebury Rock, to the south, and Ankerdine Hill to the north – through the Knightsford Gap – to head east by south-east towards the Severn.

It flows past Lulsley, Broadwas, Leigh, Bransford and Upper Wick – making a series of large bends and receiving the waters of Leigh Brook en route – before reaching Powick. Here, by the old power station just above Powick Old Bridge, Laughern Brook empties into it.

From Powick it is only just over a mile to the confluence with the River Severn, with one very large meander – in danger of creating a new, abandoned ox-bow lake – on the way. The by now sluggish Teme flows between low muddy banks to its mouth, about one mile south of Worcester Cathedral – an area which can see quite spectacular flooding after heavy rainfall.

The Stage Maps

The entire route is covered by stage maps – two per stage of the walk. The numbers which appear along the route on these relate to the same numbers within the main text.

The maps are not strictly drawn to scale but are generally at a scale of about 1½ inches to 1 mile. I have expanded this scale where the amount of detailed information to be shown requires this.

The maps are in no way intended to be a substitute for the Ordnance Survey maps of the route which should always be carried when undertaking the walk.

Public Transport

Brief details of Public Transport available at intermediate points are given in the text. The following is an overview of the position as regards the main Stage start/finish points.

WORCESTER is on the main Rail Network (use Foregate Street Station) with direct trains to London, Birmingham, Cardiff and Hereford (for connections to Ludlow and Shrewsbury) among other destinations. It is also a major centre for local bus routes.

KNIGHTWICK is linked to Worcester by bus services 419, 420 and 421 (First Midland Red; Bromyard Omnibus Company).

GREAT WITLEY is linked to Worcester and to Tenbury Wells by bus service 758 (Yarranton Bros.).

TENBURY WELLS is linked to Great Witley and Worcester by bus service 758 (Yarranton Bros.) and to Ludlow by bus service 731/732 (Whittlebus).

LUDLOW is on the main Rail Network, with direct trains to Cardiff, Hereford (for connections to Worcester), Shrewsbury (for connections to Knighton and Birmingham) and Manchester among other destinations. It is linked to Tenbury Wells by bus service 731/732 (Whittlebus), to Leintwardine and Knighton by bus services 738/740 (WhittleBus), and to Hereford and Birmingham by bus service 192/292 (First Midland Red; Pete's Travel).

LEINTWARDINE is linked to Ludlow and Knighton by bus service 738/740 (WhittleBus).

KNIGHTON is on the Heart of Wales Railway Line, part of the national Rail Network (Wales & Borders Trains), with direct trains to Swansea and Shrewsbury (for connections to Newtown, Birmingham, Manchester, Ludlow, Hereford and Cardiff). It is linked to Leintwardine and Ludlow by bus service 738/740 (WhittleBus) and to Felindre by a very limited bus service 774 (Owens Motors).

FELINDRE is linked to Knighton by a very limited bus service 774 (Owens Motors). A rare bus runs to Newtown.

NEWTOWN is on the main Rail Network, with direct trains to Shrewsbury (for connections to Manchester, Ludlow, Hereford and Cardiff), Wolverhampton and Birmingham.

Useful Telephone Numbers.

Centro 0121 200 2700
Herefordshire County Council 01432 260948
National Rail Enquiry Line 08457 484950
Powys County Council 01597 826642
Shropshire County Council 01743 253036
Traveline (National Public Transport Information Service) 0870 608 2608
Wales & Borders Trains 0870 9000 772
Worcestershire County Council 01905 768416

Accommodation

Stage 1: Worcester: Contact Worcester Tourist Information (01905 726311).

Knightwick: The Talbot Hotel (01886 821235) was the only accommodation in Knightwick at the time of publication. Alternatively contact Worcester Tourist Information (01905 726311) or Malvern Tourist Information (01684 892289).

Stage 2: Great Witley: Contact Worcester Tourist Information (01905 726311).

Stage 3: Tenbury Wells: Contact Tenbury Wells Tourist Information (01584 810136) in season (April to September), or Ludlow Tourist Information (01584 875053).

Stage 4: Ludlow: Contact Ludlow Tourist Information (01584 875053).

Stage 5: Leintwardine: Apart from the Lion Hotel (01547 540203) accommodation in Leintwardine is very limited. Contact Ludlow Tourist Information (01584 875053). Alternatively use Ludlow.

Stage 6: Knighton: Contact Offa's Dyke Centre/Knighton Tourist Information (01547 528753).

Stage 7: Felindre: See 'Felindre' note in main text. Alternatively contact Offa's Dyke Centre/Knighton Tourist Information (01547 528753).

Stage 8: Newtown: Contact Newtown Tourist Information (01686 625580).

Publishers' Note

Every care has been taken in the preparation of this book. All sections of the walk have been independently checked and are believed to be correct at the time of publication. However, no guarantee can be given that they contain no errors or omissions and neither the author nor the publishers can accept any responsibility for loss, damage or inconvenience resulting from the use of this book.

Please remember that the countryside is continually changing: hedges and fences may be removed or re-sited; footbridges and river banks may suffer flood damage; footpaths may be re-routed or ploughed over and not reinstated (as the law requires); concessionary paths may be closed. If you do encounter any such problems please let the publishers know, and please report any obstructions to rights of way to the appropriate local authority.

About the Author

A resident of Birmingham for over thirty years now, David Milton was born in Worcester in 1949 and spent the first eighteen years of his life there before joining Customs & Excise, for whom he worked for almost thirty years, taking early retirement in 1997 to concentrate on his main interest – walking.

His interest in walking began young – sometime between five and ten years of age – with the Worcester & Birmingham Canal and Worcestershire's Abberley Hills providing early challenges. During the 1970s he walked almost the entire canal system of England and Wales and has since walked widely in Cornwall, the Derbyshire Peak District, the Lake District, Yorkshire and the Cotswolds, in the U.K., and abroad in the Greek Islands, Malta, France, Madeira, Spain and India. His declared 'favourite' walking area however is that region around Ludlow where the counties of Herefordshire, Worcestershire, Radnorshire (Powys) and Shropshire mingle. He is a dedicated 'non-driver'.

Photo by permission of Worcester Evening News

Since his retirement David has divided his time between walking for pleasure, leading walking groups - mainly in the Welsh Marches - and writing. The designer of many 'day walks', *A Teme Valley Walk* is his third long distance walk and book. His first, *The Elan Valley Way*, was published by Meridian Books in 1999 and describes the route of a 128 mile walk from Birmingham to Mid-Wales based around the Elan Valley Aqueduct; his second book *The Riversides Way* (Meridian Books), published in 2001, concerns a 72 mile circular walk in the Welsh Marches. A booklet - *The Riversides Way Clun Extension* (aRTy Publications) concerning a 19 mile extension loop to the main Riversides Way route, from Knighton to Clun and back, was published late in 2001.

David also writes poetry, under the pseudonym R. Tomas. His first collection of poems - *Past Landscapes* (KT Publications) - was published in 2002.

The Route of the Teme Valley Walk

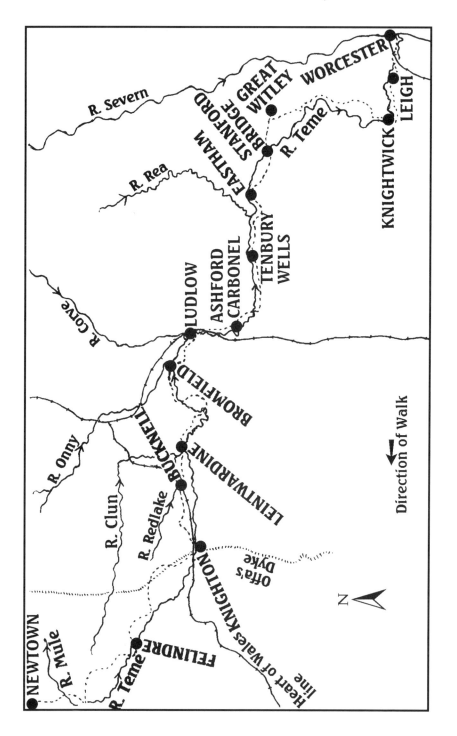

Worcester to Knightwick

Mileage: 13 Miles
(From Worcester: 3 miles to Powick; 6 miles to Bransford Bridge; 8 miles to Leigh)
O.S.Maps: 1:50000 (Landranger): 150 (Worcester & the Malverns);
                    1:25000 (Explorer): 204 (Worcester & Droitwich Spa)

Starting at the statue of Sir Edward Elgar, the route rounds the west end of the Cathedral to drop down onto the bank of the River Severn which is followed the short distance upstream to Worcester Bridge. Crossing the river the route turns south, again riverside, to reach the confluence with the Teme.

A riverside path along the Teme takes the route to Powick. Field paths, tracks and another riverside section then lead to a first crossing of the river, at Bransford. A delightful riverside walk follows with the route making its first crossing of the disused Bromyard railway line before a short road section brings it to the interesting settlement of Leigh. More field paths and a long track section lead to Lulsley, crossing the disused railway on three more occasions en route. From Lulsley Court a path leads through the river gap below Osebury Rock to a final short road section into Knightwick. The stage ends with a second crossing of the Teme via the old bridge there.

This section is very flat throughout, the only noticeable climb being a gentle one through fields after Leigh.

! Part of this stage of the walk – especially between Worcester and Powick, around the confluence of the Rivers Severn and Teme – may become impassable because of flooding after periods of heavy rainfall. The situation should always be checked beforehand and the walk not attempted if there is any doubt regarding conditions.

The walk starts at the statue of Sir Edward Elgar at the end of High Street, opposite Worcester Cathedral. If travelling to Worcester by rail leave the train at Worcester Foregate Street Station. Outside the station turn left to walk the half mile to the start of the walk – along what is first The Foregate, later The Cross and finally becomes the pedestrianised High Street.

If arriving by bus then travel to the bus station and leave this up the slope into Angel Place. Continue straight ahead along Angel Street to a crossroads, with the large former church of St. Nicholas immediately opposite. Turn right here to walk along The Cross and the pedestrianised High Street, again a total distance of about half a mile.

En route to the start, from either bus or railway station, the walker will pass two buildings of interest. The first is the former church of St. Nicholas, situated on The Cross. Now a wine bar/club, this imposing building was built between 1730 and 1735, the architect being Humphrey Hollins but the design of its tower being based on one by Gibbs and featuring an octagonal stage and lantern.

Further along, on the right-hand side of the High Street, is Worcester's magnificent Guildhall. Built, between 1721 and 1723, in the Queen Anne style of architecture, it is one of the finest civic buildings of its time in England. Its architect was Thomas White, a local man. Inside is the Assembly Room, a beautifully decorated Italianate room. Part of the building now houses a Tourist Information centre. On either side of its main doorway are statues of the kings Charles I and II. On the pediment above is a statue of Queen Anne.

Over the doorway is a head which appears to be pinned up by its ears. Generations of Worcester children, including myself, have been brought up to believe that this is a representation of the locally despised Oliver Cromwell. Unlike any known portrait of the Civil War Parliamentarian leader, the head is fashioned to resemble the Devil in order to perpetuate a local legend that it was only by selling his soul to Satan, in nearby Nunnery Wood, that Cromwell was able to defeat the Crown at the Battle of Worcester (1651).

Old leather fire buckets hanging on the wall of the Guildhall's Lower Hall – possibly visible through the left window of the recessed part of the building – recall the fact that Worcester had no fire brigade in the eighteenth century. The idea was that volunteers to tackle any blaze in the city would only be sought after hearing Worcester's fire alarm, the bell of St. Andrew's church. The buckets were provided by the Corporation for use in these circumstances.

Those walking to the start from Foregate Street railway station will also pass Berkeley's Hospital – situated on the right-hand side of The Foregate, just after Shaw Street (left) – one of Worcester's better kept secrets.

A group of almshouses, set in a garden haven and with a chapel at their centre, Berkeley's Hospital was built in 1710, in the Dutch style of architecture – the result of a bequest from Robert Berkeley of nearby Spetchley Park. Intriguingly, his will specified that the almshouses were to be for 'twelve poor men and one poor woman'! Just a few yards further along The Foregate was the site of the actual Fore Gate through the old city walls. No trace of either it or the walls remain – except for a plaque on the wall of a building (right).

The statue of Sir Edward Elgar – where the walk commences – was unveiled by HRH. Prince Charles, the Prince of Wales, on 2nd June 1981, the 124th anniversary of the composer's birth. It shows him at the age of fifty-four, in the robes of a doctor of music which he often wore when conducting.

Worcester

Worcester takes its name from two words which together mean 'the Roman town of the Weogora tribe'. The Weogora name itself probably originates from a Celtic river word meaning 'winding river' – the same name has also survived as 'Wyre', as in nearby Wyre Forest.

The site of the present city would always have been attractive to settlers – being a natural promontory formed by the confluence of the River Severn and Frog Brook (later absorbed into the Worcester & Birmingham Canal) on the east bank of the former. The attractiveness of the setting was further enhanced by the existence of a ford across the river and of sand and gravel terraces above its flood level.

The early Roman conquerors built a road along the east bank of the Severn which ran about 150 yards to the west of the present High Street but, as yet, no evidence has been found on the ground to suggest that a fort was sited here – although a possible Roman marching camp site has been identified at Perdiswell, north of the current city. However by the second century, during the reign of the Emperor Hadrian, a large Roman industrial settlement involved in iron smelting had been established. The iron slag resulting from this industry was used for roads and other engineering projects locally and the piers of Worcester's medieval bridge were found to be so composed when it was demolished in 1781 – giving rise to the theory that a Roman bridge may once have occupied the site.

In the seventh century the area was annexed into the kingdom of the Hwicce, a Saxon buffer state between the more powerful Mercia and Wessex, and in AD680 the see of Worcester was created, with Bosel as its first bishop. It was he who established the first cathedral church, on the site of the present building – St. Peter's.

The settlement name is first recorded in AD691 as Weogorna Civitas, Weogornaceaster or Weogernaceaster. In AD717 it is named as Wigranceastre and, in AD736, Castra Weogernensis. By the time of Domesday Book (1086) it was known as Wirecestre.

The thriving Saxon settlement was fortified in the ninth century and in AD960 Bishop Oswald (later Saint Oswald) built a second cathedral church (St. Mary's) alongside the first and founded a Benedictine monastery.

The Saxon settlement suffered a setback in 1041 when it was burnt by forces of the Dutch king Hardcanute, in retaliation for the murder of two of his tax collectors. The citizens fled to safety on Belvere Island – in the

River Severn to the north of the modern city – where they were able to defend themselves successfully.

In 1069, after the Norman Conquest a castle was built to the south of the cathedral by the Sheriff of Worcester, Urse d'Abitot, and in 1074 a new cathedral – the current building – was begun under Bishop Wulfstan (a Saxon bishop who had sworn allegiance to William the Conqueror and had so retained his office). The adjacent Bishop's Palace may also date from this period.

The twelfth and thirteenth centuries saw the city involved in the turbulent politics of the day – such as the Civil War between Stephen and Matilda – with possession of its strategic river crossing the cause of several sieges and skirmishes. After this period the importance of Worcester's castle waned and by 1540 it was recorded as being 'clene downe'. The city had, however, been fully walled by the early thirteenth century.

Worcester received a Royal Charter from Richard I in 1189 and this encouraged its commercial development. By 1377 its population numbered 3000 and this rose to 8000 by the sixteenth century by which time it was involved in an enormous variety and number of trades and industries, with cloth manufacture dominating.

Perhaps more than any other settlement Worcester suffered as a result of the Civil War of the seventeenth century. As in the earlier civil war the city's strategic importance was not lost on either side and both the first skirmish (Powick Bridge, 1642), and the final decisive battle (Worcester, 1651) took place just outside the city. In between the city had been besieged and taken by Parliamentarian forces – in 1646. Its support for the Royalist cause earned Worcester the title of the 'Faithful City' – incorporated into its motto – but at great cost, with much destruction of property taking place and the city not having fully recovered as late as the eighteenth century.

A newspaper, *Berrows Journal*, was started in Worcester in 1690 and survives to this day – the world's oldest. The city's population numbered 10000 in 1678 and had doubled by 1821.

The eighteenth century saw much hardship and unemployment in the city and it was partly to counter this that a Dr. Wall and his partners founded the Worcester Porcelain Works, in 1751.

Between 1790 and 1820 Worcester became an important centre for glove making, with 150 separate manufacturers employing vast numbers of workers and turning out an estimated 7,500,000 pairs a year. The removal of the import duty on foreign gloves, in 1826, effectively marked the beginning of the decline of the industry in the city, with only eleven manufacturers remaining by 1855. Shoe manufacturing companies were to employ many of the redundant glove workers, similar skills being required, while the former importance of the glove making industry is today remembered through the name commonly applied to the city's prominent landmark, the spire of the old St. Andrew's church – 'the Glover's Needle'.

Other industries were drawn to the city – especially after the opening of the Worcester & Birmingham Canal in 1815. These included iron founding, corn milling, brick making and vinegar manufacturing – the Hill Evans Vinegar Works being founded in 1830, with, at that date, the largest vat in the world (114821 gallons).

Another famous Worcester company and product – Lea & Perrins Worcestershire sauce – was also established in the nineteenth century, being first produced in the 1830s and based on a secret recipe brought back from Calcutta.

The River Severn and its commercial traffic remained important to the city and the construction of a weir at Diglis, in 1844, helped deepen its channel from Gloucester upstream to Worcester.

The railways came late to Worcester, a narrow gauge line reaching Shrub Hill in 1850 – by which time the city had been effectively marginalised on a loop line between Wolverhampton and Oxford. A line across the Severn – to Malvern and Hereford – followed in 1860.

Modern Worcester offers all the facilities one would expect of a city of its size and importance. It would be impossible for a walking guide, such as this, to do justice to all its attractions but, briefly, in addition to the Cathedral and other places of interest passed en route – for which there are separate notes – there are:

(1) Royal Worcester Porcelain

There is a Visitor Centre situated in Severn Street, near the Cathedral. The museum here houses the most comprehensive collection of Worcester porcelain in the world. The factory was founded in 1751 and is world renowned in its field. The company received its royal warrant from George III in 1788.

(2) The Greyfriars

In Friar Street, near the Cathedral. A timber-framed merchant's house of 1480, with seventeenth and eighteenth century additions, which was rescued from demolition at the time of the Second World War and has been restored and refurbished by the National Trust.

The Elgar statue

Further along Friar Street is the house from which Charles II made his escape after the battle of Worcester. Nearer the Cathedral is Worcester's oldest pub, the Cardinal's Hat (*circa* 1482).

(3) The Commandery

In Sidbury, near the Cathedral. Founded as a small hospital just outside of the city walls, by Bishop Wulfstan in 1085, from the thirteenth century its masters were known as commanders – hence the building's present name (it was formerly known as St. Wulfstan's Hospital). The present building dates from the late fifteenth century. It has a magnificent galleried hall, with original windows and an Elizabethan staircase. During the battle of Worcester (1651) the building served as the Royalist headquarters and today it houses a museum devoted to the English Civil War.

(4) The Edgar Tower

Situated at the entrance to College Green, behind the Cathedral. A thirteenth century gateway, so named because it was previously thought to date from the reign of the tenth century king, Edgar. It was formerly known as St. Mary's Gate.

(5) Huntingdon Hall

Situated behind the Crowngate Shopping Centre – to the right off High Street, *en route* to the start of the walk. Now converted into a concert hall but with its interior little changed as regards furniture and fittings, this was the church of a late eighteenth century non-conformist religious sect – the Countess of Huntingdon's Connexion – founded by Selina Hastings, née Shirley (1707 -1791), Countess of Huntingdon, a former Methodist. The building dates from 1804, with 1815 additions. It contains a fine, locally made Nicholson organ.

Starting at the Elgar statue, and facing the same way as Sir Edward, cross Deansway – with care – and walk towards a large war memorial (The Boer War, 1899-1902, in which the Worcestershire Regiment was involved in some of the bloodiest fighting) in front of the Cathedral. On reaching the memorial bear right into College Yard. Follow this around to the main (north) entrance door/porch to the Cathedral.

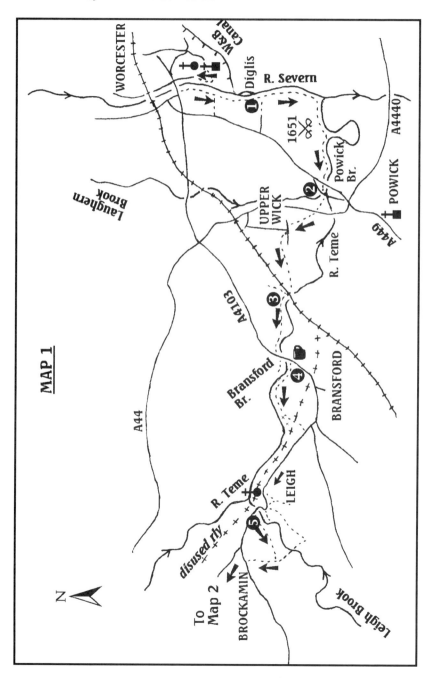

If not visiting the Cathedral bear right from the porch to pass through iron gates and out onto a terrace above the River Severn. Bear left, along the west end of the Cathedral, and then right – down steps to the edge of the terrace. Here bear left to pass down more steps and under an arch, between ruins, to reach a lower terrace. Walk straight ahead along this and then, on reaching its corner, bear left to follow a short section of wall to a iron gate. Pass through this and go straight ahead to reach more steps, through another small iron gate. Go down these steps and at the bottom bear right to pass through an arch and gateway onto the bank of the river. Turn right to walk along the metalled Kleve Walk which runs riverside here.

Passing through the gateway pause to examine the collection of food-level marks set into the wall on the left. Floods of the twentieth century are well represented, including a couple from the 1990's which would seem to bear out some global warming theories. However the floods of December 1960 and 1965 are shown to have reached a higher level (I remember the latter flood quite vividly as I, then a teenager, would cycle down through the city most evenings to see how far the waters had risen, safe in the knowledge that our own house – in the Barbourne area of the city – was well above even the upper flood plain level. Worcester's newly built Swan Theatre really lived up to its name during that flood, being almost cut off by the water!).

Higher still are the tablets showing the flood levels of 1852, 1924 and 1946 while significantly above these is one for May 1886. Approaching the top of the

Sir Edward Elgar

Born at Upper Broadheath, just over two miles to the west of Worcester, Elgar (1857-1934) rose from humble beginnings to become England's best known classical composer. His father ran a music shop at Number 10 High Street, Worcester (near where the Elgar statue now stands), and the family later moved to the city. Here Edward was sometime organist at the Roman Catholic Church in Sansome Street. Organist, violinist, music teacher and conductor, Elgar was a largely self-taught composer. From the beginning of the twentieth century his compositions brought him international fame. He is best known for works such as the *Enigma Variations, the Pomp & Circumstance Marches* (Number One of these was given words as *Land of Hope and Glory*), two symphonies, a violin concerto and a cello concerto. For many his music seems to be inspired by and to reflect the English countryside, especially that around the Malvern Hills. He himself said 'Music is in the air all around us'. He was knighted in 1904.

Master of the Kings Musick, from 1924 until his death ten years later, in later life he composed little, his heart having been effectively broken by the events of the First World War and, more significantly, by the death of his beloved wife, Alice. During his last few years he made several pioneer recordings of his own works, as conductor. He was also very much associated with the annual Three Choirs Festival which is held in turn at Worcester, Hereford and Gloucester (and was started in Worcester in 1717). He died in Worcester on the 23rd February 1934. A memorial tablet commemorating his life was laid in front of his statue to mark the fiftieth anniversary of his death.

wall is a marker for March 20th 1947, the floods that year presumably the result of one of the severest winters of recent times which saw parts of the country brought to a standstill, by ice and snow, for weeks. Even this marker cannot compete with the highest on the wall however, a metal plaque which commemorates two floods - the first in 1672 and the second, and highest of all the flood-levels recorded, that of November 1770. The height reached by the severe floods of late 2000 was, as yet, unrecorded at the time of publication of this book.

The gateway is known as the Water Gate and dates from 1378, although the extant structure is late fifteenth century in origin, and the superstructure much later still. In medieval times the tidal river would have flooded it twice a day, allowing small boats to unload underneath. The grooves for a portcullis may still be seen in the stonework - the gateway piercing Worcester's thirteenth century town walls, the finest remaining stretch of which is hereabouts.

There has been a river crossing at this point for 4000 years and the dwelling above the Water Gate originally housed the Cathedral ferrymen. A seasonal ferry – summer weekends only – still operates to a point across the river from the foot of the steps down to the water here.

Walk along Kleve Walk, the river on the left, towards Worcester Bridge. *En route*, on the right, is a concrete pillar bearing a bronze sculpture of a swan,

Worcester Cathedral

The imposing cathedral dates from 1074 and was begun under Bishop Wulfstan, (later Saint Wulfstan). Two earlier Saxon cathedral churches were destroyed during its construction – St. Peter's, (built around AD680), and St. Mary's, (AD960). Remains attributable to these have recently been discovered near the Chapter House and cloisters of the present building. There is a stone carving of Wulfstan dedicating the cathedral high on the north wall of St. Andrew's Chapel, near the north-east corner of the chancel.

The building was largely completed by 1375. Until the Dissolution, in the sixteenth century, it was at the heart of a Benedictine monastery but thereafter has maintained an independent existence. There is much to see inside.

The superb crypt is Norman and dates from 1084, the earliest part of the building.

In the chancel is the chantry/tomb of Prince Arthur – son of Henry VII and elder brother of Henry VIII. Arthur's heart is actually buried in St. Laurence's church, Ludlow – in which town he died, aged 15, (see note on Ludlow at Stage 4).

The other famous, or infamous, 'royal' buried here is King John who died at Newark but demanded he be buried at Worcester between two saints, St Oswald and St Wulfstan – both former bishops of Worcester. The tombs of the saints have long gone (destroyed at the time of the Reformation, under Henry VIII) but the Purbeck marble tomb of John, dating from 1216, remains – situated in the Quire.

Also to be found in the Quire are thirty-seven finely carved oak misericords, dating from 1379.

There is a memorial window to Sir Edward Elgar, situated in the north wall of the nave, at its western end.

In the cloisters, the east walk is home to five of the cathedral's old bells, two of which date from 1374. The south walk includes a Window of the Millennium, installed in February 2000, which depicts the last thousand years of the history of the Cathedral, Worcester and Worcestershire and reflects Christ's teachings. The most attractive approach to the Cathedral is via the Close and the cloisters.

The Chapter House, entered from the east walk of the cloisters, dates from the early twelfth century and is built of green sandstone and white limestone. It was the first circular chapter house in Britain and has a single central pillar. Originally used by the Benedictine monks for meetings it now plays host to exhibitions, lectures and concerts.

The cathedral tower rises to a height of 170 feet and dates from the fourteenth century. It may be climbed for superb views over the city and its surroundings. It was used for that same purpose by the Royalist commanders during the Battle of Worcester (1651) – see separate note.

The view of the building from across the river to the west is one which is well known the world over by cricket fans, being that obtained from the Worcestershire County Cricket Ground which many overseas teams traditionally visit early on their tours. Both the Cathedral and Sir Edward Elgar are now even more familiar, featuring (at the time of writing) on the reverse of the Bank of England twenty pound note.

which commemorates Worcester's 'twinning' with the German town of Kleverburger – presumably from where the Walk gets its name. Here, beyond the wall on the right is the old Palace of the Bishop of Worcester. Further along, also on the right, is the tower and steeple of the old St Andrew's church – known locally as the 'Glover's Needle'.

Beyond some newly installed (2001) fountains, where Kleve Walk becomes a road – South Parade – continue along the pavement on its left-hand side, still riverside, to reach Worcester Bridge. Remaining on the same pavement, cross the bridge.

While crossing the bridge look right (upstream) for a view of the railway bridge and new footbridge beyond and left (downstream) for a classic view of the Cathedral.

The Bishop's Palace

The former Bishop's Palace became the Deanery in 1842. Most of the exterior as seen today dates from the eighteenth century when the building was much added to by two Bishops of Worcester, Hough and Johnston, but within are parts dating back to the thirteenth century when Bishop Giffard was granted licence to crenellate the palace.

A story concerns King George III's stay at the building in 1788, while at-tending the Three Choirs Festival. The king, known as 'Farmer George', apparently loved to meet his subjects informally – being, in that respect, some years ahead of the current Royal family. It is said that, rising early in the morning, he climbed out of a first floor window of the Palace, slid down a roof to the ground, and then wandered about the city streets talking to the citizens – and all this while still in his bedclothes!

The railway bridge – an ugly girder construction – dates from 1905 and replaced an earlier, and more elegant, two arched structure which caused the opening of the railway to be delayed until 1860, when its original design had been strengthened.

Across the bridge, bear left to walk along Bromwich Parade, a substantial compacted dirt track alongside the river which is accessed through metal gates. (Do not go down the steps to the very edge of the river.)

Follow the track along the river, which is on the left.

Just after reaching Bromwich Parade look left across the river for a good view of the Glover's Needle. A little further on one gets the classic views across the river of the west end and tower of the Cathedral, although these may be somewhat restricted by foliage in summer.

Worcester Bridge

The current bridge, its approach roads and quays were designed by John Gwynn (1730-1786). Construction began in 1771, using sandstone which was shipped down the Severn, and the bridge was opened in 1781. Neighbouring Bridge Street was completed in 1792, six years after Gwynn's death. The bridge was widened and reconstructed in 1932.

Gwynn's bridge replaced a medieval structure which was sited about 150 yards upstream of it, at the bottom of what is now Newport Street. Originally thought to date from 1313, when it was demolished – in 1781 – the bridge was found to be supported on piers of iron slag, possibly of Roman origin.

Continue along Bromwich Parade, passing the point – across the river – where the route emerged from the Cathedral grounds, through the Water Gate, onto Kleve Walk.

Ignore a footpath going off right (signed for Bromwich Road and St. John's) but remain on the riverside track (signed Diglis Weir and Weir Lane, Half Mile).

The Glover's Needle

This is the tower and steeple of the old church of St. Andrew, demolished in 1950. The fifteenth century west tower of the church, and its eighteenth century steeple, were spared and provide the city with an unmistakable landmark. The surviving structure rises to a height of 75 metres/246 feet, of which 46 metres/150 feet is the actual steeple. This was rebuilt on at least seven occasions during Georgian times, (the last in 1751, by Nathaniel Wilkinson), when it constantly suffered from storm damage and lightning strikes. Its common name derives from the glove making industry which has been based in Worcester over the years.

Good view to be had across the river to the Cathedral from the bottom of the ferry steps. Half-left ahead the Malvern Hills make their first appearance.

Continuing along Bromwich Parade, across the river large lettering on a brick wall announces the Diglis Hotel. Ignore a gate giving access to Chapter Meadows on the right of the track.

Chapter Meadows are managed to safeguard their wildlife and are traditional river meadows, subject to regular seasonal flooding. Throughout their history the meadows have been cut for hay – by the Romans, monks and later Worcester Cathedral – and are then grazed by cattle for the rest of the summer and autumn. Formerly the property of the Dean & Chapter of Worcester Cathedral the meadows passed to the Duckworth Worcestershire Trust in October 1998.

Standing at the gate into the Meadows, the adjacent playing field on the right belongs to the King's School while beyond that can be seen the Worcestershire County Cricket Ground.

Continue along the riverside track. The entrance locks to the Diglis basins of the Worcester and Birmingham Canal will be seen across the river while a large sign alongside the track warns boaters of the imminent approach and dangers of Diglis Weir on the river. The remains of Diglis Docks (across the river) and Diglis Island are reached, closely followed by the weir itself. Approaching the weir the track is bounded by a high wire fence on its right with a stand of pine trees beyond. Beyond these is a sewage works.

In my youth, Diglis Weir was a renowned fishing spot for eels, including the young elvers. Just below the weir there appears to be some sort of outflow into

The Worcester & Birmingham Canal

Completed in 1815, the Worcester & Birmingham Canal runs for 30 miles between the two cities which give it its name, with a link from its basins to the River Severn through the two barge width locks seen. All other locks on it are of narrow-boat width – 7 feet. It is the most heavily locked canal in the country with 56 narrow locks in its next 15 miles to Tardebigge, west of Bromsgrove – a total rise of 433 feet from the Severn to that point, after which it is level all the way to Birmingham. The Tardebigge flight alone is of thirty locks within 2½ miles, the top one of which, with a rise of 11 feet, is one of the deepest narrow locks in the country – the result of a failed experiment with a canal lift at this point. There are also five tunnels on the canal, the longest being that at Wast Hills, just to the south of Birmingham – 2726 yards long.

The bill for the canal was passed in 1791, at the height of the so-called 'Canal Mania'. The new venture was fiercely opposed by both the Staffordshire and Worcestershire Canal Company – who saw the likelihood of their longer route from the industrial Midlands to the Severn, via Stourport, being compromised – and the Birmingham Canal Company – who feared both loss of trade and of water to the new venture. The latter's opposition to the bill resulted in the construction of the infamous Worcester Bar at Gas Street Basin in Birmingham – a physical barrier between the two waterways over which any through goods had to be lifted. This was only replaced, by a stop lock, in 1815.

By 1807 boats could reach Tardebigge from Birmingham. Here work stopped for a few years while the cash-poor company considered cheaper ways of completing its line. One of these was to construct the canal with narrow locks instead of the broad ones originally envisaged. The experiments with the vertical boat lift also stemmed from this need to save money. The company's new engineer, John Woodhouse, was a great exponent of such lifts and proposed reducing the number of locks down to Worcester from an envisaged 76 to 12 by this means. The experienced engineer, John Rennie, called in to give his opinion on the experiment was not so impressed and the idea was abandoned, although the proposed total number of locks was subsequently reduced to its current 58.

On opening, in 1815, the venture had cost £610,000, many thousands of pounds over its original estimate. It was never as commercially successful as its supporters hoped and by the middle of the nineteenth century was already seeing its traffic threatened by the new railway lines.

In 1874 the canal was bought by the Sharpness New Docks Company, in a bid to preserve through traffic from Birmingham and down the Severn.

Among the last commercial users of the canal were Cadburys whose narrow boats used it to reach their sites at Blackpole, to the north of Worcester, and Bournville. Threatened with closure in the 1960's, the canal now has an assured future as a leisure facility.

River Severn

The River Severn is the longest river in Britain – at almost 220 miles. Known to the Romans as Sabrina and in Wales as Afon Hafren, it rises on the Plynlimon plateau in mid-Wales and plunges eastwards through the Hafren Forest before reaching Llanidloes, the first town of any size along its course. Continuing through Newtown (the destination of this walk) and Welshpool it enters England, then flowing through Shrewsbury, Ironbridge, Bridgnorth, Bewdley, Stourport, Worcester, Tewkesbury and Gloucester on its way to the Bristol Channel and the sea. It is now accompanied on much of its travels by a long distance footpath – the Severn Way – which runs for 210 miles from its source to Severn Beach.

Although there is now no serious commercial traffic remaining on the upper river, in its heyday the fortune of many riverside settlements depended on it. At the end of the seventeenth century the Severn was the second busiest river in Europe, after the Meuse, while the late eighteenth century saw it linked to an increasingly industrial Midlands via the growing canal system. The Staffordshire & Worcestershire Canal was opened in 1772, creating the brand new canal town of Stourport where it joined the river, and the Worcester & Birmingham Canal, with its more direct but heavier locked route followed in 1815. The construction of the Gloucester & Sharpness Canal – completed in 1827, to ship canal standard – resulted in more reliable navigation, bypassing the lower river and the shifting shoals and sandbanks south of Gloucester, that town becoming an important inland port as a result. The Severn Commission was formed in 1842 to maintain the river as a commercially viable route – by means of a programme of lock and weir-building and canalisation – and by 1888 the river had a minimum depth of 6 feet up to Stourport.

Regular commercial traffic to Worcester lasted through the 1960's – in the form of oil barges, which unloaded in a basin just above Diglis river locks. This trade was killed off by pipelines and the river now carries leisure traffic in the main. The only remaining regular commercial boats using the river are two grain barges which operate from Sharpness Dock to a mill at Tewkesbury.

the river, possibly connected with the neighbouring sewage works. This would explain why our fishing expeditions here were so successful!

Beyond the weir Bromwich Parade narrows to path width and takes on a more stony surface, passing the tail of Diglis Island. The wire fence, and coniferous plantation beyond, continues on the right.

When the wire fence and main path bear right (signed Weir Lane, Bromwich Road) continue straight ahead over a stile to follow a riverside path through a field (signed River Teme, Powick Bridge ¾ Mile), (SO847532). ❶

Look behind here for a good view, upriver, over Diglis river locks to the Cathedral and Glover's Needle in the distance. Over to the right superb views across to the Malvern Hills open up on a good day, while in the foreground may be seen the square tower of Powick Church. The whole chain of the Malverns should be visible – from End Hill and North Hill, (398 metres/1305 feet), on the right, along past Worcestershire Beacon (425 metres/1394 feet), and Herefordshire Beacon to Midsummer, Hollybush and Chase End Hills on the left.

The Malverns take their name from the Welsh 'Moel Frynn' meaning 'bare hills', a very apt descriptive name.

Walk along the riverside path through the field. On reaching its far boundary cross a stile into the next field and continue riverside. At the end of this very long field pass through a gap in the boundary ahead, a redundant stile alongside on the right, into another field. Again follow the riverside path here.

Crossing another stile into a further field again continue riverside to reach a triangular concrete Worcester City boundary post on the bank, a footpath sign nearby indicating that it is one mile back to Worcester Bridge (behind) and the footpath to Powick Bridge now taken (right).

Continue ahead for the few yards along the riverbank beyond the concrete boundary post to view the actual confluence of the Teme with the Severn.

Turn right to walk across the field, bearing slightly left to reach the bank of the River Teme.

Follow the indistinct riverside path along the Teme, the river on the left.

Directly ahead is the squat, bulbous topped chimney of the old Powick Power Station (see note below).

Indian Balsam is prolific along these lower reaches of the River Teme, as it is along the neighbouring Severn. Fortunately that other great nuisance of a colonising plant, Japanese Knotweed – also Severnside – has not yet managed such progress on the Teme.

Reaching the end of the field cross a stile/hurdle into the next, remaining on the riverside path through this. On reaching a fence at the end of the field ignore a stile into the next field ahead but instead bear right, along the fence for about 30 yards, to reach the river bank again. (The two points on the Teme at either end of this short section of fence are over half a mile apart by water, such is the meander the river makes hereabouts!)

Turn right to walk along the riverside path.

Worcester Cathedral and the Glover's Needle appear ahead in the distance. Don't despair, this is purely an aberration caused by the meandering Teme!

The path passes a redundant stile. Continue riverside, leaving the field into a smaller one, via a stile. Through this field, exit over metal bars/stile, to the left of a metal farm gate. In the next field continue to follow the river.

The span of Powick road bridge appears ahead, with the old power station chimney beyond. Approaching the bridge there are good views of the Malvern Hills, half-left – the whole chain again visible. Directly to the left is the tower of Powick church.

On reaching Powick road bridge follow the path through the flood arch on the riverbank.

Notice what appears to be quite substantial towrope wear in the sandstone supports of the flood arch.

Powick Old Bridge appears ahead. Remain on the riverside path to reach it. At the end of the field cross the facing wooden boundary fence, via a stile, to reach a quiet road by the chimney of the old power station (SO835525). Turn left along the road to the bridge.

 Turn right along the quiet road to reach the A449. Various bus services run along this into Worcester – including the 44 and 46 (Mondays to Saturdays) or 144 (Sundays).

The Battle of Worcester

The fields around the confluence of Teme and Severn were the site of the Battle of Worcester which took place on September 3rd 1651 and was the final and decisive battle of the English Civil War – with the largely Scottish army of Charles II defeated by Parliamentarian forces under Oliver Cromwell and Charles Fleetwood.

The Parliamentarian 'Roundheads' occupied the east bank of the Severn and the west bank to the south of the Teme, with the Scots to the north of that river and a Royalist force also occupying the city, its artillery at Fort Royal there. The Roundheads heavily outnumbered Charles's force – about 30000 as against between 12,000 and 17,000.

Cromwell and Fleetwood used two bridges constructed of boats – one across the Severn and another on the Teme – to move troops and thereby support each other during the fighting. Fleetwood's force crossed the Teme – via the bridge of boats and also over nearby Powick Bridge – and drove the Scots back towards the city while it was Cromwell who delivered the final onslaught from the south-east.

The battle marked the end of any Royalist aspirations of restoring the Monarchy by force, leaving its army shattered – with over 3000 dead, 10,000 prisoner and the remainder, including Charles, as fugitives.

A long distance walk based on the route taken by Charles II as he escaped after the battle of Worcester is the subject of *The Monarch's Way* by Trevor Antill. A total of 610 miles in length, from Worcester to Shoreham, a guide to the walk is published, in three volumes, by Meridian Books.

The site of the bridge of boats over the Teme is thought to have been about 25 yards from the confluence, just beyond where the footpath reaches the riverbank.

At the near end of the bridge a memorial stone commemorates the many Scots who died – so far from home – during the battle of Worcester. It was erected to commemorate the 350th anniversary of the battle in 2001.

Cross only the first two arches of the bridge (NOT the river). After the second arch, only part way across the bridge, turn right onto a stony track which initially forms part of the driveway to premises on the right – a cattery at the time of writing. Ignore a turning to the right – the entrance to the cattery – but continue ahead along the track, crossing a stile to the left of a metal farm gate on it.

Beyond the gate the track loses its stony surface and bends slightly to the right, the A4440 road appearing both ahead and over to the left. Follow the obvious track which crosses a sturdy bridge over a mill stream. **2**

Across this bridge, ignore paths going left and straight ahead but follow the main track which bears right. Ignore a further footpath option going right off it.

The track passes under trees. Here, at a Y-junction, take the left option which bears left towards the A4440 – a wooden fence, and watercourse beyond, on the right. Reaching the road it passes under it via a high rounded concrete under-bridge, lined with metal

Powick Church

The church – not visited on this walk – is dedicated to St. Peter and St. Lawrence. Dating from the twelfth century, only the walls of the north and south transepts survive from this period. A new chancel, slightly at a skew to the rest of the building, was built in the thirteenth century while the church tower is fifteenth century in origin, as is the font. During the battle of Worcester the tower was used as an observation post by Parliamentarian gunners and marks made by musket balls are still visible on its walls.

Powick Power Station

The station was opened in 1894 by Worcester City Corporation who had bought the old Powick Mill for this purpose. It was the first commercial scale hydro-electric power station in the world and was operated using four water driven turbines backed up by three steam engines. Superseded by a larger generating station (situated on the bank of the Severn just upstream of Worcester Bridge, and itself now long gone), it closed in the 1950s and the building then became a laundry (the Metropole). This undertaking ceased in the 1970s and the site has now been restored as part of a housing development.

Powick Bridge

Powick Bridge carries the A449 Worcester to Malvern road. A single span structure of iron on sandstone it also has two flood arches – one on either side of the river – used by riverside tracks. It was built in 1837 to bypass the adjacent Powick Old Bridge. The span bears a coat of arms which includes (at the top) a beehive, a sailing ship and a horn of plenty (cornucopia) – presumably signifying the rewards of industry and commerce. At the bottom are what appear to be the coats of arms of Bewdley (left) and Kidderminster (right), although as to why these should be included here I have no idea and would welcome any suggestions! Interestingly, the original architect's plans show the span bearing the Worcester coat of arms. The architect was William Capper.

inside. Emerging from this bridge follow the right-hand boundary through the field so entered. A small patch of woodland beyond the boundary on the right conceals a pond.

Continue to follow the boundary to the far right-hand corner of the field. Here cross a stile over a five barred wooden fence to enter the next field. From the stile bear half-right across the corner of the field to reach two stiles with a concrete bridge over a small stream between them. Cross these into the next field which appears to have been an orchard in the past – with a scattering of trees remaining. Here go half-left – to maintain direction – up a slight slope, passing just to the right of the corner of an enclosure within the field/orchard which contains farm outbuildings. Approaching the far side of the field the path runs immediately alongside, and to the right of, the boundary fence to the aforementioned enclosure.

On reaching the far side of the field/orchard cross a stile, to the right of a metal farm gate, to emerge onto a quiet road in the small settlement of Upper Wick. Turn left along the road. At a road junction ignore a turning right (Upper Wick Lane) but continue straight ahead (Tan House Lane).

About 30 yards after the junction leave the road, right, along what is signed as a Public Footpath to Bransford. It leaves the road just after a green corrugated metal farm outbuilding, on the right, is passed. Initially metalled, within a few yards it becomes a stony track which almost immediately bends to the left and is joined by another track from the right.

Follow the obvious wide, stony track across a large field, eventually passing around a barrier across it to continue along it through the next field. The

The Battle of Powick Bridge

Powick Old Bridge was the setting for the first skirmish of the English Civil War (which technically began with the raising of the royal standard at Nottingham on August 22nd 1642) – the battle of Powick Bridge, on September 23rd 1642. A Royalist force, under Prince Rupert, blundered into a Parliamentarian contingent of about the same size, under Colonel John Brown, and in the ensuing confusion the Royalists mounted a successful cavalry charge which routed their enemies.

A memorial stone, erected in September 1992 – across the river at the far end of the bridge – records both this event and the later battle of Worcester, when the bridge was one of the crossing points used by the Parliamentarian force under Charles Fleetwood in its advance against the Scots to the north of the river – see note on battle of Worcester above.

Powick Old Bridge

The bridge dates from the fifteenth century and is built of red sandstone. It consists of five arches in total. The first two of these (in the direction of this walk) carry it over the waters of the mill race and Laughern Brook, which enters the Teme here. The remaining three arches cross the main river. A record of 1336 records an earlier bridge across the river hereabouts.

There was formerly a small quay adjacent to the bridge – technically the head of navigation, although with the co-operation of the various mills upstream of here it would be possible for vessels of a limited draught to make headway further upriver. The bells for Shelsley Beauchamp church were transported this way in 1790 (see note at Stage 2).

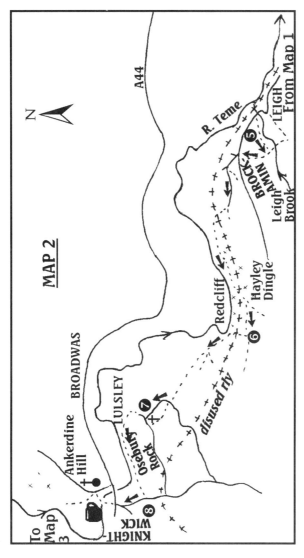

track maintains a steady westwards direction.

At the end of the field the track suddenly narrows to footpath width and becomes much less distinct on the ground. It bears slightly right to enter a more enclosed area, with an orchard on the right and a field beyond a hedgerow on the left. Follow the narrow path to reach a stile which gives access to railway lines (Worcester to Malvern and Hereford). Cross the lines, with care, and another stile.

Over the stile from the railway, ignore another stile – immediately on the right – but instead turn left along a narrow path which initially runs alongside the railway lines (which are now on the left). ❸

Some plum trees growing wild hereabouts were in fruit as of early August and were sampled, and the fruits found to be delicious.

Follow the narrow path, which becomes indistinct and wet underfoot in parts, to reach the bank of the River Teme. The railway crosses the river just to the left.

Bear right to follow the riverside path, the river on the left. The path may be overgrown and indistinct in late summer but is kept passable by anglers along this stretch of river. (Explorer Map 204 shows the path leaving the riverbank to cut off a bend in the river at one point but on all my visits to this stretch the adjacent fields have been under crops with no sign of the path passing through them. The actual riverbank path has always been passable however.)

Crossing a stile and a small footbridge, over a seasonal watercourse, continue along the path. The river bends to the left – the aforementioned point where the Explorer map shows the path leaving it.

Continue to follow the path, eventually reaching a makeshift stile – made out of pallets and a convenient large willow tree at the waters edge. Cross this to enter another field and continue to follow the riverside path through this to emerge over a stile, to the left of a metal farm gate, onto the busy A4103 road. Turn left along this to reach Bransford Bridge.

A few yards along the road to the left is a lay-by where there is often a mobile café cum 'burger-bar' parked.

There was a bridge across the river at Bransford in 1338, built by Wulstan de Bransford – who was born locally and became Bishop of Worcester in that year. Old maps show a wooden bridge here in the seventeenth century and one is re-corded as being destroyed by the Scottish army in 1651, prior to the battle of Worcester. A three arched brick bridge was replaced by the present uninspiring

The Bromyard Railway

The disused railway, crossed several times on this stage of the walk, was the line from Worcester to Bromyard and thence to Leominster, which left the extant Worcester to Hereford line at Bransford Road Junction.

This was a classic case of a rural branch line, planned during the years of 'Railway Mania', which never fulfilled the expectations of its supporters. It was constructed by three different companies. In 1861 the Worcester, Bromyard and Leominster Railway was incorporated to construct a through line from Bransford Road, on the Worcester & Hereford Railway (later the West Midland Railway), to Leominster, on the Shrewsbury & Hereford Railway. It was given five years to complete the line.

The company was plagued by financial hardship and by 1869 – after two time extensions – the route had only been built from Bransford as far as Yearsett, some three miles short of Bromyard. The company then applied to abandon the planned Bromyard to Leominster section and obtained a new act enabling them to complete the line to Bromyard. The line was not fully open to Bromyard until 1877.

Disillusioned by the lack of progress at the Leominster end of the route a separate company – the Leominster & Bromyard Railway – was formed in 1874 with the aim of building a line between those two towns. This company had its own financial struggles and could only finish four miles of the line from Leominster, as far as Steens Bridge, by 1884.

In 1888 both companies were absorbed into the Great Western Railway's empire and that company then set about completing the missing link, between Steens Bridge and Bromyard. The through route was finally opened in 1897, its 23¾ miles having taken 36 years to build.

The line was never more than of local importance. It was closed in the same piecemeal fashion as it opened, the section from Leominster to Bromyard in 1952 and the Bromyard to Bransford Road Junction length in 1964, a Beeching casualty.

Both steps and stiles hereabouts look as if they may have been made from old railway sleepers.

single span concrete structure in 1936 – the pier bases of the old bridge may be seen just upstream of the present bridge.

 Very limited bus service 421, to Worcester in the one direction and to Leigh and Knightwick in the other, runs along the A4103 here.

Just beyond the bridge, on the left, is the Fox Inn.

Ignore a footpath going right off the road and along the riverbank just before the abutments of the bridge but instead cross the bridge and then the road to take a path which also goes off to the right, and again riverside, at the far end of the structure. The path drops down a couple of steps from the bridge abutments into a field. Follow the riverside path, the river on the right. **4**

The narrow path along the river is bounded by a wire fence on the left, the field beyond. Over a stile, the path leaves the fence behind and emerges into an open field – a low bank over to the left concealing a small reservoir. Continue to follow the riverbank.

Indian Balsam of all shades from deep 'sunset' pink to white along this section, one August. A short, idyllic section of riverside walking now commences.

River and path make enormous bends, first left and then right – a section with the path running along the very top of the riverbank. Rounding the second of these two bends, the raised banks of the reservoir are much closer at hand on the left.

On reaching the end of the open field section of riverbank, cross a stile and bear slightly left up some wooden steps with handrail. At the top of these bear right to follow a path alongside the boundary fence – on the left – to what appears to be part of a plant nursery, with various ornamental shrubs planted in rows. To the right of the path is woodland with the river beyond and below that.

At the end of this section the path bears left to reach a stile. Cross this and descend a flight of wooden steps with handrail to reach duckboards across a disused railway track bed (Bromyard line), here in a cutting. At the far side of this climb up a longer flight of wooden steps, again provided with a handrail, to cross a stile at the top into a field.

Emerging into the field follow the boundary on the right, a large pond over to the left which seems to have been a fairly recent creation. (At the time of writing there had also been a recent attempt to plant saplings along the path so it may be that walkers in years to come may find themselves confined on a narrow path by trees.)

Follow the boundary to the corner of the field. Here cross a stile into what appears to have been an orchard in the past. Here again follow the boundary on the right, the path soon confined between this and another boundary on the left. Woodland continues beyond the boundary on the right. Crossing another stile the path passes beneath trees, entering a more overgrown area and bearing slightly to the left. Emerging from the trees cross another stile into a field. Here bear left to follow its boundary hedge to the near corner where a stile gives access onto a road. Turn right along the road.

Due left from the first section of road the Malvern Hills make their first appearance for some time. Directly ahead in the distance is Ankerdine Hill, just beyond and below which lies the stage destination of Knightwick.

Leigh

Leigh (pronounced 'Lie') is first mentioned in three tenth century charters. One of these, dated AD972, concerns the grant of land hereabouts to Pershore Abbey. The name of the settlement here has been variously spelled as Leah, Leyghe, Lega and Ley and is derived from the Saxon word meaning a 'woodland clearing' or 'glade'.

The parish was well established by the time of Domesday Book (1086) probably because of its abovementioned connection with Pershore Abbey, the Benedictine monks of which would have cleared the forest and cultivated the land.

Its church is dedicated to St. Edburga, a Saxon princess – the granddaughter of King Alfred the Great and daughter of Edward the Elder (king of Wessex from AD900 to AD924) – who became an abbess at Winchester. There was a chapel dedicated to her at Pershore Abbey to which her remains were transferred in about AD972, having been purchased at a great price by an English nobleman named Egilwade. The unusual dedication of the church at Leigh followed from this and legend has it that some of Edburga's bones were buried under the building here at the same time. (Others are reputed to lie beneath St. Edburgha's church at Yardley, Birmingham.)

The church is Norman in origin, dating from around 1100, and built on the site of an earlier monastery, the main building of which probably lay in the grounds of the extant Leigh Court. The oldest surviving part of the current building is the nave and the western end of the chancel while the four bay arcade, separating nave from the south aisle of the church, dates from about 1180.

The thirteenth century saw the extension of the south aisle and of the chancel to the east while the church tower was added in about 1380. The extant timber entrance porch to the building dates from the fifteenth century and was probably moved to its present position, to the west of the tower, from an earlier doorway in the south wall of the building. Inside it is a stone basin supported by a carved stone gryphon, thought to have come from within the church

Inside the church, the bowl of the font dates from the twelfth century and features a carved chevron band and scallops. The font stem and base are more modern.

In the chancel, against the south wall, is the tomb of Edmond Colles, the first Lord of the Manor after the dissolution of the monasteries wrested control of Leigh from Pershore. He died in 1606 at the age of 76. His recumbent tomb effigy has what appears to be a dog at its feet – or is it a lion? Opposite, against the north wall of the chancel, is the tomb of his son, William Colles (died 1615) and wife Mary. Their effigies kneel under a painted canopy while below their feet their twelve children are also depicted kneeling in prayer.

Nearby is the tomb of Walter Devereux, Viscount Hereford, and his wife – the latter, wearing a gown and lace cap, beside her husband under an arch carved with flowers. On the wall above this tomb is a monument to their eldest son, Essex Devereux, who drowned in the Teme – see below.

The south aisle has some fifteenth century floor tiles (near the old south door of the church), and a carved wooden screen of the same period which was heavily restored in the nineteenth century. It is decorated with Tudor roses and separates the east end of the aisle –

the Lady Chapel – from the remainder of it.

The Lady Chapel itself contains what is perhaps the crowning glory of this ancient and interesting building, a carved stone figure of Christ which was formerly in a niche on the outside north wall of the nave. The life-size figure was removed from its outdoor position and restored under the auspices of the Victoria and Albert Museum, London, in 1970. It was then exhibited in London before being returned to its new position inside the church. The V&A dated the carving as being from about 1100 although the architectural historian Sir Niklaus (Nicholas) Pevsner disagreed, arguing that the carving is an effigy from a coffin lid and dates from about 1220. Whichever is correct the carved figure of Christ, hand raised in blessing, is an undisputed treasure.

The Nicholson organ, installed in 1997, came from the church of St Nicholas, Worcester – now a wine bar/club and possibly seen en route to the start of this walk. (See separate note.)

Leigh Court stands alongside the church. Most of the extant building dates from a major rebuilding by Sir Walter Devereux in the seventeenth century of what was the stable block of the previous manor house here, the existence of which can be traced at least as far back as the end of the twelfth century.

After the dissolution of the monasteries under Henry VIII the former Pershore monastery lands at Leigh were leased by William Colles. By 1590 they were in the ownership of his son Edmond (Edmund) Colles and on his death, in 1606, they passed to his son, another William. When he died, in 1615, he was succeeded by his son, another but more notorious Edmund who became so deep in debt that he

was forced to sell all his lands to Walter Devereux.

Many tales surround this unfortunate Edmund Colles. So badly in debt was he that he is said to have lain in wait for, and ambushed, a friend of his who was travelling to Leigh from Worcester with a large sum of money. The friend fought off his unrecognised assailant, striking him with his sword. On arriving home he found a severed hand still gripping his horse's bridle with, on one finger, the signet ring of his friend Colles. Another story tells of Colles murdering a man and bricking up his body in a cellar.

A local legend concerning Edmund Colles has his ghost driving a coach and four through Leigh, taking to the air over the tithe barn and disappearing into the River Teme. An apparition it might be well worth seeing!

Sir Walter Devereux, Viscount Hereford, became M.P. for Worcester in 1625. It was he who oversaw the rebuilding of Leigh Court to the state in which we see it today.

On 20th February 1639 tragedy struck the family when Sir Walter's elder son, Essex, and a friend – George Freke – were drowned in a boating accident on the Teme. A memorial to Essex Devereux is on the wall above the tomb of his parents, in the chancel of the church (see above), while a tablet above the font commemorates Freke.

The property passed, via marriage, to the Martin family of Cambridgeshire and in 1724 was purchased by James Cocks, M.P. for Ryegate. Several further changes of ownership later, in 1898, it came into the possession of the Gabb family – interestingly enough descended from the original owners, the Colles family.

In the grounds of the Court stands Leigh Tithe Barn. This, the largest cruck-built medieval tithe barn in England, dates from the end of the thirteenth century and was built by the Abbots of Pershore for storage of the parish tithes. Over 150 feet in length and 33 feet wide it rises to a height of 34 feet. Its roof, of red tiles, covers an acre and is supported by nine full cruck trusses and two half-hipped trusses at either end. There are two gabled wagon bays on the side facing the church, each of which contain two further cruck trusses.

The building is under the care of English Heritage (01604 730320) and is open to the public from 1st April to 30th September, 10am to 6pm, Thursday to Sunday.

It is currently home to a horse-drawn cider mill and press.

Tomb of William and Mary Colles, Leigh church

After about two-thirds of a mile the road reaches the name-sign for Leigh. It dips and makes a large bend to the left. On the right of the road at the bend are Leigh church, Leigh Court and a Tithe Barn.

Note the very attractive oast house conversion on the right, just past the bend in the road.

 Very limited bus service 421 to Knightwick in the one direction and to Bransford and Worcester in the other, runs through Leigh. Can be boarded outside the church.

Medieval stone carving of Christ, Leigh church

Remain on the road through Leigh, ignoring a footpath going off to the left on the first bend. After this first right-angled bend left, the road then bends right. Ignore two footpaths which leave it, left, here.

The road bears slightly to the left and then makes another more significant bend right. Ignore yet another footpath going left here.

The road next makes a pronounced bend left to reach a substantial bridge over Leigh Brook, en route to its nearby confluence with the Teme.

Immediately after crossing the bridge leave the road, left, for a public footpath which runs up the main drive to a dwelling called The Barn (SO781535). **5**

Walk up the drive and pass to the immediate right of the house. Continue straight ahead to reach a stile in the top right corner of the grassy area behind. Cross this and continue straight ahead through a paddock area, a wooden fence immediately on the right and a metalled drive, to another dwelling, beyond that.

Where the wooden fence (right) is replaced by the wall of the aforementioned dwelling keep straight on alongside it (the dwelling on the right), to reach a stile in the top right-hand corner of the paddock. Cross this into a field.

View of the Malvern Hills half-left on entering the field – from a somewhat different angle to previous views obtained on this stage of the walk. Here one sees the north of the range only, with North Hill hiding most of the remainder of the chain. By the time the next field is entered the view is superb.

Follow the right boundary hedge through the field, a slight climb at first which becomes more noticeable as progress is made. There is a significant drop away to the land on the left.

View back to Leigh church over the left-hand shoulder.

Cross a stile into the next field, continuing to follow the right-hand boundary hedge.

About 30 yards before reaching the next stile look right, on a good day, for distant views of two large wooded hills. These are Woodbury Hill (left) and Abberley Hill (right) which will be seen at much closer quarters towards the end of Stage 2 of the walk. Well to the left of these can be seen Ankerdine Hill.

Reaching another stile cross it into the next field, this time following the left boundary to reach a stile at the far side. (This field may be subdivided into two by an electric fence but a crossing point is provided if this is the case.)

More good views to the right of Abberley and Woodbury Hills. There is woodland (mainly ash trees) in the dip beyond the left-hand boundary in both this field and the next.

Crossing the stile, continue to follow the left-hand boundary through the next field to reach its far left-hand corner. Here cross a stile to emerge onto a dirt track and turn right along this. The track is bordered by hedgerows on both sides. After an initial slight rise it begins to descend gently. Ignore two farm gates leading off it, right, but remain on the track which then swings left and climbs slightly. At a Y-junction in it go right, although both arms reach a quiet road in a matter of yards. Turn right along the road, through the small settlement of Brockamin.

At the first road junction go left – indicated as a No Through Road and signed as Dingle Road. Almost immediately, at a Y-junction, go left – passing to the left of a house called Brockton, a picture of two badgers on its nameplate. Ignore a minor road going off to the right – may be roughly marked as leading to Riverlands – and a footpath going left about 50 yards afterwards but remain on the quiet road which meanders along passing isolated dwellings.

One of the isolated dwellings passed, on the left of the road, is called The Sett. The Sett, Brockton and the name of the settlement itself – Brockamin – would seem to have badger connections. Is this a particular badger stronghold?

Continue on the road. About half-a-mile after the start of the road (at the junction signed Dingle Road), and just after passing some farm buildings, right – Little Brockamin Farm – it loses its metalled surface at a Y-junction (SO767535). Here take the right track ahead – the left is marked 'Private. No Through Road'. Follow the obvious wide stony track.

A short distance along the track a settlement will be see in the distance ahead, on the other side of the river valley. This is Broadwas, on the busy A44 road. An ancient settlement, in AD786 it was given to the church at Worcester by King Offa (of Dyke fame!) and remained under ecclesiastical control until 1776. Its church – dedicated to St. Mary Magdalene – stands beside the river, along a quiet lane from the village, and dates from about 1200.

The track descends to pass under a red-brick bridge – the second crossing of the disused Bromyard railway line on this stage of the walk. Beyond this it bends sharply left and then eases right.

The track continues to undulate and meander along, finally dropping to skirt the edge of the wooded Hayley Dingle. It passes between two large wooden gateposts (no gate), crosses a small stream (culverted) and swings left then right and begins to climb through woodland. Passing between the red-brick abutments of a former railway overbridge – actually a short viaduct, and the third crossing of the disused Bromyard line – it swings right. Here ignore a footpath going left ahead but remain on the main track (SO761543).

The railway to Bromyard crossed Hayley Dingle via a brick viaduct of six arches, 107 yards long and up to 70 feet in height.

Almost immediately the track leaves the woodland into a large open field, still a very gradual climb underfoot. Follow the now more grassy track through the field, a boundary hedge to the right. A level section commences.

Half-left ahead are the Suckley Hills. Further to the left are the Malvern Hills, the first view of these for some time.

Nearing the far side of the field the track passes through the boundary hedge (right) but continues to run alongside it. On reaching the far side of the field DO NOT pass out of it through the metal farm gate ahead – beyond which a track is signed as a Bridleway – but instead bear 90 degrees right to follow the boundary (now on the left as it is walked) within the field – signed as a Public Road. ❻

Walking along the boundary, look half-left ahead – into an adjacent field – to see the low grassy embankment of the disused railway line.

On reaching the corner of the field pass through a wooden farm gate and go straight ahead to cross a bridge over the disused railway track – the fourth and final crossing of it. Over the railway the track bends right and then immediately sharp left. Ignore paths going off into the woods to the right at this point.

Divert a few steps along the paths into the woods on the right here and look down through the trees, left, for a glimpse of the River Teme which is here about to pass below what is marked on Explorer Map 204 as Red Cliff.

The track descends through woodland, typical railway boundary fences on its immediate left. It continues to descend and narrows, with a more stony surface. It now runs nearer the edge of the woodland (left) with a large field – often under hops – to the right. Soon it levels out.

At a Y-junction of sorts – where the path widens to track width – keep right on the main track, the field immediately on the right of it, ignoring the left arm where two footpaths depart (SO752546).

The track is now only separated from the field on its right by an incomplete hedge and tree boundary. There is still woodland to the left of it. After having a mainly dirt surface – which can cause it to be very muddy after wet weather – it now becomes stonier again. It passes between two large wooden gateposts (no gate), the left-hand of which was definitely a railway sleeper in a former life – the holes where the rails were attached being clearly visible. A short 'tunnel-like' section of overhanging trees is followed by a more open section, the track meandering along.

The track finally rises to a T-junction with a quiet narrow road (SO748554). Turn right along this.

Distant view of the spire of Broadwas church, right.

The road bends left, passes the interesting buildings of Upper Court (left) and climbs – slightly sunken – to a road junction. ❼

Here turn right, onto a quiet road/metalled track which passes through metal gates (may be open). Ignore a turning off it to the left, into a farm, but continue along it.

The farm is named 'Cold Place' – not a comment on temperatures hereabouts but a reference to the Colles family, its former owners, previously encountered on this stage of the walk at Leigh Court.

The road/metalled track bends left, between high hedges containing several horse-chestnut trees (almost an avenue of sorts). It approaches the half-timbered Lulsley Court. Nearing this, bear left at a Y-junction – the right arm leads to the house – the metalled surface underfoot now replaced by a gravel one. The resulting track approaches some outbuildings recently (2002) coverted to dwellings.

The privately owned Lulsley Court is an attractive half-timbered building with large chimneys. It dates from the sixteenth century.

At another Y-Junction again go left – the right arm leading into the forecourt of the aforementioned outbuildings. Continue along the gravel section until reaching a wooden farm gate – the converted outbuildings/dwellings alongside on the right. Here leave the gravelled track, left, through a small wooden gate.

Through the gate, follow a wooden fence (right) along – passing through/over one or possibly two facing paddock boundary fences – to eventually enter a field. (Note: At the time of publication the route through Lulsley Court was affected by the conversion of its outbuildings to dwellings. An official diversion of the Right of Way was pending and the description of the route to the field, above, reflects this. The walker may find minor changes, on the ground.)

Bear half-right across the field to a corner where there appears to be a gap in the boundary hedges. Here cross a stile, to the left of a metal farm gate, into the adjacent field. Follow the left-hand (top) boundary through this field. The path runs along a grassy ridge, the field to the right sloping down to the bank of the River Teme below.

Ankerdine Hill is to the right across the river.

Continue to follow the boundary through the field, at one point passing below some springs which can make the going wet underfoot. The field narrows towards the far side, increasingly hemmed in between the river and the mass of Osebury Rock, ahead left.

At the far end of the field cross a stile (to the right of a metal farm gate) to walk along a narrow path ahead between the Teme, now immediately on the right, and the wooded slopes of Osebury Rock.

Osebury Rock, called Rosebury until the early twentieth century when the 'R' was dropped, is a large wooded rocky outcrop which forces the Teme to make an enormous bend – confined between the Rock and neighbouring Ankerdine Hill in what is known as the Knightsford Gap. Unfortunately for the

Knightwick

Knightwick is more properly the settlement to the south of the Teme, the detached part to the north of the river perhaps being more correctly termed Knightsford Bridge. An old settlement, there are records of it being given to the monks of Worcester by King Edgar in AD964.

Fifteenth century accounts speak of a wooden bridge across the Teme hereabouts, probably near where the Talbot Hotel stands. The age of the hotel itself is difficult to guess. Re-fronted with brick in the eighteenth century parts of the building date back certainly to the sixteenth century, possibly the fourteenth. There was formerly another public house on the other side of the river bridge – the Flying Horse – but this is now a private dwelling.

By the late 1950s the old bridge over the river by the Talbot had become very weak – the locals tell horror stories of buses arriving at one side having to unload their passengers who then walked across the bridge to be followed, gingerly, by the vehicle! It was replaced by the new Knightsford Bridge just downstream, with the A44 realigned accordingly. The old road crossing was then converted into the footbridge seen today. This seems to have done the Talbot no harm at all as it now finds itself on a quiet backwater of a road instead of on a noisy racetrack, but still able to meet the needs of modern travellers.

The establishment brews its own beers – Teme Valley Brewery – and uses much locally grown produce in the meals on offer.

Note the old stone cider press in the garden/car-park of the hotel.

Just along the road from the Talbot (B4197) is the church of St. Mary. It was built in 1855-6 at a cost of £200. Note the stone marking the height reached by the Teme floodwaters here on 14th May 1886 – set in the wall of the entrance porch, just above the step.

peace and tranquillity hereabouts, the gap is also used by the busy A44 Worcester to Bromyard/Leominster road. Osebury is designated a site of special scientific interest. Its lower slopes are covered with masses of white ramson flowers in season, making the very air smell of onions!

The path emerges from the wooded area below Osebury Rock over a stile (situated to the right of metal farm gate) into a field. Here bear half-left, away from the river, following but not actually alongside the boundary with the woodland on the left, and heading towards a stile in the right-hand boundary of the field – situated to the left of a metal farm gate.

Cross the stile onto a road and turn right along this – now on the route of the Worcestershire Way. **8**

Views, right, of Osebury Rock and, half-right, of Ankerdine Hill from the road.

Follow the road to where it makes a T-junction with another. Here turn right to reach, within a few yards, another T-junction – this time with the busy A44 Worcester to Leominster road.

The modern Knightsford Bridge, opened in 1958, is just along the A44 to the right.

Reaching the A44, there is a good view of Osebury Rock to be had, right. Its summit now bears a mobile phone mast.

Go straight across the road – with care – and pass to the immediate right of a bus shelter opposite, past a Worcestershire Way signpost. Here bear right along a stretch of superseded main road – signed Worcestershire Way North.

The old road leads, past a Surgery on the left, to a footbridge over the Teme – formerly the old road bridge. Over the bridge, along a further short section of road, is the Talbot Hotel where this stage of the walk ends.

Old stone cider press outside the Talbot, Knightswick

Knightwick to Great Witley

Mileage: 10 Miles
(From Knightwick: 3 miles to Berrow Green; 5 miles to Ham Bridge; 6½
miles to Shelsley Beauchamp)
O.S.Maps: 1:50000 (Landranger): 150 (Worcester & the Malverns);
138(Kidderminster & Wyre Forest)
1:25000 (Explorer): 204 (Worcester & Droitwich Spa)

*The route leaves Knightwick via low-level tracks but soon climbs,
through woodland, onto the neighbouring ridge and a viewpoint at
Collins Green. A quiet road and fieldpaths lead to the settlement of
Berrow Green before farm tracks take the walker back down to the
Teme at the delightful Kingswood Nature Reserve. A short riverside
walk, through fields, leads from here to Ham Bridge and the halfway
point on the stage.*

*From the bridge the route uses low level, part riverside, fieldpaths
and tracks to reach Shelsley Beauchamp church. The main climb of
the stage then begins – first up a quiet road and ancient sunken path to
reach Camp Lane and then, after a short road section, over Walsgrove
Hill on woodland paths. Descending from the hill the route drops
down through the grounds of Abberley Hall School to reach Great
Witley.*

A short diversion to Abberley Clock Tower is included.

Starting outside the Talbot Hotel, facing its car park/garden, turn left and
walk to the corner of the building. Here turn left, off the road, onto a
metalled track indicated as a Public Footpath.

*The rear of the Talbot, as seen from the track, gives a better idea of the true
age of the building than does its frontage (see note at end of Stage 1).*

Over to the right is the mass of Ankerdine Hill.

Follow the track to reach a group of farm buildings – Ankerdine Farm –
where the metalled surface underfoot ends. Ignore two tracks going left – one
into fields the other to the main farm buildings – but bear very slightly right
ahead to pass between outbuildings. Beyond the farm buildings the track, stony
underfoot, bears right and the Teme now comes alongside on the left. The way
soon passes beneath trees in a short wooded section.

Remain on the obvious track which, as the river bends away left again,
reaches a metal farm gate. Cross a stile to the right of the gate and continue
along the track, now in open fields again and on a long straight section. In the
distance, directly ahead, another group of farm buildings will be seen –
Horsham Farm.

The track passes through a wooden farm gate (may be open) with a stile to
its right. Still forging straight ahead it reaches a further farm gate, again a stile
alongside to the right.

A fine half-timbered house some distance to the right of the track here was, sadly, in a ruinous state at the time of writing.

Beyond the gate the very straight section of track ends as it bends left to approach the buildings of Horsham Farm.

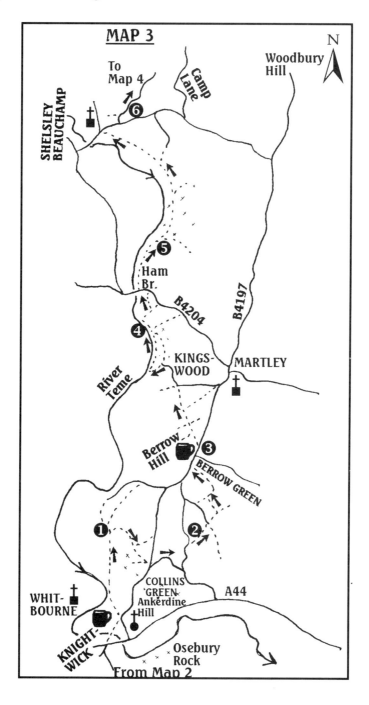

Whitbourne

A moated site adjacent to the church here was where the Bishops of Hereford had their summer palace. Whitbourne is not mentioned in *Domesday Book* (1086) but a letter from Gilbert Foliot, Bishop of Hereford, dated 1163 survives and concerns a dispute between two priests, each of whom claimed the living of Whitbourne as his own.

The nave of the extant church, dedicated to St. John the Baptist and dating from 1180, is very large for size of the local settlement – as befits a place of worship with a bishop often in residence nearby.

Buried in the church is Bishop Francis Godwin, Bishop of Hereford from 1617 until his death here in 1633. Ironically Godwin is best remembered for his novel 'The Man in the Moon' which was published in 1638, after his death, and is often claimed to be the world's first science fiction story. In it Godwin tells of a man who trains four swans to tow him, in a wicker basket, to the moon.

On reaching a point just before the first of the farm buildings (the farm house itself) on the right, and a pole carrying overhead wires, on the left, leave the main track – sharp right – onto a grassy track which climbs alongside the farmhouse boundary hedge (which is now on the left) following the poles carrying the overhead wires (SO735576). It is signed as a Public Footpath. ❶

This is the start of a climb up onto the ridge which ends above Knightsford Gap with Ankerdine Hill.

Passing the first pole, the grassy track reaches a wooden farm gate with a stile alongside to its right. Cross this and continue on the track which itself still follows the poles.

As the track bends left look behind, across the river, for a distant view of the church tower at Whitbourne.

The track bends left. Just beyond a double pole it reaches a metal farm gate, again with a stile on its right. Beyond this it continues to climb, with an old orchard area (mainly damson trees) to its right. Slightly 'sunken' in parts and still following the overhead wires, the track reaches a wooden farm gate, yet again a stile on the right. Over this climb straight ahead, the track now less distinct, following the NEARER of two overhead lines (on the left). Bear half-right, with the indistinct track, to pass just to the right of two poles in succession to enter woodland.

Good views behind across the Teme valley during the final climb to the woods. The woodland is known as Hay Wood.

Once among the trees the track becomes more distinct again. Remain on it – still with the overhead wires, their poles on the left – as it quickly reaches more open terrain, the main area of woodland to its right. Skirting the woodland the track approaches the small settlement of Collins Green. A dwelling appears up to the left and the now much narrower track reaches a wooden farm gate with a stile alongside it on the right.

Cross the stile to reach another track at a T-junction. Turn left up this, passing another dwelling – Laurel Cottage – which is on the right. Just beyond this the track emerges onto the B4197 at Collins Green.

Go straight across the road and down a narrow grassy path between two dwellings opposite to reach, within a few yards, a quiet road (SO740573).

Pause here, on a clear day, to take in the stunning view across the lower Teme and the Severn valleys which is suddenly revealed. It extends to the Cotswold Hills and includes the route of Stage 1 of this walk.

The Malvern Hills are half-right while, on a very clear day, Worcester Cathedral and the city may be visible slightly to the left ahead. Again visible on a good day, the long hill mass straight ahead in the distance is Bredon Hill, an outlier of the Cotswolds which lie beyond it.

The route is at a height of about 130 metres/426 feet hereabouts, having climbed from a starting height of 35 metres/115 feet at Horsham Farm.

Turn left down the narrow road.

Good views of the Malvern Hills on the right, with more of the chain appearing.

The road descends and bends right. Ignore a footpath going off left at the apex of this long bend – just opposite a property called the Gatehouse. Passing Easinghope Farm (on the left) the road starts to bend left and reaches a junction.

Further superb views of the Malverns over to the right, approaching the road junction. A marker post, on the small grass triangle at the junction itself, informs the walker that this is the route of the Worcestershire Way.

Turn left at the road junction. The road descends and bends first left and then right. After about 200 yards on the road leave it, right, over a stile into a field – as shown by the Worcestershire Way signs. ❷

Over the stile and pausing for a drink, one August morning, I was accosted by two enormous Great Dane dogs whose owner only appeared some five minutes afterwards. Fortunately the pair were as friendly as they were large but even in their welcome posed something of a threat – with water bottle and sack scattered far and wide!

Good views of the Malverns, over to the right, while crossing this field.

In the field, bear half-left over its highest point, following the poles for overhead lines but keeping well to the left of them. Reaching a wire boundary fence, cross a stile into the next field and continue straight ahead through it. On reaching the far side of this field cross a stile – to the left of a farm gate – to emerge onto a quiet, narrow road.

Go straight across the road and over a stile into another field. Here follow the right boundary hedge to its bottom right-hand corner.

The prominent hill seen on the left from this part of the field is Berrow Hill.

Look right just before reaching the bottom corner of the field to see an old metal 'Climax' wind pump in the adjacent field. Made at a factory in Worcester these pumps were exported all over the world.

On reaching the corner of the field follow the boundary hedge around to the left to walk along its bottom boundary. Do NOT pass through the metal farm gate just after the corner despite the fact that it bears more than one footpath sign.

Continue along the field boundary to reach a wooden footpath gate through a boundary fence ahead.

At the time of writing the route of the Worcestershire Way through this and the subsequent fields had recently been provided with new wooden footpath gates with a clever top-lever opening mechanism. It will be interesting to see how these wear, although they certainly get my vote!

Through the gate, continue to follow the boundary (right) through the next field for about 30 yards and then turn right to pass through that boundary via another footpath gate. In the new field follow the right-hand boundary.

Berrow Hill is now half-left ahead.

Follow the boundary across the field until almost at the corner and then turn right to pass through the hedge via another footpath gate. Through this, turn left and follow the boundary hedge (left) to the corner of the field so entered. Here pass through another footpath gate, the top of an old railway truck adjacent on the left.

Through the gate walk straight ahead along a short length of grassy track to reach the B4197 road. Turn right along the road, remaining on its right-hand side.

The road passes through the settlement of Berrow Green.

There is a telephone box on the left of the road, just beyond the turning for Broadwas and Broadheath, and just beyond this a public house – the Admiral Rodney.

At a road junction ignore a turning right, signposted 'Broadwas 3, Broadheath 4', but continue on the B road. Ignore a footpath which leaves the road, right. The road begins to bear right and starts to descend gently. It passes Tuckers Hill Farm House (right).

Just as the road is about to descend more steeply, alongside a barn on the right of it, cross it and leave it, left, for a footpath which initially uses the entrance drive to a property called Tabwell. Worcestershire Way signs point the way (SO749586). ❸

After about 25 yards leave the tarmac drive, right, and bear left – around a tree – and over a stile into a field, the garden of another dwelling on the right. From the stile head straight down the field, aiming towards a post carrying overhead wires.

Entering the field, the views ahead open up. Ahead in the distance the high wooded hill is Woodbury Hill. Two lower hills will be seen in the foreground. These are Pudford Hill, left, and Penny Hill, right.

Pass to the left of the post to reach a stile in the facing boundary. Cross this and continue straight ahead to reach another stile, just to the right of a wooden farm gate in the boundary ahead. Cross this stile to reach a metalled track and go straight ahead, from the stile, along this.

Crossing the stile onto the metalled track look left for a good view of Berrow Hill which, it can now be seen, bears a beacon. The hill rises to a height of 183 metres/600 feet and also has an Iron Age hill fort on its summit. There is no Public Footpath up it.

The metalled track is initially straight. As it bends slightly left leave it – dropping off it on its right to walk along the field edge there, soon separated from the metalled track by a boundary hedge (left). A Worcestershire Way marker post indicates the point where the track is first vacated.

Follow the edge of the field to reach another metalled track running left to right ahead – which the original track to the left has itself just reached at a T-junction. Turn left along this track for a few yards to round the corner of a property called Tarragon and then, by a large pole at the entrance to that property, bear right off the metalled track into a field. Here follow the boundary hedge – which should be on the RIGHT – along a grassy track.

On reaching the far corner of the field go straight ahead through a gap in the boundary hedge, ignoring a footpath going right at the same point. Head straight across the next field.

Look over the left shoulder behind for probably the most impressive view yet of Berrow Hill. Over to the right the tower of Marley church should be visible.

On reaching a 'crossroads', with a metalled track going left – 'White Cottage, Private Road' – and a minor road to the right and straight ahead (SO747596) go straight ahead up the quiet, narrow road.

Within a few yards the road bends first sharp right and then sharp left before straightening and climbing steadily. It soon reaches the top of its climb and begins to descend, bearing slightly left.

Note the old stone cider press – similar to the one outside the Talbot at Knightwick (Stage 1) – in the garden of Peak Cottage.

The road descends past a dwelling on the left – Peak Cottage – and then bends to the right. Look out for a sign announcing Kingswood Nature Reserve, on the left of the road about 45 yards after the bend. Here leave the road, left, through a wooden farm gate – signed as a Public Footpath (SO745598). (The Worcestershire Way continues for a few yards further along the road and then leaves it, right.)

Through the gate, walk down a dirt track which descends into the nature reserve, skirting woodland (below, right). Narrowing to path width as it goes, the way is initially confined between a hedgerow (left) and a wire fence (right), later between wire fences. It begins to bend right and finally makes a right-angled bend right, following a corner in the wire fence on that side. The reason for that bend is the presence of the River Teme which is now immediately alongside, on the left.

Follow the main riverside path through the nature reserve, ignoring minor paths which join and leave it. Beyond a section which has obviously been affected by land slips a rough seat has been provided.

Kingswood Nature Reserve is privately owned/run and is a delightful spot. Pause for a while at the seat provided, by what is usually a shallow fast flowing section of river with rapids and a gravel bar opposite – a wonderful place for lunch. I rarely stop here for very long without seeing at least one kingfisher. Deer tracks are also present but the animals remain elusive. I am told, however, that there are muntjac deer hereabouts.

Just beyond the roughly hewn wooden seat look out for the similarly makeshift carving of a man with an axe – a real guardian of the forest!

The riverbanks hereabouts – and all the way down to Knightwick and beyond for that matter – are prone to be undercut by the river. Land slips are quite common – as evidenced by the riverside path through the reserve.

Wooden carving in Kingswood Nature Reserve

From the seat, continue along the riverside path, ignoring another path joining sharply from the right – the route of the Worcestershire Way rejoining. The path finally reaches a wooden footbridge over a small side stream. Cross this to emerge out of the woodland (and Kingswood Nature Reserve) into an open field. **❹**

In the field, continue to follow the riverside path, bearing left with the river bank. The path crosses a seasonal side stream, via a primitive 'bridge' (planks) to reach a field boundary which is crossed via a stile.

Over the stile, continue to follow the riverside path through the next field until reaching a large notice board which proclaims that there is no right of way along the riverbank from this point. Here bear half-right across the field to its far boundary, farm outbuildings beyond this (Hambridge Farm).

On reaching the boundary bear left along it. (The Worcestershire Way goes through a gap in the boundary hedge straight ahead and is NOT taken.)

Follow the boundary along to the corner of the field. A gap through the boundary hedge here was blocked by a low wire fence at the time of writing but this could be easily stepped over. (The perpetrator of this footpath blockage had actually attached one end of the wire to the marker post showing the existence of the right of way!)

Into the next field, continue to follow the boundary hedge on the right. This bends around to the right to reach another field corner, a dwelling just beyond. On reaching this corner bear left to continue to follow the field boundary, the aforementioned dwelling and its garden now on the right, beyond that boundary. Continue to follow the boundary hedge until the garden of the dwelling is no longer beyond it. Look out for a flight of wooden steps leading up through the boundary on the right and climb these to reach a stile which gives access to the busy B4204 road, here between Martley and Clifton upon Teme (SO739609).

Turn left down the road, initially remaining on its left-hand side where there is a wider verge but crossing it as soon as it is safe to do so after a rough parking spot opposite, where it bends left. Remain on the road to reach Ham Bridge over the Teme. Do NOT cross the bridge but instead leave the road, right, just before its abutments to pass though a farm gate (may be open) into a field.

The present bridge here was built in 1842, the road having crossed the Teme at this point since 1769. Before then there was a crossing point about a mile down river, at Kingswood – first a ford and then later a bridge.

Were it not for the busy road the bridge would be an ideal place to spend some time gazing into the river. The riverbanks hereabouts are often busy with anglers and I once passed the time of day here watching an enormous fish, identified from its whisker-like mouth appendages as a barbel, under the bridge.

The structure is also popular with house martins which nest beneath its span.

 Limited bus services 310, 311, 312, 313 and 314 run along the B4204 at Ham Bridge. These run to Martley and Worcester in the one direction and to Clifton upon Teme in the other. The even more limited service 309 also passes this way, linking Martley with Worcester via Stanford Bridge (Stage 3 of the walk) and Shelsley Beauchamp.

Entering the field aim across it to cut off a shallow bend made by the river (left), almost reaching the water's edge by its far side. Here locate and cross a stile in the boundary, about 10 yards in from the riverbank. Cross a second stile – ahead across a short grassy break – into the next field.

Go straight ahead from the stile to eventually walk along the riverbank, following an obvious path through this long, narrow field. Approaching a line of willow trees, ahead, bear slightly right towards the right end of these (the right boundary of the field) where there is a footpath marker post. Continue past the willows, following the right boundary of the field to its far corner.

On reaching the field corner pass through a gap and walk up an obvious dirt track, bearing slightly right, to a point where it makes a sharp bend to the right, narrowing to path width (SO739621). Here, at the apex of the bend, go left over a makeshift wooden stile (simple bars) – situated to the right of an old metal farm gate – to enter woodland. **❺**

From the stile follow an obvious path which meanders through the woods, soon beginning a gradual descent – the river just below and to the left, through the trees. Ignore a path going off and up, right, but continue on the main path which meanders and undulates along, sometimes between low banks and larger trees. (A lower, parallel, path runs some yards to the left, along the riverbank. Do NOT venture onto this.)

On reaching a Y-junction, with a wet area beyond, go left – passing between two gateposts (no gate), and through the aforementioned boggy area. Keep to the left side of this to find the driest route underfoot.

The path emerges into the corner of a very large field.

Entering the field, views up the Teme valley open up ahead. Directly ahead in the middle distance is Shelsley Beauchamp church.

In the field, follow the right (top) boundary hedge – a slight climb.

Look directly left, across the river, to see a prominent grassy mound – the Motte of Homme Castle.

On reaching a metal farm gate through the right-hand boundary hedge pass through it – the buildings of Lower House Farm ahead and above. Through the gate turn left to follow the boundary hedge (left) along – the actual footpath running in a dip alongside that boundary, although this may be so overgrown as to necessitate climbing out of it and walking along its edge.

Ignore two metal farm gates through the boundary but continue to follow it along to the far left-hand corner of the field.

The River Teme is now right over at the far side of its valley, left.

On reaching the corner of the field pass through a metal farm gate onto a dirt track. Go straight ahead along this – orchards on the right and fields on the left – heading directly towards the tower of Shelsley Beauchamp church.

The rolling wooded hills and valleys to the left across the river have some wonderful names – such as Devil's Den and Hell Hole. The marked dip almost due left, as the church is neared, is Witchery Hole. Look behind for a good view of Lower House Farm (just passed), and the ridge of Rodge Hill above and beyond.

Follow the wide, obvious track to a T-junction with a road. The lychgate entrance to Shelsley Beauchamp churchyard is just opposite.

 A very limited bus service 309 (at the time of writing running once daily each way on Tuesdays and Fridays only) runs through Shelsley Beauchamp to Stanford Bridge (Stage 3), Shelsley Walsh and Martley in the one direction and to Martley and Worcester in the other.

Shelsley Beauchamp church

Shelsley Beauchamp

Only the red sandstone tower survives from the original fourteenth century church of All Saints, Shelsley Beauchamp. By the nineteenth century the remainder of the building was in such disrepair that a complete rebuilding was considered necessary and this was completed in 1847 at a cost of a little over £1500. The architect was James Cranston of Birmingham, whose very different secular work we shall see in Tenbury Wells.

Inside, the font is fourteenth century as are two crude oak chests in the nave.

In the churchyard is the base of an old preaching cross which was converted into a sundial in the sixteenth century. The pointer (gnomon) of this survives in the vestry.

Interestingly the six church bells, cast in 1790, were brought to Shelsley Beauchamp from Gloucester via the Rivers Severn and, perhaps more surprisingly, Teme. This could only have been done with the co-operation of all the millers downstream on the river as it has never been technically navigable above Powick Old Bridge.

Notice the old gravestones just inside the lychgate, on the right. The inscriptions on most have been rendered indecipherable by weathering over the passage of time but one bears the dates 1697 and 1705.

Shelsley Beauchamp takes its name from the Beauchamp family who owned land here in the twelfth century. There are actually three Shelsleys – Beauchamp, Walsh and Kings. Like Shelsley Beauchamp, Shelsley Walsh takes its name from local landowners; Shelsley Kings, however, is so called because it was part of the royal manor of Martley. The origin of the 'Shelsley' prefix is not so easy to identify but probably means the clearing of someone called Scyld or Sceldwa.

Fourteenth century oak chest in Shelsley Beauchamp church

Shelsley Walsh and Southstone Rock

Across the far side of the Teme Valley to Shelsley Beauchamp is the neighbouring settlement of Shelsley Walsh – about one mile distant by road. (Turn left on reaching the road from the track, cross the river via New Mill Bridge and then turn right onto the Stanford Bridge road. Its church is situated along an entrance drive, left, after about half a mile on this road.)

Best known for its hill climb – the world's oldest motoring event – it is well worth a detour to visit the little church of St. Andrew there, accessed up the drive to the adjacent Court House – the hill climb course on the other side of this.

Entering the nave of the church through the Norman doorway – the oak door and its lock are medieval – one is confronted by a small stained glass window high in the wall opposite, depicting St. Andrew. The stained glass was installed in 1860 but the window aperture dates from the twelfth century as does the remainder of the nave.

The chancel is thirteenth century in origin. It is separated from the nave by a superb fifteenth century oak screen – carved with vine leaf, fruit and tendrils – which also forms a side chapel on the south side of the building. Above the screen is a fifteenth century carved Rood beam which supports a Celtic cross, this latter dating from 1859 when restoration work was carried out on the building. The roof timbers are also particularly impressive.

In the chancel – near the screen – some fifteenth century tiles survive while, above, the plank ceiling is decorated with painted gold stars.

In a quiet corner of the chancel, to the left of the altar, is the wooden tomb chest of Sir Francis Walsh who died in 1596. Its panels bear the Walsh Coat of Arms. On the other side of the altar is a fourteenth century carved stone coffin cover, let into the floor.

The font dates from the early twelfth century and is of sandstone.

Discovered in the churchyard, it was restored to its rightful place in 1908. A metal fixture on the roof timbers above it was so mounted to enable the cover of a Victorian font – installed in 1859, during the restoration of the church – to be raised. This font, like most of the 1859 internal restoration, was later removed and broken up. The reason for this action is unknown. An enlargement of a contemporary print, which hangs on the west wall of the nave, shows what the church looked like before 1859 and the scale of the restoration work carried out.

The church is built of locally quarried travertine blocks (from Southstone Rock) – see note on Eastham church at Stage 3. (A footpath leading to Southstone Rock leaves the Stanford Bridge road – into a field, left – about a mile beyond the entrance drive to Shelsley Walsh church, the unusual large rock formation being situated in Rock Coppice at SO708639. As with Shelsley Walsh church a diversion well worth making!)

Shelsley Walsh takes its name from the Walsh family – a John Walshe being recorded as holding land here as early as 1211. The family lived at Court House, adjacent to the church, and it was from here, in November 1605, that Sir Richard Walsh (as High Sheriff of Worcester) rode out to supervise the capture of the Gunpowder Plotters – at Holbeach House, near Stourbridge, where they had fled from London after Guy Fawkes had been caught literally red-handed in a cellar underneath the Palace of Westminster.

The point where the track reaches the road by the church is, in fact, almost a 'staggered crossroads' with another road departing almost straight ahead from a junction in front of the lychgate (signposted 'Stanford 2, Great Witley 3'). To continue with the walk, however, turn right on reaching the road from the track (signposted 'Martley, Hillside 1½').

Walk up the road, passing the Rectory – on the left. Just before the next dwelling on the left turn left at a road junction – indicated as a No Through Road. ❻

Passing a semi-detached dwelling (right) within 100 yards this minor road makes a right-angled bend to the right. Ignore a metalled drive going left at the same point. After this the road meanders and undulates along, gradually making height through rolling countryside, before beginning to climb more steeply.

This is the start of the final, and main, climb of this Stage of the walk – initially up to Camp Lane and then over Walsgrove Hill. The starting height at Shelsley Beauchamp church is about 40 metres/131 feet while Camp Lane runs along at about 145 metres/475 feet. The summit of Walsgrove Hill is about 262 metres/860 feet in height.

At the end of a particularly steep section of road, on a bend and just before reaching an isolated dwelling called Leys (right) look left for a superb view up the Teme valley. On a clear day this extends as far as Titterstone Clee Hill. In the middle distance the church at Stanford on Teme is prominent on its hill.

Remain on the quiet, narrow road. It ends just to the right of a large weeping willow tree, around which the metalled drive of an isolated dwelling on a hillock to the left (Red Hill) goes left. Here bear very slightly right ahead to walk up a short section of track between two wire fences which gives access, via an old metal farm gate (likely to be open) onto a narrow sunken path. The narrow path climbs steeply, confined between tree-lined banks. Much used by horses, it can be very muddy. Follow it up to a T-junction with a quiet road, Camp Lane.

The steep, often muddy, path can be quite hard going – even for horses! On one occasion I found no less than three discarded horseshoes here.

The path is obviously of some age but I have been unable to discover its origins. It may have marked a boundary of some sort or was possibly a route used by the local population to reach Shelsley Beauchamp church. It may even be connected in some way with the Iron Age hill fort on nearby Woodbury Hill.

Towards the top of the narrow path look out for a substantial tree house, in a large tree on the left. Surely built by 'older children'!

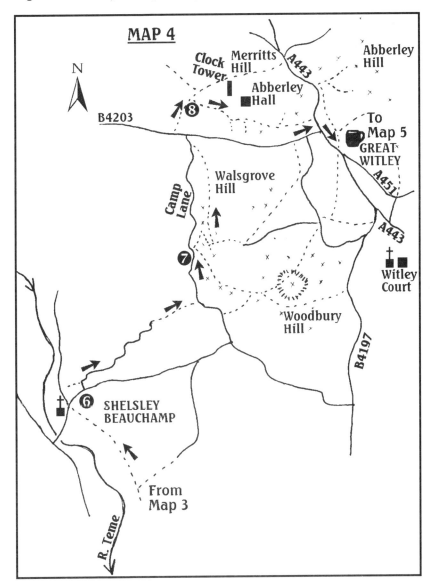

A good spot for buzzards hereabouts. If not seen during the climb up the narrow path and subsequent walk along Camp Lane then their cries will almost certainly be heard.

Emerging onto Camp Lane look left, through a gap in the hedgerow just on the left, to see the isolated dwelling on Red Hill and the Teme valley beyond. Look slightly to the left of Red Hill to see the settlement of Shelsley Walsh across the river, its church on the left.

Turn left along Camp Lane. The quiet road runs along at a high level above the Teme valley.

From the initial section on Camp Lane there are good views back down the Teme valley. Shelsley Walsh is also visible, across the river, opposite.

The road makes a pronounced bend right and climbs slightly. Levelling out it bends left.

Views now, on a clear day, half-left ahead up the Teme valley and as far as the Clee Hills in the distance. The large building seen in the foreground, overlooking the valley, is Hillside Farm. Beyond that, and just to the left of it, are the distant twin summits of Brown Clee Hill – Abdon Burf (540 metres/1772 feet), and Clee Burf (510 metres/1673 feet) – and to the left of that, and much more prominent, Titterstone Clee Hill (533 metres/1748 feet). Further still around to the left, in the middle distance, is Stanford on Teme church.

Continuing to bend left the road climbs slightly. Reaching the top of the climb it begins a gentle descent and bears right before climbing, more steeply this time, and bearing left once more. At the top of this climb it starts to bear right, passing the entrance to a dwelling on the right – Woodlands. Ignore a footpath going off sharp right up the drive of this – the Worcestershire Way's route.

Ignore also a track going left here – the drive to Hillside Farm.

Just past a garage to the dwelling on the right (1, Hillside Cottages), and about 20 yards beyond where the further of the two arms of the drive to Hillside Farm joins the road, left, leave the road – turning right onto a footpath which commences just to the right of a metal farm gate, as indicated by a Worcestershire Way marker post (SO741646). ❼

The path leaves the road with a wire fence to its left and the boundary of the garden of 1, Hillside Cottages on its right. Up a couple of steps, it enters woodland and swings left – beginning to climb.

Nice views of the Clee Hills in the distance, to the left through the trees, as the climb through the woods begins.

Follow the narrow but obvious path up through the woods. Reaching a Worcestershire Way marker post it bends sharply around to the right – almost back on itself – to continue its climb to the top of the ridge.

At the top, ignore a minor path going right just before reaching a stile over a fence, but instead cross the stile into a field and turn left. Walk about 30 yards along the fence to reach another stile over it and cross this, back into the edge of the woods.

While climbing over the stile into the field look right, on a clear day, for a good distant view of the Malvern Hills.

Before crossing the next stile, back into the woods, walk a few yards out into the field for superb views on a clear day. Far in the distance the two main summits of the Clent Hills may be seen – over 15 miles distant – while the settlement in the foreground is Great Witley, with the large Hundred House prominent towards the left. The large wooded hill mass behind the village is Abberley Hill, which rises to a height of 283 metres/928 feet. The large wooded hill over to the half-right is Woodbury Hill (276 metres/905 feet).

From the stile bear right to walk along a narrow ridge-top path towards the summit of Walsgrove Hill. The woodland initially obscures any views off the ridge either side.

Crossing a stile, the path emerges onto a more open section of hillside, although still with a high hedge boundary on the right.

Owain Glyn Dŵr and Woodbury Hill

Camp Lane takes its name from the nearby Iron Age hill fort at the summit of Woodbury Hill. In 1405, during the Wars of Welsh Independence under Owain Glyn Dŵr, this site was famously re-occupied by a combined Welsh and French force which had penetrated as far as Worcester before being confronted by the English under Henry IV.

The English force set up its own camp on the neighbouring Abberley Hill and the two armies were then involved in eight days of stalemate, with some light skirmishing, jousting and the capture of some English supply wagons the main highlights. After this the Welsh/French force retreated to Wales – this episode marking the the pinnacle of Glyn Dŵr's success in his ongoing struggle.

In truth both armies were probably too exhausted to engage in full battle, the French being additionally hampered by the fact that they had lost most of their horses during their sea crossing to Wales.

An interesting postscript to these events is that one of the French leaders, Jean de Hangest, was captured by the English and confined at Wichenford Court – just over three miles to the south-east of Woodbury Hill. Here he is supposed to have refused the amorous advances of the lady of the house, Lady Washbourne, who then murdered him. A brown stain on the floor of the house bears testament to this deed while de Hangest's ghost is said to walk Wichenford Court by night.

Other ghosts – those of French troops drowned in the river during the retreat from Woodbury Hill – reputedly haunt the Teme valley hereabouts.

Woodbury Hill Camp was again re-occupied some 78 years later, in 1483, by a force under the Duke of Buckingham who was in conflict with Richard III – the latter having just had, reputedly, the 'Princes in the Tower' murdered to secure his hold on the Crown.

Buckingham set out from the Welsh Marches, with his followers, intending to cross the Severn and then march on London. He arrived to find the river in flood and its main crossings – at Worcester, Gloucester and Bridgnorth – fortified against him. He set up camp on Woodbury only to find his supporters deserting the cause and leaving him no option but to flee. He was captured and later executed.

Superb views to the left and half-left ahead from the section just after the stile. On a clear day Titterstone Clee Hill is particularly prominent, half-left – about twelve miles distant. Further over to the left the hills of Mortimer Forest, above Ludlow, may be visible.

Looking up the Teme valley, in the direction of Titterstone Clee Hill, one or two of the settlements there are seen – such as Eardiston and Lindridge (with its tall church spire).

Over to the left, on a very good day it may be possible to see as far as Hay Bluff and the Black Mountains, over and beyond the low hills bordering the Teme valley.

Slightly further along the path a look back over the left shoulder should provide the first view of Shelsley Beauchamp since the climb from it began, although the church there is likely to be hidden by trees. Shelsley Walsh is also visible across the river from its neighbour. The very keen eyed may be able to make out the top of the spire of the church at Clifton upon Teme, over and beyond the top of the wooded hills across the river – look at a point between and above the two Shelsleys. Despite its name, Clifton is some distance away from and above the river. Its modern name is actually derived from the 'Cliston ultra Tamedam' (recorded in AD934), 'ultra' meaning 'beyond'.

Another stile takes the walker onto a more enclosed section with high bushes on both sides of the path, which continues to climb imperceptibly towards the summit. Approaching another stile, this one with a dog gate provided, the climb becomes more noticeable. Over this stile the path emerges onto the open top of the hill, the summit just ahead. Go straight ahead from the stile.

Walking out onto the open hilltop, one is immediately confronted – straight ahead – by a superb view of Abberley Clock Tower, with the adjacent Abberley Hall and school buildings just in front of and below it.

Walk straight ahead past a large ash tree to visit the very top of Walsgrove Hill.

The ash tree near the summit of Walsgrove Hill is a good place to pause and admire the views. To the right of the clock-tower is the long wooded mass of Abberley Hill while working left from it one sees the Clee Hills, Teme valley and the hills above Ludlow and those along the eastern edge of the Vale of Wigmore beyond – as far as Croft Ambrey. Further to the left Hay Bluff and the Black Mountains may be visible beyond the low rolling hills on the western side of the Teme valley.

Over to the left, a piercing whistle or a cloud of steam may reveal the presence of a miniature railway situated in a field, alongside one of a number of dwellings set above the Teme valley hereabouts. I first noticed it in operation on Boxing Day 2000.

From the very top of Walsgrove Hill look right for views which have been largely obscured by trees and bushes during the climb along the ridge to date. In the middle distance Witley Court may be seen, the tower and cupola of the adjacent church prominent – see under main note on Great Witley. It is about 1¾ miles distant.

Look further right for a view of the wooded Woodbury Hill and (further right again, in the distance) the Malvern Hills.

Abberley Clock Tower

Abberley Clock Tower dominates the views for miles around. Situated in the grounds of Abberley Hall, on top of Merritts Hill, at a height of 215 metres/705 feet, the building is itself some 49 metres/161 feet high.

Abberley Hall was built, on the site of an earlier residence, for John Lewis Moilliet, a banker of Birmingham and Geneva. In 1845 Moilliet died and, in the same year, the building was badly damaged by fire. Moilliet's widow, Amelia, supervised its rebuilding and lived at the hall until her own death in 1857, when she was succeeded by her son, James.

In 1867 the property was sold to Joseph Jones, a cotton magnate from Lancashire and when he died, in 1880, it passed to his cousin John Joseph Jones.

John Joseph Jones carried out improvements to the hall and its estate. These included adding a west wing and stables to the hall and building a system of waterworks and reservoirs on neighbouring Abberley Hill which can still be seen there to this day, although they are no longer used for domestic drinking water supply.

He seems to have been a man of strong opinions and a sense of self-importance. For example, he erected a flagpole on top of Abberley Hill from which he insisted a flag be flown whenever he was in residence at the hall.

It is probably against this background that his decision to build the clock tower on the top of Merritts Hill should be considered. Several theories exist as to why Jones had it built – the choices encompassing grief, love, greed and envy! One idea is that it was a memorial to his late cousin, from whom he had inherited Abberley Hall. Another is that it was a tribute to his wife, Sarah Amelia (Amy) – who used a room near the top of the tower for sewing, and who laid the foundation stone of the structure with her husband on 4th May 1883. Another suggestion is that it was built as a clock tower in order that none of his employees might have an excuse for arriving late for work. A final idea – which seems not unlikely given the man's character – is that it was built in response to the grandeur and wealth of his neighbour, the Earl of Dudley at nearby Witley Court, so that Jones could look down on him. Total construction costs were about £12,000.

Also known as 'Jones's Folly', the clock tower is a strange mixture of thirteenth and fourteenth century Gothic styles and resembles a large grandfather clock rising out of the ground. It used to contain a carillon of bells which played a selection of forty-two tunes as well as striking the hours and quarters.

Despite selling off the adjacent hall and grounds – in 1916, for use as a school – the Jones's retained ownership of the clock tower until 1939. In the summer of that year the carillon and sixteen of the tower's twenty-one bells were removed and sold to Taylor's of Loughborough for scrap.

Seen from the track below, the tower is most impressive. Note the chain strung across the platform under the clock face, presumably protection for anyone needing to work on it.

The tower bears four mosaic clock faces in total, one on each side, as well as a sundial. Also present, above its doorway, is the coat of arms of the Jones family.

There is an interesting postscript regarding John Joseph Jones which again bears out the character of the man. The parish boundary between Great Witley and neighbouring Abberley passes through the actual building of Abberley Hall. The story is that Jones was on bad terms with the vicar of Abberley over some matter and, on falling ill, elected to die in the part of the hall which lies in Great Witley parish so that his burial service could be conducted there!

To continue with the walk take a narrow path which goes off half-left, just before the ash tree, to contour its way down the hill – initially heading in the general direction of the clock tower.

Follow the narrow but obvious path down the hill, heading towards a large white house which will be seen alongside a road (B4203) below. Passing a Worcestershire Way marker post, part of the way down, the path bears slightly left towards a hedge boundary and a stile – which will be seen to the left of a metal farm gate in that boundary.

Cross the stile to rejoin Camp Lane. Turn right down this to reach a T-junction with the B4203, where the aforementioned white house stands. Turn left along the busy B road, crossing it as soon as it is safe to do so.

The white house, at the road junction, is a former toll house.

Walk up the B4203 to reach the large metal gates to Abberley Hall School – on the right. Leave the road here, turning right to pass through the smaller of the gates on that side. From the school entrance gates walk straight ahead along the obvious stony track, immediately passing a lodge/gate house (left). The grounds of the school lie to the right of the track and initially consist of playing fields and then tennis/basketball courts. Beyond these – half-right ahead – are modern school buildings and the old Abberley Hall behind them.

Continue along the track to reach a point just before the corner of the first of these buildings – with very large windows at its end nearest the track and which closer inspection will reveal to be an indoor swimming pool.

Here leave the main track, turning right onto a wide path which passes to the right of, and alongside, the swimming pool building. ❽

Diversion to Abberley Clock Tower:

A quick diversion to the base of this well-known landmark is possible by remaining on the main stony track beyond the swimming pool building. The track reaches a five-way junction, with two paths going into the school grounds (right), a track going left (used on Stage 3 of this walk) and a continuation of the main track straight ahead, which is the route now taken.

Walk about 150 yards along the track ahead to reach the base of the clock tower, which stands on a rise to the right of the track. Retrace the route to the indoor swimming pool building and there turn left to rejoin the main route. ❽

Deer are often to be seen grazing in the large field opposite the clock tower. These are farmed for venison.

Back on the main route, walk up the wide path which runs alongside and to the right of the indoor swimming pool.

Past the pool building, the path climbs gently and bears first right and then left, other modern school buildings on its left and the hall beyond these. On reaching a point below the corner of the old hall go right at a Y-junction of sorts – the left arm only going into the buildings there.

Follow what is now a stony track as it passes through a short rocky cutting, descending gently. Ignore a track going left and then immediately, at a

Abberley Clock Tower

Y-junction, go left (the right arm leads to what looks like an all weather playing court).

The stony track continues to descend. At another Y-junction go left again. The track passes a walled garden (below, right).

Look straight ahead between the 'arms' of the Y-junction for a distant view of Witley Court. Surprisingly good views, looking across the walled garden to the right. On a clear day Worcester – some 12 miles away – may be seen with the long shape of Bredon Hill – another 10 miles beyond that – in the far distance behind.

Looking more to the right Walsgrove Hill and Woodbury Hill can also be seen. At certain times of the year one of the fields over in this direction may appear to be covered in white … Geese being reared for Christmas!

Great Witley

The modern settlement of Great Witley is spread over quite a large area. Apart from refreshments/accommodation at the Hundred House and the petrol station/shop passed at the end of the walk there is also a small post office/shop further along the A443 road, which is the right arm of the Y-junction just beyond the Hundred House. There is a telephone box just before the Hundred House on the opposite side of the road.

The Hundred House in its present form dates back to the eighteenth century when it was built, on the site of an earlier inn, by Lord Foley of Witley Court.

The settlement probably takes its name from two old English words – 'whit', meaning a curve or bend in a steam, and 'leah', a clearing. Various spellings of its name occur in documents over the years – Vicelage, Witlega, Wittlaeg, Witlege and Wytele, this latter dating from a document of 1275 when the prefix 'Magna' (Major or Great) was added to distinguish it from neighbouring Little Witley (Parva Wytele).

Little is known of the origin of the manor of Great Witley and its history prior to the thirteenth century, although *Domesday Book* (1086) mentions one Urso as holding land at Witlege.

By the thirteenth century the most influential family locally were the Cookseys, who held the manor of Great Witley until 1498, when it passed to Robert Russell of Strensham. The Russells held it until 1655. During the Civil War Sir William Russell, High Sheriff and Governor of Worcester, and a Royalist, lived in a mansion in Witley Park – a predecessor of Witley Court.

Sir William spent most of his fortune in the cause of the Crown and in 1655 sold the manor and his residence to Thomas Foley of Stourbridge, whose wealth was based on the family iron founding business.

Under Thomas Foley's grandson, another Thomas, the residence was largely rebuilt and subsequent generations of the family continued with this work, it becoming known as Witley Court at the time of the first Lord Foley, early in the eighteenth century.

By the late eighteenth century the Foleys had lost much or their wealth and in 1837, after 182 years as their main residence, Witley Court was sold to the trustees of William, eleventh Baron Ward and later first

Earl of Dudley, who was at that time still a minor. The selling price was £890,000, a not inconsiderable sum of money in those days.

Under the Dudleys Witley Court was transformed into one of the finest country houses in England, visited by royalty and dominating and largely supporting the local economy and community. In 1883, two years before the death of the first Earl, the Dudley estates covered 25,554 acres, of which 14698 were in Worcestershire – placing the Earl twenty-ninth in a table of noblemen by acreage owned, but seventh by virtue of the income earned by those estates – much of this wealth attributable to the considerable coal mines on Dudley property.

Royal visitors to Witley Court began with the dowager Queen Adelaide, widow of William IV – who actually lived in the building as a tenant from 1843 to 1846. The royal connection continued through the reign of Queen Victoria and royal visits reached a peak towards the end of the nineteenth century when Edward, Prince of Wales (later Edward VII) was a frequent visitor.

The early twentieth century and the First World War saw Dudley fortunes adversely affected and in 1920, after the sudden death of his wife, Lady Rachel Dudley, the second Earl sold Witley Court to Herbert Smith, whose fortune came from the Kidderminster carpet industry. Much of the grandeur and glamour of the Dudley era disappeared under the new ownership.

On the evening of Tuesday 7th September 1937 fire broke out in the building, gutting the centre and east wings – including its enormous ballroom – but sparing the west wing

and the adjoining church. The building was never lived in again and 1938 saw a sale of the salvaged contents, fixtures and timber. Over subsequent years the building was much vandalised and partly demolished, the very existence of the ruins being threatened, but in 1970 it was listed as an Ancient Monument and has since passed into the care of English Heritage who now care for it as 'England's finest country house ruin'.

It is open all year but admission times vary with the season. Telephone 01299 896636 for more information. It lies alongside the A443 Worcester road about 1½ miles beyond the Hundred House.

At the peak of its fortunes Witley Court was surrounded by superb landscaped gardens and grounds, the work of William Nesfield (1795-1881). Nesfield laid out the Witley Court gardens in the Italian Style, arranging them around two enormous fountains – the Perseus and Andromeda fountain and the Flora or Triton fountain. The former of these is some twenty-six feet in height and is said to be the largest block of sculpture in Europe. It was capable of shooting jets of water 120 feet high. The fountains have recently been restored and are the subject of occasional test firings.

Adjacent to Witley Court is St. Michael's church, built for the Foleys and completed in 1735. Generally reckoned to be one of the finest examples of Baroque architecture in Britain, the interior contains superb ceiling paintings by Antonio Belluci (1654-1726) which originally graced the ceiling of the chapel at Cannons, the Middlesex residence of the Duke of Chandos. The stained glass windows, stucco work and church organ came from the same source.

The stony track continues its gentle descent through woodland. At another junction ignore a track going right – marked as Private Property and leading to the walled garden – but keep left.

The track makes a significant bend left before straightening again and reaching a pond, left. Ignore a track going off to the left immediately beyond this but bear right to reach a metal farm gate with a stile alongside it on its right.

The pond on the left of the track was a renowned spot for finding grass snakes, in my youth. Sadly they no longer seem to be in residence.

Over the stile – which was somewhat the worse for wear at the time of writing – continue to follow the track to a T-junction with the busy A443 road, here between Worcester and Tenbury Wells.

Cross the road – with great care, it is on both a long bend and steep hill here and is very busy indeed – and turn right down it, on a pavement. After about 70 yards, at a junction where the B4203 Bromyard road goes right, remain on the A road. About 20 yards beyond this, on the left, is a petrol station which has a well-stocked shop on its premises.

Remain on the pavement of the A road. A further 180 yards beyond the petrol station, and also on the left of the road, is the Hundred House where this stage of the walk ends.

On Walsgrove Hill

by R. Tomas

The distant head of Titterstone
Above the clouds, in sunlight, rears;
Across these miles and counties, I
Gaze out in awe. The world appears
So small and petty, set below:
A tapestry of greens and browns,
Laced with the grey of early mist
Come creeping off the River Teme.

The loud geese in the fields behind,
Fattened and ready for the feast,
So soon will disappear leaving
White feathers, blown about like
*   ghosts.*

Another year is turning fast,
Another coming in the east
So quickly dying on the hills;
A cold wind tugs at thin brown
*   grass.*

The niggard ash tree sheds a leaf,
Now almost naked, bent and old;
Defiant, stands beside the stumps
Which were its fellows - dead and
*   felled.*
The clock tower chimes the
*   quarter-hour,*
A pale sun cast upon its face;
We turn upon our steps, descend,
And let the spirits claim this place.

Stage 3

Great Witley to Tenbury Wells

Mileage: 13½ Miles
(From Great Witley: 3 miles to Stanford Bridge; 8½ miles to Eastham; 11¼ miles to Rochford)
O.S.Maps: 1:50000 (Landranger): 138 (Kidderminster & Wyre Forest)
 1:25000 (Explorer): 204 (Worcester & Droitwich Spa); 203 (Ludlow)

Reversing the last half-mile or so of Stage 2, the route climbs out of Great Witley through the grounds of Abberley Hall School. (The short diversion to visit Abberley Clock Tower included at Stage 2 of the walk is an option here also.)

The route then uses fieldpaths and tracks to drop back into the Teme Valley, crossing the river at Stanford Bridge. From here a short road section, followed by fieldpaths and tracks takes the walker up into the rolling wooded hills to the west of the river.

Woodland paths take the route westwards, finally dropping down onto a low ridge nearer the river again. Fieldpaths and a short road section then lead to Eastham and its twelfth century church.

Fieldpaths, a short section of quiet road and then a riverside path bring the walker to Rochford, and another twelfth century church. A longer section of quiet road then leads to the final approach into Tenbury Wells, which is via a footpath alongside first the Teme and then its tributary, Kyre Brook.

The first half-mile of this stage is the close of Stage 2 in reverse.

Starting outside the Hundred House, facing the A443, turn right to walk up the road, using the pavement on the right-hand side. After about 200 yards, and just after the petrol station/shop on the right, at a road junction ignore the road going left – the B4203, signposted for Bromyard and Stanford Bridge – but remain on the A road, now beginning to climb.

Walking from the Hundred House to the B4203 junction, look left for views of the wooded Woodbury Hill and, to its right, the partly wooded Walsgrove Hill – the latter of which was climbed towards the end of Stage 2.

After a further 70 yards cross the road – with care – to take a track which goes off left. This is signed as a Public Footpath and leaves the A road between Holly Cottage (Number 16) and the garden of its neighbour (Number 17).

Walk up the stony track to reach a metal farm gate with a stile – the worse for wear at the time of writing – on its left. Cross this and continue on the track, which bears right. At a Y-junction, with a pond between the two arms, go left. The track bends left and begins to climb through woodland. Ignore several minor paths which leave the main track as it bends first right and then left, climbing steadily all the time.

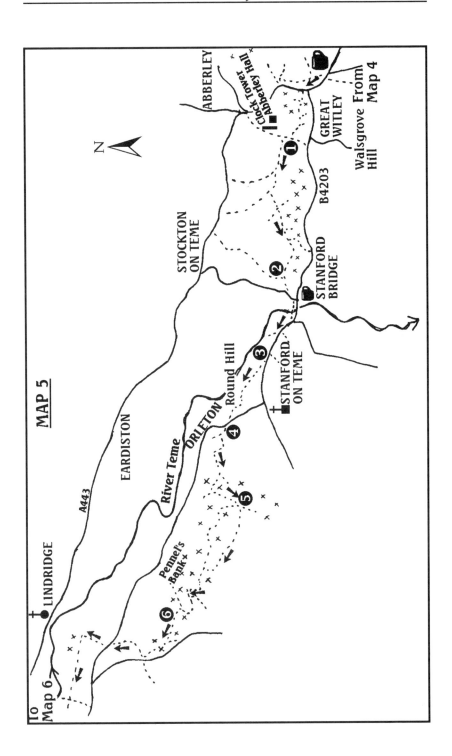

At a junction go straight ahead, ignoring a track going left and marked as Private Property. The main track passes a walled garden (left).

Look across the walled garden for views of Worcester, and Bredon Hill beyond, on a clear day. Look half-right across the garden for views of Walsgrove Hill and, beyond that, Woodbury Hill.

Continue up the stony track. At another junction ignore an arm going left but bear slightly right ahead. At yet another junction bear right – the left arm this time leading to what looks like an all weather playing court. Immediately ignore a track going off right.

The track climbs through a short rocky cutting. At the top of this ignore a short track going right – to school buildings – but bear slightly left on the track. Remain on it as it passes along the left-hand side of a school building with large windows – an indoor swimming pool – and reaches a T-junction with another track. Turn right along this.

In just under 100 yards, at a five-way junction of tracks – with two arms going right into the school grounds, the track straight ahead and another going left – take the track left. It is signed 'Menagerie Entrance' (SO744665). ❶

Diversion to Abberley Clock Tower:

A quick diversion is possible from this junction to the base of Abberley Clock Tower. Go straight ahead at the junction, along a stony track, for about 150 yards to reach a point directly below the tower (right). Retrace steps to rejoin main route, turning right at the five-way junction.

See Stage 2, page 61, for notes on Abberley Hall and Clock Tower .

From the five-way track junction walk down the stony track.

Good views, right, of the clock tower. The adjacent field on the right often contains deer which are farmed for venison.

The track passes through a large high gate (may be open) and reaches the buildings of the menagerie (right).

The menagerie resembles the many urban farms which have sprung up in cities over the past few years, which allow children to handle animals. The walker often passes here under the stare of an owl in one of its cages, while one's arrival at the adjacent dwelling is usually greeted by a chorus of barking!

Remain on the track past the menagerie. It passes through a metal farm gate, a stile alongside on the left (gate may be open), and continues down an avenue of trees bounded by fences, bearing slightly right.

Where the track makes a more noticeable bend right – a sign alongside it saying 'Private Road. Farm Access Only' – leave it, left, either through a metal farm gate (may be open), or through the remains of a kissing gate (to the right of the farm gate) into a field. (Note: This effectively maintains the direction of travel followed since the menagerie.)

In the field, follow a boundary on the right – a wire fence with a small stand of trees beyond – immediately bypassing a redundant stile. On reaching a boundary ahead cross it either through a gap or, if this is blocked (electric fence), over a stile (a little the worse for wear at the time of writing) just to its right. Crossing a dirt track (and possibly another electric fence), go straight ahead through the next field, following the remains of a boundary, (right) – as evidenced by the very slightly higher ground/low ridge to the right – towards a lone tree.

Nearing the tree, there is a noticeable dip in the field. About 50 yards beyond this look out for the remains of a wooden stile – a survivor from the old boundary fence on the right – with a pole carrying overhead lines and small woodland area just beyond it (SO737671). On reaching a point level with the stile turn left to walk across the field and locate a stile (very much the worse for wear at the time of writing) over the boundary there. Cross this into the next field.

Bear slightly right from the stile, towards either a red-roofed dwelling or the left corner of a group of trees, if the former is not immediately visible. On reaching the far boundary of the field, an electric fence, cross it over the protector provided. In the next field maintain direction – passing just to the left of the group of trees – which conceal a pond.

Passing the left corner of the pond maintain direction, towards the wall of a second (nearer) dwelling which should now have appeared ahead, passing the corner of an adjacent field on the right en route. (A stile leading into this field is ignored.)

Pass just to the right of the aforementioned house wall and then bear slightly right to exit the field onto a track, via a metal farm gate. Go straight across the track and through another metal farm gate, opposite, into a field.

Crossing the track look left for a fine view of Walsgrove Hill. A good distant view of the clock tower, and Abberley Hill beyond, also to be had over the left shoulder.

Go straight ahead from the gate, towards the nearest of a few isolated trees across the field – a footpath sign under it. On reaching a field boundary, another electric fence, again cross it via the protector provided – situated just to the left of and under the tree.

(Note: the electric fences hereabouts are always liable to be repositioned. Use the isolated trees as a navigation aid if in doubt.)

Passing under the branches of the tree, maintain direction, very slightly downhill – heading towards a distant stile. Aim to pass just below and to the left of a second isolated tree.

The woodland down to the left is Ellbatch Wood. Abberley Clock Tower is directly behind at the stile.

Cross the stile (it incorporates a protector for an electric fence) – over a fairly insignificant boundary fence – and maintain direction ahead, gradually losing height. Head towards a dip, slightly to the left, the distance to Ellbatch Wood (left) decreasing. Pass just to the right of a group of trees to locate a stile in the boundary ahead and make for this. (Note: Explorer Map 204 shows the path running alongside a triangular patch of trees as it approaches the stile at SO729666. This is not such dense woodland as the map might suggest.)

On reaching the stile cross it into the next field. Head half-left across the field, eventually aiming for an isolated tree in it. (Note: On every occasion I have tried to walk this path the field has been under crops with – unusually for these parts – no path through them. If this is the case then on entering the field turn left to follow the boundary around its edge, rejoining the right of way at a point just after passing the aforementioned isolated tree, which is just out into the field.)

Aim to pass just to the left of, and beneath the branches of, the isolated tree – (a detached length of hedgerow to its right, beyond) – and then maintain direction to reach the main field boundary. Bear right along the boundary, Ellbatch Wood beyond it.

Follow the boundary (left) through the large field. Ignore a path going into the woods, left.

Look half-right across the Teme valley to see the church at Stanford on Teme. Look slightly to the right of this, out in the valley, to see a small isolated tree-covered rounded hillock – Round Hill – which the route rounds later. Due right in the distance is Titterstone Clee Hill.

At the time of writing the farmer hereabouts seemed to be particularly walker-friendly as regards clearing the rights of way through his fields when they are under crop. He cuts great, wide swathes through them which can be walked five or six abreast. One almost wants crops to be present as it makes the navigating so much easier!

Continue to follow the boundary to the bottom left-hand corner of the field, ignoring a second path going left into Ellbatch Wood. Approaching the corner bear right to follow the field boundary – here a wire fence with trees and bushes beyond – around.

Beyond a point where there is a large oak tree in it the boundary bends right. Here drop down, left, through a gap in the boundary (by a lone gatepost) and onto a track. Bear right along the track to emerge into the corner of another field, a large red-brick farmhouse half-left below at its far side (Lower Crundelend Farm).

Entering the field, bear slightly left to leave the track – aiming in the general direction of the outbuildings adjacent to the aforementioned farm. On reaching a point where the farmhouse is directly on the left bear left, down the field, towards it.

Pass to the left of the corner of the farmhouse garden, where there is a footpath marker post. Follow the boundary (right) down the field – passing the farmhouse (right).

Stanford on Teme church is directly ahead.

Passing the end of the farm garden (right) maintain direction down the hill. Aim for a pole carrying overhead wires which will be seen below, woodland beyond it. On reaching the pole turn left along an adjacent metalled track, immediately crossing a bridge over a stream (SO719661). ❷

Continue along the track, ignoring a footpath going right over a stile. It runs along with the stream and woodland to its left and more open country to the right. Follow it to a T-junction with a quiet road – just beyond a dwelling on the left called Glen Cottage. Turn left along the road, passing a dwelling, Bank Cottage, on the left and an old water pump on the right. The road then bends left to a Y-junction, just behind the Bridge public house.

Bear right – signed as a No Through Road, and with the pub car park and a telephone box on the right – and walk towards a gap through railings ahead. Through the railings go straight ahead along a metalled path to reach and cross old Stanford Bridge over the Teme.

A very limited bus service 309 (at the time of writing running once daily each way on Tuesdays and Fridays only) runs through Stanford Bridge to Shelsley Beauchamp (Stage 2), Martley and Worcester in the one direction and to Shelsley Walsh and Martley in the other.

Across the bridge, turn right along the B4203 road – remaining on the right-hand side of the road where there is a pavement (at least for some of the way).

Across the road (left) here is a Farm Shop. Opening hours were – at the time of writing – Monday to Friday, 8.30 am to 6 pm; Saturday & Sunday, 9 am to 5 pm.

The road passes the tree-lined entrance drive to the premises of Forest (a company who make wooden fences), left. Ignore a footpath going left here. Just beyond this ignore a track going off right. A pavement recommences after this.

Remain on the road, past a short terrace of cottages on the right and some commercial premises just beyond. The road dips and bends slightly left. Just after passing speed limit signs ignore a footpath going left, over a stile. About 50 yards after the signs leave the road, right, through a metal farm gate into a field. ❸

In the field, bear left to follow the left boundary hedge – that is the boundary with the road. On reaching a boundary ahead pass through it via a metal farm gate (may be open). In the next field go slightly right from the gate, roughly towards a round wooded hill which will be seen ahead (Round Hill) – the distance to the boundary hedge on the left increasing as the field is crossed.

Crossing the field look over the right shoulder behind for a distant view of Abberley Clock Tower with, to its left, the top of the wooded Abberley Hill and, to its right, Walsgrove Hill and the ridge used by Stage 2 of the walk. Right of these is Woodbury Hill.

Stanford Bridge

Stanford means a stony or rocky ford, which sums up the importance of this site over the centuries. The first bridge recorded here was built in 1548 by Humphrey Parkington of Chaddesley Corbett. A later three arched structure collapsed into the river and was replaced, in 1797, by a single span iron bridge designed by Nash.

In 1905 Nash's bridge was replaced by one of ferro-concrete – at the time of opening the longest span of concrete anywhere in the world, at 99 feet. This is the bridge used by the walk.

Alongside it is a new bridge of 1971 which is of unusual design in that it has a curve, a camber and an incline built into it.

Nearing the far side of the field, head for its far right-hand corner. Here cross a stile – located under a large oak tree which itself stands alongside a willow – into the corner of the next field (the field on the right).

Take just a few steps in the new field and then cross the boundary fence on the left, via another stile. In the next field bear half-right towards the far right corner, the wooded hillock of Round Hill beyond. Aim to pass well to the right of the leftmost of two isolated trees in the field. (Note: Part of this field is often under hops and a direct route may not always be possible.)

More good distant views of Abberley Clock tower and Walsgrove Hill behind from the gate in the field corner.

Pass through a metal farm gate in the corner of the field and turn left along a grassy track which runs around the base of Round Hill here. Follow the track which runs between wire fences, and bracken in season.

Look left for a nice view of St. Mary's church, Stanford on Teme, standing high on its hill alongside the B4203.

The grassy track bends right, around Round Hill. Ignore a farm gate leading into an orchard straight ahead but remain on the track which now becomes much wider as the distance between its boundary fences increases. The track heads towards a grassy continuation of the hillock. As the fences on either side continue to diverge, follow the boundary fence with the orchard, left.

Follow the fence around to the left, below the grassy hillock. Where the fence is joined by a row of hawthorn and hazel trees continue to follow these left, the fence soon taking over again.

Still following the fence, the path reaches the edge of a ridge and a large oak tree.

Stanford on Teme Church

The church was built on this site in 1768-9 by James Rose as part of Sir Edward Winnington's redevelopment of Stanford Court, his residence. There was formerly a church to the south-east of the present site – on a spot now underneath a small lake in the grounds of the house. The house itself has long gone and a replacement of 1886 is now used as offices by Forest, who own the grounds.

In the church is the fine alabaster monument and tomb of Sir Humphrey Salwey (died 1493) and his wife, moved here from the old church. The Salweys owned the manor of Stanford from the fourteenth century until 1670 when it passed to the Winningtons via marriage.

Pause at the oak tree to admire the views up the Teme valley which suddenly open up from the low ridge edge. The wooded hills slightly to the left are those the route will soon cross. Just peeping out from behind them is Titterstone Clee Hill while further over to the right, in the distance, is Brown Clee Hill, with its twin summits. Straight ahead, in the middle distance is Eardiston while to the right the small settlement of Stockton on Teme can be seen. In the foreground is Orleton Court.

On reaching the oak tree ignore a gateway into the orchard, left, but continue to the left of and under the tree – along the fence – to reach a stile in the very corner of the field. Cross this onto a quiet road and turn right down it (SO699666).

The road descends, bending slightly left. After about 130 yards on it, where a significant bend to the right begins, leave the road, left (almost straight on, in fact), along a metalled track – indicated as a Public Footpath. **④**

Remain on the track as it bends 90 degrees left, ignoring a footpath going straight ahead at the bend. At another significant bend – this time right – ignore a footpath which crosses it. Just before reaching a group of farm buildings the track loses its previously concrete surface. Here bear left with the main track.

Within a few yards, at a fork in the track, take the lower option on the left – the right arm is the drive to School House. The track passes through a metal farm gate (may be open) and gradually climbs – running between a wire field boundary, left, and a hedgerow on the right, beyond which is the drive to School House.

Still climbing, the track bends slightly left and then right. Levelling out it bends right to reach two dwellings. Bear right, as if to enter the drive of the right of these (Orleton Grange), but then pass through a small wooden gate immediately to its right, under fir trees (SO693666).

Proceed straight ahead from the gate along a grassy path, bounded on the left by the wooden fence of Orleton Grange and on the right by the fence of School House. At the end of this initial narrow section pass through a wooden gate and continue straight ahead, following the right-hand boundary, a wire fence.

The path drops steeply down towards a boundary fence, beyond which is a stream. Ignore a small gate through the fence, slightly left ahead, but instead descend almost into the corner of the field to locate a wooden footbridge over the stream, accessed via a stile at either end. Cross the bridge, climb up a couple of wooden steps and bear slightly right to a stile. Cross this into a field. Here turn left to follow its boundary, left, to the corner where another stile leads into woodland.

Over the stile bear half-right, immediately climbing. Follow a steep, narrow path up through the trees – ignoring minor animal tracks – to reach a T-junction with another narrow path at a wooden fence, a small wooden hut beyond. Turn left along the path.

A right turn along the path brings the walker, within a few steps, to a stile leading out of the wood into the corner of a field. A quick diversion along here can prove very worthwhile.

Emerging into the field, look slightly right for a superb distant view of Abberley Clock Tower, Abberley Hill (to its left), and Walsgrove Hill (to its right) on a clear day.

In season – late July to early September – the hedgerow immediately to the left of, and running along away from, the stile is one of the very best I know for blackberries.

Follow the narrow path along, the aforementioned wooden fence initially on the right. The path climbs though the woods, becoming slightly sunken but then later almost running along the top of a low bank. It continues to climb steadily, a steep drop down through the trees on its left and a gully to its right.

The woodland is Wall Hills Wood.

The path climbs to an indistinct T-junction with another. Here go left. Within 5 yards it reaches another junction – with a footpath marker post indicating two options, either straight ahead or to the right (SO688668). Here go right – on a sometimes indistinct, narrow path which immediately bends left and climbs. (Note: This is probably the most important junction of this stage of the walk. A wrong turn here will lead the walker miles off course with little option to regain the route without backtracking some considerable distance. However indistinct it looks, the path to take at the marker post is the one which goes right and then bears left and CLIMBS. The option which goes straight ahead, and appears the more substantial path on the ground, is initially level.) ❺

Follow the path up through the trees. After the initial bend left it bears slightly right. Within 100 yards of the junction it reaches the edge of the wood. Pass through a gap – with a marker post alongside – into a field. Here bear very slightly left, continuing to climb, across and up the field to a stile over a boundary fence ahead. Crossing the stile, bear between half-right and due right through the next field – towards the edge of the woodland again.

Locate a gap leading into the woodland (look for a wooden gatepost) and pass through this. Walk a few steps under the trees to reach a T-junction with a path – a notice board announcing Pennel's Bank Nature Reserve adjacent. Turn left along the path, through the reserve.

Pennel's Bank Nature Reserve is cared for by the Worcestershire Nature Conservation Trust (01905 754919) and covers 30 acres of mixed deciduous woodland which was last commercially worked over 60 years ago and has been allowed to regenerate naturally.

At a Y-junction go left, ignoring the right arm which descends into the woodland. The path becomes more distinct underfoot. Ignore two other paths, going right and half-right at the same point – by a large tree. A very gradual descent continues on the main path.

Slightly wider now, the path bends right, the descent becoming more noticeable.

The Teme valley, over to the right, is only glimpsed through trees. Where gaps in the trees permit there are views across the valley to Lindridge, with its prominent church spire, and beyond to the twin summits of Brown Clee Hill and, to its left, the slopes of Titterstone Clee Hill.

The path continues on its way through the woods, meandering and undulating, now with a drop on its right. It bends left, then right – to round a wooded chasm, right. Follow the obvious path to pass an isolated dwelling, left, the way now running along the very edge of the woodland. Ignore a footpath going left through a gate here (SO683674).

Just after passing the dwelling the path emerges onto its stony access track. Continue straight ahead along this.

The track meanders and undulates along, passing another Pennel's Bank Nature Reserve sign. It then bends left, to avoid a deep side valley. At the apex of this long detour, as the track bends right, ignore a track going sharp left into a field but continue on the main track. Just beyond this the track bends sharp right and begins to descend. Here, at a Y-junction, go left – leaving the main track – climbing very slightly to pass through a metal farm gate. ❻

Through the gate, in the field beyond bear slightly right – under a large oak tree – following a grassy track which then bends slightly left towards a farm gate with a corrugated metal building alongside and to the right. Before reaching these bear right to another metal farm gate.

Pass through this gate and walk straight ahead to reach, and pass through, another. Through this, follow a path straight ahead – a wire boundary fence on the immediate right.

Views across the Teme valley begin to open up as the tree cover thins.

Follow the now very narrow path along the fence to reach a corner, with a stile over the fence ahead and a small gate through the boundary on the right. Cross the stile ahead to enter an area of rough, open woodland. Walk straight ahead through this to reach, after no more than 10 yards, a Y-junction – a large ash tree between its two arms. Here go half-left to climb through the semi-woodland, on initially an indistinct path which runs about 10 yards from a boundary with open fields beyond, left.

Remain on the path, the distance between it and the fields on the left gradually lessening. Another path joins, sharp right. Continue straight ahead to reach a stile. Cross this to emerge into a field.

Follow the right-hand boundary through the field to reach another stile at its far corner. Cross this into the next field. Here continue to follow the right boundary hedge, some farm buildings over to the left, to a makeshift stile at its far corner. Cross this into a third field. Here again initially follow the right-hand boundary along the top of the field.

Where the field boundary bends right leave it, maintaining direction straight ahead to reach a stile leading into woodland. Over the stile, drop down straight ahead into the woods to reach – after about 20 yards – a T-junction with a wider path. Turn right along this.

Follow the path through the woods. It narrows and begins to bear slightly to the right, a quiet road down to the left. The path shuns contact with the road and emerges, over a stile, into a field on the right. Here go straight ahead, aiming towards the left-hand side of a stand of fir trees beyond the boundary below – some dwellings (Eastham Grange) and a large pond further over to the right.

Walking down through the field, head gradually towards the boundary on the left – and still towards the left of the fir trees – to locate a metal farm gate through it. Pass through this, a road beyond, and turn immediately right – NOT ONTO THE ROAD – through a wooden gate and down a metalled drive, as per a Public Bridleway sign.

Walk down the drive to join a better cared for length of it, leading to Eastham Grange – with lamps along either side. Continue straight ahead along this. Approaching the dwellings, at a Y-junction bear left – (the right option only runs a few yards). Pass along a laurel hedge (right) towards the main house of Eastham Grange and then through a brick gateway and alongside the house itself (right) and a stable block with a clock tower beyond. Continue straight ahead through a wooden farm gate, marked as being the entrance to Mill Cottage. Passing through this DO NOT follow the stony drive to the dwelling but instead bear right to leave the drive and follow the boundary hedge here – passing just to the right of a wooden garage.

Follow the hedge, through a grassy area, to reach a metal farm gate. Pass through this into a field (SO673681).

This particular farm gate will always remain indelibly imprinted in my memory. A few years ago, deciding to climb it rather than open it, I caught my foot on its top bar and took a nosedive off it and into a strategically placed clump of stinging nettles. An extremely painful experience which still hurts when I think about it although my nephew, Ian, found it most entertaining at the time!

Follow the right-hand boundary though the field – on a sunken grassy track at its edge – until almost at the first corner, here bearing left to continue to follow it along its next side, and eventually dropping down to a farm gate at the next corner. Pass through the gate onto a road. Turn left along this.

Approaching the farm gate onto the road, the steeple of Lindridge church is directly ahead across the Teme valley.

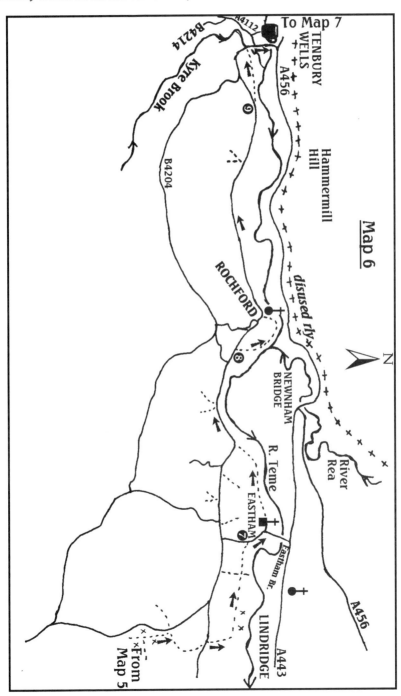

Lindridge takes its name from two old English words 'linda hryeg' meaning 'the ridge of lime trees'. A record of AD781 finds the monks of Worcester giving land here to one Wiferd and his wife, Alta. The tall steeple of the church of St. Lawrence makes it something of a landmark in this part of the Teme valley. The church is the third on this site and dates from 1861.

Walk along the road which rises and bends very slightly to the left and then right. Just before reaching the top of the rise, at a Road Narrows sign, leave the road through a metal farm gate, right, into a field.

Go straight across the field from the gate to reach its far boundary, woodland beyond this. Here bear left to walk along that boundary. On reaching the corner of the field cross a stile into the next and continue to follow the boundary (right) through this. Where the boundary bears away to the right continue straight ahead along a more open low ridge, the River Teme below to the right and the busy A443 road beyond that.

View of the whole of the long mass of Titterstone Clee Hill half-right, with Brown Clee Hill just visible to its right, in the distance.

Keep to the left of an isolated large oak tree, heading for a metal farm gate through a boundary ahead. Passing through this go straight ahead from it.

As a slight descent commences look behind – over the left shoulder – for a final view of Abberley Clock Tower and the surrounding hills.

Keep fairly close to a line of trees on the left along the ridge, now beginning to descend slightly. Bear very slightly left, aiming for a pole carrying overhead wires (the middle one of three visible ahead). Pass just to the left of the pole and around a field corner ahead to walk alongside its boundary hedge, which should be on the immediate right of what is now a track. Follow this down to a metal farm gate (SO664685).

Pass through the gate, a footpath marker post just beyond it, and walk straight ahead to reach a T-junction with a stony track. Go straight ahead, across this, to pass through a metal farm gate into a field. Here continue ahead until the land in front falls away and then bear slightly to the right, down the field, towards trees below which conceal the course of a stream.

On reaching the stream turn right along it to locate a bridge over it. Cross this and climb the short steep slope at its far side, keeping as close as possible to a wire fence on the left. At the top of the slope the path emerges into an orchard. Turn right to walk along the top of the slope past six rows of trees (left), and then bear half-left to walk between the sixth and seventh rows of trees to the far side of the orchard. Here locate and pass through a metal farm gate in the boundary hedge to emerge onto a road (SO661686). ❼

Turn right along the road. After just over 100 yards it bends left. At a junction, after a total of about 300 yards on the road and as it makes a marked bend right, leave it by turning left onto a minor road – indicated as a No Through Road and signposted to Eastham Church.

Eastham Bridge, over the River Teme, is about 400 yards further along the road if the turning to the church is not taken, a T-junction with the A443 just beyond it. *Bus service 758 runs along here, to Great Witley and Worcester in the one direction and to Tenbury Wells in the other.*

Walk along the road, past a large farmhouse on the right, and where it bears slightly left continue straight ahead to enter the churchyard through a gate. Pass along the left-hand side of the church if not visiting it.

If visiting the church the key may be obtained from the large farmhouse, passed en route. On entering the churchyard bear around to the right of the building to enter the chancel via a small door there.

Passing the south doorway of the church, at the far left end of the building, bear half-left to reach a wooden gate. Pass through this out of the churchyard and onto a track – a continuation of the 'No Through Road' walked earlier.

Proceed straight ahead along the track, passing a dwelling on the left. Ignore a footpath going left, alongside the dwelling, but instead continue past farm outbuildings, through a metal farm gate and up a track ahead. This bends very slightly to the left and can be very muddy indeed due to constant livestock usage. Ignore several gates leading off the track as it climbs.

At the top of the short track are two metal farm gates – one straight ahead and the other just to the right. Pass through the latter to enter a field. Here follow the right-hand boundary for about 25 yards to reach a gate through that boundary. Pass through this into another field.

Follow an indistinct track through the new field, initially straight ahead from the gate and then aiming to keep the hedge boundary on the right between 35 and 40 yards distant.

Eastham Church

Eastham church (St. Peter & St. Paul) dates from the twelfth century but stands on the site of an earlier Saxon church. The nave and chancel are constructed of blocks of travertine (tufa) rock quarried at Southstone Rock, some four miles to the east.

Travertine (tufa) is quite an unusual building stone – a pale calcareous rock (limestone) deposited by springs. It is porous in character, easy to cut and work, hardens on exposure and is very durable indeed. Southstone Rock is no longer marked on Ordnance Survey maps but is near where Explorer Map 204 indicates Rock Coppice, at SO708639.

Approaching the church, note the metal plaque on the outside of the east wall. This announces that the remains of one William Green, aged 69, were interred nearby on 23rd August 1754 – as were those of his widow, Catherine, who died, aged 82, on 9th November 1776.

Still outside, note the projecting south doorway – twelfth century in origin – simply decorated. The arcading above this may be a surviving remnant of the earlier Saxon building.

To the right of the doorway, above a church notice board, is a carved stone cherub or angel. Much higher on the wall above this are two much weathered carvings representing Leo and Sagittarius. Inside the church on the same (south) wall of the chancel are two corresponding carvings – this time of an Agnus Dei (Lamb and Cross) and a lion with one head and two bodies. All of these four carvings would appear to be the work of the same group of twelfth century masons.

A description of the church from 1816 states that the chancel and nave were separated by a Norman arch and the base of one of the pillars to this can still be seen through an opening situated just behind the lectern. The wooden lectern itself dates from the late sixteenth or early seventeenth century and has a base with four carved lion feet – reputed to have been part of a four-poster bed in a previous life.

The existing chancel arch has above it a painting of the Royal Arms of the House of Hanover. From the time of the Reformation it was compulsory for churches to display the Royal Coat of Arms but by the reign of the first Hanoverian king, George I, the legal requirement to do so had been removed. The display of the Coat of Arms here almost certainly shows the strong preference of the local populace for the Protestant House of Hanover as opposed to the Catholic Jacobites. A similar situation will be encountered at Rochford church, to be visited later on this stage of the walk.

The church contains some fine seventeenth century panelling behind the altar while the panelling of the pulpit is of a similar date.

There are also two fine 'Priest's chairs'.

In the south wall of the chancel is an interesting blocked Leper Window. Just to the right of and above this an oval brass plaque, a memorial tablet to an infant from 1789, bears the words, 'The little stranger began to sip the Cup of Life, but, perceiving the bitterness, turned away his head and refused the draught.'

The large basin shaped font, at the western end of the nave, dates from the twelfth century with a more modern base. Nearby, over the south doorway, is a painting of the Crucifixion – probably of the seventeenth or eighteenth century. Strangely its upper portion is well executed while the lower part is very crudely done – presumably repainted at some stage.

Outside once more, in 1830 the old bell turret of the church was dismantled and replaced by the extant red-brick tower which looks somewhat out of place with the rest of the building.

The place-name 'Eastham' literally means 'east settlement' or 'enclosure' 'in the bend in the river'.

Good view of Eastham church to the right during the early part of this field. Nearing the far side of the field a glance behind will reveal that the tower of Eastham church and the distant spire of Lindridge church are directly in line.

Proceeding through the field, bear gradually right to eventually reach its far right-hand corner, the course of the River Teme now clearly visible below on the right. Pass through a metal farm gate into the next field and here follow the right-hand boundary hedge. During the latter stages of this long field a small area of woodland lies beyond the hedge.

On reaching the far right-hand corner of the field cross a four-bar wooden fence – no stile at the time of writing – into an orchard area (SO648685). Go straight ahead through this, keeping as close to its right-hand boundary as is practical – not easy given the steep slope down to that boundary. Ahead will be seen a dwelling (Boat House) and an oast house.

Continuing straight ahead, drop down to the far boundary of the orchard to locate and cross a five-bar fence/barrier there which bears a notice warning, 'Beware dogs running loose' – (possibly an empty warning). Cross this to emerge into the garden of Boat House, a pond on the right and a bridge over a stream just to the left.

Entering the garden of Boat House one rainy September afternoon I disturbed a heron from the pond. On another occasion there were swans on it.

Bear slightly left to cross the bridge over the stream and then walk across the garden lawn, passing to the right of the house and up a couple of steps onto its tarmac drive. Bear half-left up this to reach metal gates leading onto a quiet road, at a bend on it. Turn right along the road.

(Note: The walker may find the gates leading onto the road closed and locked. If this is the case then walk back down the drive, rounding an old oast house (left) and bearing left along a short length of stony track – bounded on the right by the garden hedge of the house and on the left by the boundary fence of a field. Pass through a metal farm gate in the boundary fence on the left to enter the field. From the gate head half-left up a steep slope, the aforementioned oast house immediately to the left, to reach a metal farm gate in the top boundary of the field. Cross a stile – very much the worse for wear at the time of writing – situated just to the right of the gate, under a damson tree, to reach the road. Turn right along it.)

The road runs initially straight and level – the River Teme one field distant to the right, its course marked by a line of trees. A slight bend right heralds a section where river and road come very close together, although the former is largely hidden from the latter by trees and high boundary hedges hereabouts.

It is to be hoped that the large number of dead toads I encountered on the road hereabouts, one September afternoon, was indicative of a large local population rather than a mass – almost lemming-like – loss of collective road sense on their part.

The road passes the entrance drive to Newhouse Farm, left. Ignore a bridleway going left off the road here (which uses the drive) and a footpath going off left just afterwards. As the road passes a dwelling, right, the river is at its closest but is again not clearly seen due to tree cover.

At a junction ignore a road going left – to Upper Rochford – but continue straight ahead. Shortly after this the road passes Lower House Farm, which is on the right. About 250 yards after the farm leave the road, right, over a stile which is immediately to the right of a farm gate into an adjacent field. **❽**

Walking hereabouts in late September I passed fields in which the hops were still being harvested. With hop-picking nowadays a largely mechanised procedure, the area no longer sees the vast army of pickers who used to arrive from Birmingham and the Black Country via the railway station at Newnham Bridge. September is the main month for the harvest and the passing of that month makes a great difference to the views and landscape seen when walking the first three stages of the route.

Cross the stile into a field and follow the left-hand boundary fence through it. On reaching a boundary fence, ahead, pass through it via a farm gate and continue to follow the boundary on the left to reach the riverbank. Here pass through the boundary, left, via a metal farm gate, to walk alongside the river.

Walking through the first field, riverside, depending on the tree cover and season it may be possible to make out the confluence of the Rivers Rea and Teme, opposite.

The River Rea is formed by the amalgamation of several streams, including Rea Brook, to the north-east of Titterstone and Brown Clee Hills. It flows south past Cleobury Mortimer and then south-west to Newnham Bridge – just over half a mile to the north-east of where the route currently is – before reaching the confluence.

Rochford

There is some difference of opinion as to the origin of Rochford as a place name. Some see it, very literally as deriving from 'Rock ford', the ford near a rock above the river – there is an overhanging bluff of red sandstone rock some 200 yards upstream of the church. Others maintain that the name comes from the old English word 'raecces', a roche or hunting dog – the name thus meaning 'the ford of the hunting dog'.

The church of St. Michael is twelfth century in origin. The chancel and the greater part of the nave survive from this period. The building is of old red sandstone and is surmounted by a shingled spire.

Outside, above a now blocked north door, the tympanum has the only Worcestershire example of a shallow-carved Tree of Life – unfortunately, after some 800 years, now so worn as to be almost unrecognisable. This motif appears on several churches in neighbouring Shropshire and Gloucestershire and it is likely that the same travelling band of stonemasons was responsible for all of them.

The Norman chancel arch bears chevron carving and dates from about 1150.

Two of the nave windows are its original Norman apertures – set high in the thick walls. The window at the east end of the church, in the chancel, is more modern but no less interesting, containing as it does stained glass work by William Morris. This Victorian work commemorates a death in 1863 and the design and pastel colours of the glass are unmatched by anything done in England or abroad during this period.

Above the blocked north door, inside the church, are the Hanoverian Arms – probably indicative of the strong support felt by the local populace for that cause as opposed to the Jacobites, a similar situation to that encountered at Eastham church, earlier.

On the north wall of the nave is a tablet which reads 'On the other side of this wall, by her own desire, are deposited the remains of Sarah relict of Edward Downes of Sutton Sturmey, who died September 2nd, 1802.' Outside in the churchyard there is no sign of a grave.

The church organ dates from about 1810 and is surmounted by a double-headed golden eagle.

Leaving the church, via the south door and porch, glance left to see the gravestone of John Cheese 'Elder of this parish who departed this life the sixteenth day of May in the year of Our Lord 1704, aged 88'. The stone bears carvings of a grim looking skull, an hourglass with the sands of time run out and a pick and shovel. Charmingly gruesome!

For those in need of more than spiritual relief there is a toilet situated outside the church, against its north wall.

To the north of the church, between it and the Teme, is a grassy mound which is thought to have been the site of a wooden fort which once guarded the ford here.

Gravestone of John Cheese, Rochford Church

Reaching the end of the field cross a stile into the next and continue to follow the riverside path.

The spire of Rochford church appears half-left. The busy road across the river is now the A456, which joins the hitherto riverside A443 at Newnham Bridge.

On reaching the end of this field again cross a stile into the next and continue to follow the river. Again, at the end of this field cross another stile into the next. Here again initially remain alongside the Teme, now bearing towards Rochford church.

The noisy A456 apart, this is a very pretty section of riverside walking, with the Teme living up to its reputation as being particularly fast flowing.

Nearing the end of the field, bear left away from the riverbank, heading for a metal farm gate through the boundary ahead. Passing through this gate, DO NOT walk along the obvious track towards another farm gate ahead but instead head directly towards the church, and just to the right of some farm outbuildings. Pass just to the right of a steel pylon carrying overhead wires and head for a birch tree. Cross a stile beneath this and walk a few paces along a fence to enter the churchyard via a gate. Walk along the path to the entrance porch of the church.

If not visiting the church then on reaching its porch turn left along a stony path to pass through a metal gate and up steps and through a second gate, out of the churchyard and into a field. Go straight ahead from the second gate, a wire fence on the immediate left, to a kissing gate which leads out onto a quiet road. Turn right along this. The road makes a long bend around to the left and then right and descends to commence a very long straight section. It is low lying and views from it are restricted by high hedgerows. The river runs along the far side of the fields to the right, which are often under hops. Reaching the end of the straight section the road bears slightly right and begins to meander, still on the flat.

A brief glimpse of Titterstone Clee Hill may be obtained between and beyond the low hills across the river, half-right. Look over the metal farm gate across the road from where two footpaths are indicated as leaving on the left, adjacent to some outbuildings – at SO614684. The fairly prominent rounded grassy hill half-right ahead across the river is Hammermill Hill.

The road eventually reaches the isolated dwellings of Northwick Cottages – a concrete semi-detached construction with large letter 'N's' adorning its walls – on the right (SO605686).

Notice the cycle oriented sign outside Number One, Northwick Cottages. This was – at the time of writing – home to Trevor Jarvis and his wife. Trevor hand builds 'Flying Gate' bicycles, so named because of the design of the frame. The cycles were commercially manufactured between 1935 and 1955, when the company ceased trading. Trevor has resurrected the design and has been making them since 1979.

A brief tour of his workshop was followed by a refreshing glass of orange squash, one hot August afternoon. My heartfelt thanks to you, Trevor!

Note the notice outside Number Two, Northwick Cottages. A Great Western and London & North Western Joint Railway sign, it threatens anyone who fails to shut the gate with a fine of up to forty shillings (£2). If it is an original sign then it is likely to have migrated from the disused railway across the river – see note at Stage 4.

Beyond Northwick Cottages the road rises very slightly and commences a long, gradual bend left. Just over 170 yards beyond the dwellings – and about 50 yards after passing the entrance to Tenbury Wells Sewage Works, left – leave the road, right, for a stony path. There is a 'No Cycling' sign where it leaves the road. (Note: The total distance on the road from Rochford church to this point is a little under two miles.) **❾**

Just a few yards along the path the Teme flows alongside, right. The opposite bank of the river here is in Shropshire. The route of the walk stays resolutely in Worcestershire, where it has been from the start.

The path initially has a fence separating it from the river, right, and a bank with hedge on the left confining it. As a high hedge begins, right, the path reaches more open country on its left – a field there being succeeded by a playing field (Palmer's Meadow), the path separated from these by railings. Part of the way along the playing fields the stony path widens to track width and takes on a metalled surface (Rise Lane).

The sound of water again on the right announces the presence of Kyre Brook, which joins the Teme just to the north – to the right of where Rise Lane widens and takes on its metalled surface. The brook is a combination of several small watercourses which rise between Tenbury and Bromyard. Two streams, Collington Brook and Netherwood Brook, join near Pie Corner – on the B4214 near Collington – to form what is thereafter known as Kyre Brook. It flows for eight miles to reach the Teme.

Follow the metalled track to a road bridge across Kyre Brook, now among the houses of Tenbury. Do NOT cross the bridge but continue straight ahead across the road to continue to walk alongside the brook (right).

Look right, across the brook, to see the extraordinary Spa buildings or Pump Rooms – recently restored at the time of writing. Their style is best described as 'Chinese Gothic'. See main note on Tenbury Wells for their history.

Passing through a metal gate – which may be open – the metalled track reaches another road bridge over Kyre Brook. Turn right onto the road (B4204) and cross the bridge – the Crow Hotel on the immediate right just over it. Here, at a road junction with the A4112, continue straight ahead along the A road – Teme Street – on its right-hand side through the town to reach Teme Bridge over the river where this stage of the walk ends.

Walking along Teme Street note the plaque on the wall of Number 18 – The Country Restaurant, at the time of writing, and opposite Tenbury Tourist Information Office (across Teme Street), and the Library (across a side street ahead). The plaque informs the reader that the house was once occupied by the surgery of Dr. Henry Hill Hickman.

Hickman was a pioneer of the use of anaesthesia by gas during surgical operations but was unable to secure support or wide acceptance for his ideas. Frustrated, he set up his surgery in Tenbury where he died, aged 30, in April 1830. He is buried in Bromfield church – passed on Stage 5 of the walk.

Teme Bridge marks the boundary between Worcestershire, in which the walk remains for the moment, and Shropshire. Its three northern arches probably date from the fourteenth century. The remaining three are early nineteenth century replacements – built by Thomas Telford – for predecessors destroyed by floods in 1795. The bridge has a curve in it – quite unusual in England. It was widened in 1871.

The Spa building and pump rooms, Tenbury Wells

Tenbury Wells

Modern Tenbury Wells is a busy little town serving a largely agricultural community. The walker will find most useful shops and services here – from the Tourist Information Office (open April to September only), library, post office and banks to chemists, hardware shops, newsagents, bookshops, toilets, telephone boxes and supermarkets. There are also plenty of public houses. Teme Street is the main thoroughfare.

There has been a river crossing here since the Iron Age. The name 'Tenbury' originated in Saxon times, as Temebury – meaning the stronghold/fort on the Teme (*Domesday Book* has it as 'Tamedeberie'). This probably relates to the old Castle Tump which lies just north of the river and west of the current bridge and was almost certainly built to protect the river crossing – although other opinions have it as a ford marker or even as the grave of the ancient British leader Caractacus.

In 1249 the town, by now known as Temettebury, was granted a charter (by Henry III) which permitted it to hold a weekly market and an annual fair. Roger de Clifford owned the market rights and divided up what is now Teme Street into Burgage Plots which he let to traders. He also built a bridge over the river. The town has been home to a thriving market ever since.

The 'Wells' suffix was added to Tenbury's name in 1841, in an attempt to promote the mineral water springs which had recently been discovered in the town. Since the eighteenth century Tenbury has also been known as the 'Town in the Orchard', after the many cider apple orchards hereabouts.

The greater part of the town is built on the flood plain of the river – a very unusual situation and one which has caused it to suffer from serious flooding throughout its existence. The last major flood was in 1886 with water in Teme Street and Church Street reaching a depth of four feet. Since 1770 no less than twenty-two floods have flowed through the town centre.

Tenbury's first church was built by the Normans. Situated on the flood plain, like the rest of the town, it has not escaped from the flooding and the building seen today (passed at the start of Stage 4 of the walk) is the third on the site. Inside the building a plaque, situated just to the left of the Acton Adams monument (see below) records the height reached by the floodwaters on 14th May 1886.

The church is dedicated to St. Mary. Its tower survives from Norman times but most else was swept away by a great flood in 1770. The 1886 flood caused more serious damage and most of what is seen today is Victorian in origin.

Inside, near the north wall, is a fragment of the shaft of an Anglo-Saxon preaching cross, about two feet in height and carved on all four sides. Discovered during restoration work in 1864, it is thought to date from about AD880.

Across the church – to the left of the Lady Chapel – is the fine alabaster monument and tomb of Thomas Acton Adams and his wife, Mary, which dates from 1581 and was one of the few monuments to escape the 1770 flood, remaining in superb condition.

On a tomb in the Easter Sepulchre – within the rails of the high altar – is a miniature effigy of a knight, cross-legged and holding his heart. This may indicate a heart burial – with the body buried elsewhere. The figure is known locally as the 'Little Crusader' and probably dates from the early years of the thirteenth century. The detail of the carving of the knight's chain mail armour is exquisite.

Built into the south wall of the church, near the Lady Chapel, is a stone effigy known as the 'Big Crusader'. Somewhat damaged, the figure dates from the late thirteenth century.

The discovery of the mineral springs came too late for the town to challenge others, such as Bath or Leamington – even with the suffix 'Wells' added its name! The enterprise never paid its way, even in the 1840s, and subsequent attempts to resurrect the spa have all failed. It has, however, left the town with its most unusual and outrageous building, the Spa or Pump Rooms – passed by the walk as it enters the town.

A saline spring was discovered in July 1839 when a well was sunk in the garden of one Septimus Holmes Godson, at his residence near Kyre Brook – 'The Court'. Godson wasted no time in publicising the discovery

and the Tenbury Well was opened on June 1st 1840. In July 1846 a second spring was discovered close to the Crow Inn.

James Cranston, of Birmingham, was called in to design a suitable building for the enterprise and the result is the 'Chinese Gothic' concoction seen today. Cranston based his design on some green houses he had been responsible for, substituting wrought iron sheets for glass. The building is one of the earliest examples of prefabrication, with the sheets manufactured in Birmingham for assembly on site. It has recently been restored.

Cranston was also responsible for the unusual Round Market, situated in the triangular 'Market Square', at the A4112 end of Church Street. Given that he has left Tenbury with two such unusually designed buildings the residents of Shelsley Beauchamp (Stage 2) must be thankful that Cranston was of a more restrained mind when he rebuilt their church in 1846-7.

Tomb of Thomas Acton Adams and Mary, his wife, in Tenbury Wells Church

Stage 4

Tenbury Wells to Ludlow

Mileage: 10 miles
(From Tenbury Wells: 4¼ miles to Little Hereford Bridge; 7 miles to
Ashford Carbonel)
O.S.Maps: 1:50000 (Landranger): 137 (Ludlow)
            1:25000 (Explorer): 203 (Ludlow)

*Leaving Tenbury, past the church, the route runs along a low ridge
above the river for most of the way to Berrington – using a mixture of
footpaths and quiet roads. There follows a riverside section to Little
Hereford Bridge where the only river crossing of the stage takes place –
although en route there is an opportunity to take a short detour across
the Teme and back, via a footbridge, to visit Little Hereford church.*

*Over the river, tracks – one of which follows the former course of
the Leominster Canal – and a quiet road lead to the pretty village of
Ashford Carbonel, where both church and water mill are visited. From
here a low-level route – quiet road and then tracks and fieldpaths –
leads to Ludlow, which is entered riverside.*

Starting at the southern (Worcestershire) end of Teme Bridge walk along
the right-hand side of Teme Street, through the town – passing the Bridge
Hotel, a Lloyds/TSB bank and the Ship Inn, all on the right.

About 40 yards beyond the Ship Inn – just past a bus stop – turn right along
an alleyway (Church Walk) which initially runs along the side of the Regal
Community Centre. Follow this to reach a quiet back street – Church Street –
with steps leading up to a gate into the churchyard immediately opposite.

*Divert a few yards left along Church Street to find a small metal plaque set
into the wall alongside the top of the doorway to house Number 13. This
records the level reached by the water during the flood of 1886 and vividly
illustrates how susceptible Tenbury is to flooding.*

Cross Church Street and enter the churchyard. Here bear left to round the
corner of the building and reach its entrance porch.

*For notes on Tenbury church see the main note on Tenbury Wells at the end
of Stage 3.*

Bear left at the porch to exit the churchyard via its main gate – alongside a
small building bearing the date '1858'.

The small building has served as both a fire station and a mortuary in its time.

*Look straight ahead when leaving the churchyard to see Tenbury's Round
Market building.*

Leaving the churchyard, bear right to round two corners of the small
building and walk along a narrow metalled path, which initially runs alongside
the churchyard wall (right). Continue to follow the narrow path – a hedgerow
succeeding the wall on the right; the Teme about 40 yards distant beyond.
When the path reaches a bungalow development – its metalled surface

replaced by paving slabs – follow it between the first two dwellings and then continue straight ahead to emerge into the end of a cul-de-sac. Turn left along this.

After about 35 yards – alongside bungalow Number 32 – leave the road, right, to cross a footbridge over a small stream and pass through a small wooden gate into a field/orchard. Go straight ahead across this, to its far boundary where there is a gateway through the hedge. Do NOT pass through this but instead turn left to walk along the boundary to the corner of the field.

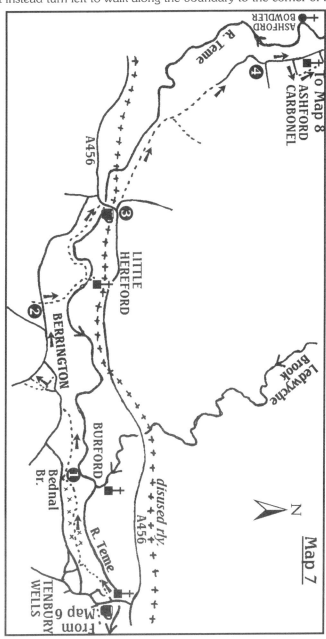

Here pass through a gap – possibly closed off by a couple of livestock barriers – and through a small wooden gate, ahead, and onto a narrow path. Follow this between the gardens of neighbouring dwellings to emerge onto a road – Berrington Road – via a kissing gate and a couple of steps.

Turn right along the road. After only about 15 yards on it – just past the first lamp post and by a dwelling called 'The Bednalls' – leave it through a metal kissing gate, right, to walk along another narrow footpath, again initially passing between gardens to reach the rear of the houses. A footpath sign – 'Bednal Bridge ¾' – points the way off the road (SO592679).

Bending left, the path runs alongside garden boundaries. Cross a stile on it to enter a rough meadow area, following the right-hand boundary through this.

Look right for a view of Titterstone Clee Hill and over the right shoulder, behind, for a distant view of Tenbury Wells with its church prominent.

Leaving the rough meadow area the path becomes confined between a high garden hedge, on the left, and a lower hedgerow, right – the river some two fields distant below. It runs along a low ridge. Follow it over three more stiles, the third of these giving access to a field. Here follow the right-hand boundary.

On reaching the far corner of the field drop down to cross another stile into a more open area of low ridge. Continue to follow the obvious path straight ahead, soon passing through a gate into a wooded section – the path running near the top edge of the trees, with a wire fence and a field beyond it on the left and a progressively steeper drop down through the trees on the right.

An attractive woodland walk with the river soon visible down through the trees on the right.

Gaining height the path emerges, left, from the trees – the fence still on the left. Just beyond this, at a break in the trees, turn right, downhill towards the river – as indicated by a footpath marker post.

Walking down the clearing, Burford House and church are directly ahead across the river. Ledwyche Brook joins the Teme alongside the house.

At the bottom of the slope, with the river ahead, bear left to reach a stile into a field – crossing a small side stream en route. In the field bear left to reach its left-hand boundary – a wire fence – and then follow this along. A grassy/dirt track soon begins underfoot.

Follow this to the far corner of the field. Here cross a stile – situated to the right of a metal farm gate.

Beyond the gate follow the obvious broad dirt track, the Teme briefly alongside on the right until the track bends away from it, left. Remain on the track to eventually pass through a metal farm gate and emerge onto a road. ❶

Turn right along the road, immediately crossing Bednal Bridge, over Bednal Brook. Within 30 yards of the bridge leave the road, right, over a stile into a field. Bear half-left from the stile up the field to reach a corner opposite that where it was entered. Here cross another stile, accessed over a plank across a seasonal water channel, into a plant nursery/field. Follow the right-hand boundary through this, a gentle climb, to reach an area with greenhouses. Continue to follow the right-hand boundary through this, a metalled track now underfoot, passing through any gates encountered.

Look between the rows of greenhouses (left) and when a red-brick house comes into view turn left off the metalled track onto a stony track which runs

Burford

Burford church (St. Mary's) contains the only Royal tomb along the entire length of the Teme – that of Princess Elizabeth, daughter of John of Gaunt, Duke of Lancaster, and sister of Henry IV. Married to Sir John Cornewall (Cornwayle) who won the right to wed her in a tournament in 1400, she died in 1426. The building itself dates from the twelfth century, with a fourteenth century extension and fifteenth century tower. It was much restored in the late nineteenth century.

The neighbouring house – built on the site of an old castle – dates from 1726 and is home to Treasure's garden centre and the national collection of clematis. The original castle here was built by Richard Fitz Scrob during the reign of Edward the Confessor and the manor then passed to his son, Osbern Fitz Richard. (The family also owned Richards Castle, to the south of Ludlow.) His descendants held the manor for a further 300 years before it passed to the Cornwall family, who occupied it for 400 years. Purchased by a William Bowles, the castle was demolished and replaced by the current house, bought in turn by the Treasure brothers in 1954.

The name Burford means 'fortified place by a ford' – that is the pre Norman Conquest castle.

between the greenhouses towards it. Beyond the greenhouses a metalled surface recommences underfoot and the track passes through a metal farm gate to reach the aforementioned dwelling (left). Beyond this it emerges onto a quiet road, a car park for the nursery (Frank P. Matthews Ltd.) just opposite. Turn right along the road.

After just over 100 yards on the road leave it, left, along what is signed as a No Through Road. (There is a Public Bridleway sign at its entrance.)

The narrow road descends from the junction, bending left to cross a stream – Cadmore Brook – and approach a house with a sign which reads 'Lancroft Labradors' – Berrington Mill. Just before reaching the house bear right, off the road, over a stile (NOT through the gate and up the path to the right of the house.)

From the stile a narrow path climbs up through a small wooded area, bending to the left and up some steps to reach another stile into a plant nursery/orchard area. (A path goes right here but is not taken.) Follow the left-hand boundary fence through this, a gentle climb. Pass through a metal farm gate in a boundary ahead and continue to climb alongside the left-hand boundary fence through the next 'field', another plant nursery area.

Just before a point where the boundary fence, left, bends slightly right look right for the best view yet, on this stage of the walk, of Titterstone Clee Hill.

Continue to follow the left-hand boundary fence to the top of the plant nursery 'field'. Here cross a stile, in its corner, to emerge onto a quiet road. Turn right along this.

The road soon begins to descend and reaches a junction. Here go left, signposted 'Little Hereford 2', passing through the small farming settlement of Lower Berrington where a gentle climb begins. On reaching another junction ignore a road going left (Field Lane) but continue straight ahead, the road still climbing.

More good views of the classic – almost 'crouching' – outline of Titterstone Clee Hill over to the right.

Reaching the top of its climb, the road begins a slight descent.

At a point on the road where there are metal farm gates on either side look half-right over the gate on the right for a first view of the pyramidal roof of Little Hereford church, across the river.

The road makes a sudden slight dip and then bends left. On the level again, and where the two arms of a footpath signpost indicate a path crossing it, leave the road, right, through a metal farm gate into a field – SO558675. (The gate is the second on the right after the dip in the road and has another gate opposite it.) ❷

Head very slightly left from the gate, the distance to a hedge boundary over to the left decreasing as the field is crossed. Nearing a point where the land ahead drops away down to the river walk alongside the aforementioned hedge (left) to locate and cross a stile over it – situated about five yards before a gate through that same boundary. In the adjacent field, bear right from the stile to reach the point where the land begins to drop away. Here turn left to walk along the edge of the field, above the river – a very steep drop to the right.

After about 45 yards the path bears half-right down into a wooded section, leaving the field. The narrow path descends some rocky steps and runs along a

Little Hereford Church

The nave and the pyramidal roofed tower of the building date from the thirteenth century, the chancel from the fourteenth. An unusual feature of the church is the remains of a second altar set high above the narrow chancel arch and accessed by a gallery – long gone – and a flight of stone stairs which can still be seen in the right-hand side of the arch. What remains of the altar is a stone cross, a piscina – or stone basin – let into the wall, and the letters 'BB' which probably represent a dedication to the Virgin Mary and stand for 'Beata Beatissima', 'Blessed, the Most Blessed'.

A second altar was not, in itself, an unusual feature in Medieval churches. Dedicated to the Virgin Mary, they were usually sited against the wall dividing the nave from the chancel but in some instances, as here, they were placed in the rood loft – the rood being the cross above. The Little Hereford example is one of the few remaining rood loft altars in the country. It is thought that the altar may have been so positioned here to avoid flood damage.

Just inside the door of the church, on the south wall of the nave, is a memorial tablet recording the loss of sixteen local children, aged between 10 weeks and 14 years, to a diphtheria epidemic in 1870. Adjacent to this is a new Millennium window which represents air (wind), water, fire and earth and is the work of Jennifer Davies of Ludlow.

Walking towards the chancel arch look left to see a plaque on the north wall of the nave which reads 'Here lieth the body of Roger Dansey of Little Hereford in the County of Hereford Esquire who deceased 25th day of August Anno Domini 1658 Aged 74.'

A tomb recess in the north wall of the chancel dates from the fourteenth century and has a well worn contemporary effigy – probably of a female figure – carved in it.

short section just above the water, protected by a wooden handrail. Reaching the end of the woodland cross a stile into a field.

Crossing the stile the route leaves Worcestershire, in which it has been from the start, to enter Herefordshire.

Follow the riverside path through the large field – the river on the right. Part way through the field the path reaches a footbridge across the river which leads to the church of St. Mary Magdalene, Little Hereford – a short, very worthwhile diversion.

To reach the church cross the footbridge and then follow an obvious path, slightly to the left, to a gate into the churchyard. The entrance porch lies half-right from this.

Leaving the church, return across the river, over the footbridge, to continue with the route of the walk.

I shared a late October visit to the church with a field mouse.

Continue to follow the riverside path through the field until reaching a point where a side stream (West Brook) enters the river. Here bear right to leave the field and cross the stream, via a high footbridge. Again follow the riverside path through the field so entered – an isolated dwelling (Westbrook Cottage) over to the left and just beyond the field boundary.

On reaching the far boundary of the field pass through a small metal gate to enter an orchard area. Continue to follow the riverside path through this – a caravan park beyond the boundary fence on the left. On reaching the far side of the orchard cross another high-level footbridge, over a side stream, to enter another orchard. Again, follow the riverside path through this.

The modern, concrete Little Hereford Bridge, carrying the A456 road across the river, appears half-right ahead.

Reaching the far side of the orchard cross a stile to emerge onto a rough parking area alongside the A456. Walk across this to the road and turn right along it (signposted 'Tenbury Wells 3') to cross the river via Little Hereford Bridge. There is a pavement on the right-hand side of the road here. Just beyond the bridge, on the right of the road, is the Temeside Inn.

 Bus Service 731/732, Tenbury Wells – Ludlow, runs along the A456 here.

Over the bridge, cross the road to a pavement which now commences on its left-hand side, passing a black-painted building of wood and corrugated metal (left).

Just beyond the black-painted wood and corrugated metal building a disused railway track crosses the road. This was the line between Woofferton, on the extant Shrewsbury to Hereford line, and Bewdley, on the preserved Severn Valley Railway (see the note on 'Tenbury's Railways').

As the A456 road bends right leave it, left, at a junction – signposted 'Middleton, Bleathwood'. After about only 40 yards on this road, as it bends right, leave it straight ahead to walk along wide dirt track – SO547684. ❸

Joining the track, look behind for a distant view of Little Hereford church.

During the early stages on the track notice the grassy embankment running through the field on its right – the course of the old Leominster Canal.

Continue along the obvious, wide dirt track, crossing a small stream which runs across it via a footbridge (on the right-hand side of the track). When the track reaches a metal farm gate pass through this into a field. Here follow the hedge boundary on the left – along a section which can be very muddy after wet weather.

The long, narrow nature of this field betrays its former life as the course of the old Leominster Canal.

Continue to follow the left-hand boundary hedge through the long, narrow field. Where that boundary bends away left continue straight ahead, eventually

The unusual surviving second 'high altar' in the rood loft,
Little Hereford church

Tenbury's Railways

A railway line from Woofferton to Tenbury Wells was constructed by the Tenbury Railway Company between 1859 and 1861. Leaving the Shrewsbury & Hereford Railway Company's line at Woofferton Junction it ran for just over five miles to a station situated to the north of the river, and main settlement, at Tenbury. Short sections of the, by then, drained bed of the Leominster Canal – see note below – were used for its route.

The extension of the line from Tenbury to Bewdley was undertaken by the Tenbury & Bewdley Railway Company between 1861 and 1864. From Tenbury the line ran through Newnham Bridge and then to the east of Cleobury Mortimer to pass through Wyre Forest and so to Dowles Bridge, over the River Severn, and a junction with the Severn Valley Railway just to the north of Bewdley station – a distance of some 14 miles. This line also made use of the drained canal – over a 3 mile section between Tenbury and Newnham Bridge.

Throughout its life the route was never more than locally important. It served several small collieries in the Wyre Forest area – such as the pit at Bayton, linked to a siding near Cleobury Mortimer station by an aerial ropeway.

Cleobury Mortimer station was also the junction for a line serving the dhustone quarries on Brown Clee Hill, via an incline – the Cleobury Mortimer & Ditton Priors Light Railway.

The two railways were also in part promoted to serve in the development of the new spa at Tenbury itself while another, very seasonal, traffic was of hops – and of the vast army of hop pickers from the industrial Midlands required to harvest them.

By 1869 the Tenbury Railway had passed into the joint ownership of the Great Western Railway and the London & North Western Railway and in the following year the Tenbury & Bewdley Railway became the property of the Great Western.

The line between Woofferton and Tenbury was closed in 1961 and passenger traffic on the remaining Tenbury to Bewdley section ceased in the following year. All traffic ceased in 1965 and the track along the entire route had been lifted by 1966.

Some railway features remain – notably the piers of Dowles Bridge, in the Severn just north of Bewdley, and Newnham Bridge station.

climbing a short slope to reach a dirt track and a metal farm gate. Pass through the gate and follow the track ahead from it.

On reaching another metal farm gate pass through this into a field. Here follow the right-hand boundary.

The cluster of radio masts at Woofferton appear half-left in the distance. The old canal aqueduct over the Teme was situated at the far (left) side of this field – at SO537687.

Continue to follow the right-hand boundary through the field, ignoring a footpath which departs, right, over a stile at a bend in that boundary. Upon reaching a facing metal farm gate in the boundary pass through it into the next field, here following the left-hand boundary (which is effectively the same boundary as was followed through the previous field). On reaching the far

The Leominster Canal

The Leominster Canal or, to give it its full title, the Kington, Leominster and Stourport Canal was an ill-conceived project of the 'canal mania' years of the late eighteenth century. Promoted from about 1789, the canal was planned to join the three towns of its name and to link the area with the important trade route of the River Severn, and so with the industrial Midlands. Of more local significance, it was also planned to serve several small collieries in the Mamble and Pensax areas.

The proposed route was 45 miles in length and would require several major engineering features – three tunnels (the longest of which, at Pensax, would be 3850 yards), three aqueducts (one over the Teme near Little Hereford, another over the Rea at Newnham Bridge, and a third over the Lugg at Kingsland), and a flight of seventeen locks to raise the route 200 feet from its junction with the Severn.

An Act of Parliament for the undertaking was obtained in 1791, empowering the promoters to raise £150000 capital, with a further £40000 if required. It was decided to build the section from Leominster to the Severn first, in order to generate revenue for the balance of the route to Kington.

By 1794 the canal was open from Woofferton as far as Marlbrook Wharf, to the east of Newnham Bridge, from where a tramway served Mamble collieries. An immediate effect was the supply of cheap coal to Tenbury.

The project was, however, already suffering from a shortage of funds and poor workmanship. The opening of the next section of canal –

from Woofferton to Leominster – was delayed because of difficulties with Putnal Field tunnel while to the east of Marlbrook, on the section towards Stourport, another tunnel – at Southnett – collapsed burying three workmen.

By 1796 the canal was open between Leominster and Marlbrook but was in poor condition and had substantial debts. £93,000 had been spent in constructing just 18 miles of the projected 45 mile route.

By 1803 all construction work on the undertaking had ceased and, despite various plans to raise additional capital and to substitute tramways and inclined planes along the remainder of the route, no additional mileage was opened.

The canal company struggled on until 1858 when it was purchased by the Shrewsbury & Hereford Railway, who had initially intended to use its bed between Woofferton and Leominster for their tracks but later decided against this. They did however sell sections of the drained canal to both the Tenbury Railway and the Tenbury & Bewdley Railway for use in the building of those lines – see note above.

Given the years since its closure, and its use in part for the lines of the subsequent railways, a surprising number of canal features remain. These include a fine wharf house at Marlbrook – the headquarters of the canal company – and a now crumbling single arch aqueduct over the River Rea, near Newnham Bridge. The Teme Aqueduct still stands although its centre span was blown up as part of a wartime military exercise in 1939.

left-hand corner of the field cross a stile, situated to the right of a small metal gate, and walk straight ahead to reach a stony/dirt track.

Crossing the stile the route leaves Herefordshire to enter Shropshire.

Walk along the stony/dirt track, which runs along between hedges and eventually bends left to approach the large green, corrugated metal outbuildings of Aberkirk Farm. Remain on the track which passes to the left of these and takes on a metalled surface to become a quiet road.

The road descends very slightly past isolated dwellings. Ignore a dirt track going left off it – signed as a Public Bridleway. A right bend leads to a crossing of a small stream and the road then bends left and rises, meandering to eventually reach a road junction – with a seat and a walnut tree on a small grassy island. Here turn left, crossing the road to its right-hand side where there is a pavement. ❹

The road runs through the village of Ashford Carbonel. It crosses a small stream and then passes a handsome half-timbered dwelling (right) – Brook House – and the thatched Candlelight Cottage (left). Beyond this, again on the left, is the village hall and stone war memorial. Just after passing the war memorial, at a junction, turn right off the road along Donkey Lane.

Donkey Lane takes its name from the animals which were used to transport goods along the trade route which formerly crossed the Teme via the ford just to the west of Ashford Carbonel. At times of flood, when the ford was impassable, the animals were corralled hereabouts.

Walk up Donkey Lane, ignoring a turning left (The Hayles). Passing Meadow House (right) the road bears 90 degrees left, past the entrances to two further dwellings – The Old Coach House and The Avenue. With another dwelling (Sunny Bank) on the left it then bends 90 degrees right to become the entrance drive to The Leys. At this bend leave the road straight ahead along a narrow grassy path, confined between a hedge on the left and a wire fence boundary to a field on the right – SO526709.

There is a very good view of the whole of Titterstone Clee Hill to be had, over to the right, from the path to Ashford Carbonel church and from the churchyard itself.

Ashford Carbonel

The village of Ashford Carbonel takes its name from the Norman Carbonel (Carbonell) family, members of which came to England as part of William the Conqueror's invasion force in 1066. Ashford comes from the old name of the manor which was Esseford and refers to a ford across the River Teme, near ash trees.

The ford was somewhat downstream of the current Ashford Bridge and is thought to have been situated on an ancient trackway from the Midlands to Wales, possibly a salt-way. Across the ford from Ashford Carbonel is Ashford Bowdler.

At the time of Domesday Book (1086) the manor of Esseford was held by Osbern Fitz Richard of Richards Castle and Burford. Sometime between 1174 and 1185 Osbern Fitzhugh, his son, granted the manors of 'Hesford and Huvertune' (Ashford and Overton) to William Carbonel and his heirs in return for ongoing services under arms.

Walk up the narrow path to reach Ashford Carbonel church. Here, at a Y-junction, take the path which enters the churchyard – through a wooden gate – rather than the one which skirts to the right of it.

Just inside the churchyard on the right is the grave of Arabella Yate, its marker a rare cast-iron tomb cover dating from 1806.

At an immediate junction of paths go right to walk along the right-hand side of the building and leave the churchyard through another wooden gate, ahead. (Go left at the junction if visiting the church.)

Look over to the left, just before leaving the churchyard, to see a gravestone dating from 1882 which bears the lines:

'A sudden shock –
I in a moment fell;
I had not time to bid my friends farewell.
Beware! Death happens unto all;
This day I fell – tomorrow you may fall.'

It commemorates a Mrs. Lancett who was struck and killed by a train on the line just south of Ludlow while picking up nuts.

Passing through the gate out of the churchyard, turn left down a quiet road which descends to a T-junction with the main road through the village, Ashford Carbonel Primary School on the corner, right. Turn right along the road.

Notice the old bell on the rear wall of the school. The front of the building bears the date 1872 and two plaques – a diamond with three dog heads on one and a stag on a shield on the other (the coats of arms of the Downes and the Hall families – local Lords of the Manors).

After about 60 yards on the road leave it, left, over a stile – situated to the right of a wooden farm gate – into a field. Follow the left-hand boundary of the

Ashford Carbonel Church

The church of St. Mary Magdelene, Ashford Carbonel, is sited above the village in a roughly circular churchyard which suggests a religious site of far greater age than the current, mainly Norman, building – a fact reinforced by the presence there of five ancient yew trees, two of which have a girth of some thirty feet and have been estimated as being 1500 years of age.

The church dates from Norman times with later additions and restorations up to Victorian times. About half of the chancel and two-thirds of the nave are early Norman. The chancel was doubled in size in about 1200 and the western third of the nave was added about 100 years after that.

The oldest objects inside the church are a decorated stone tomb slab situated in the floor to the left of the altar – dating from the late fourteenth century – and the basin of the font which is twelfth century in origin.

A window next to the pulpit contains fifteenth century stained glass at its top – a decorative rose at its centre – while on its sill is a delightful little piscina.

The chancel roof was renewed during the restoration of the church in 1883 but that in the nave dates from 1600. The pyramidal roofed timber belfry dates from the mid fifteenth century. It houses three bells, two of which date from around 1320.

Just inside the door, on the right, are two early views of the church, both water-colours, the one dating from 1791 and the other from between 1820 and 1840.

Outside, the Priest's Door in the south wall of the chancel dates from the second half of the eleventh century while a blocked doorway to the nave on the north side of the church dates from about 1210.

At the west end of the church the surround of the lancet window bears the carvings of two stone heads – the church's only medieval sculpture.

field to its far corner and then turn right to follow the far boundary along to the next corner, the river below on the left. (Note: The public footpath sign at the stile from the road points half-right from the stile to the opposite corner of the field, which is in fact the corner now reached. While Explorer Map 203 does show a path running diagonally across the field the Right of Way is indicated along the field boundaries, as above.)

On reaching the corner of the field cross a stile to drop down into an orchard area. Go straight ahead through this, under apple trees. Ashford Mill and its semicircular weir will be seen half-left ahead. Remain well to the right of the building while crossing the orchard (small footpath marker posts show the way). On reaching a track to the mill turn right along it to reach a metal farm gate with a stile situated just to its left. Cross the stile to emerge onto a road and turn right along this. ❺

The mill was built in about 1819. Technically still capable of operating (and unique on the Teme in this respect), it is no longer used to grind corn for human consumption because of health regulations. The weir, just upstream, is a good place to pause and watch salmon leaping.

Quite an ornithological crossing of the orchard, one late October afternoon, with a heron disturbed off the weir and a buzzard in among the apple trees themselves. I also spent some time watching a wren on a pile of logs by the mill.

To the left along the road, beyond the orchard, is Ashford Bridge, which crosses the Teme just upstream of the mill. Designed by Thomas Telford and built in 1797 at a cost of £830 the single span brick bridge here was quite revolutionary in its day in that Telford decided to make the spandrels hollow in order to reduce weight. The bridge has a span of 81 feet. It was partially rebuilt under Thomas Groves in 1877. There is a good view of the weir to be had from the bridge.

Go left at the road, crossing Ashford Bridge and – later – a railway bridge, to reach Ashford Crossroads on the A49, in a little under half a mile. Bus service 731, Tenbury Wells to Ludlow, stops here. The occasional bus on this route runs into Ashford Carbonel village.

On reaching a crossroads go left onto a quiet, narrow road – indicated as a No Through Road. It runs along, fairly level, initially between high hedgerows. Remain on it until it eventually reaches railway lines and comes to an end – an isolated, line-side dwelling on the left.

Walking along the narrow road, the hills over to the left are those of Mortimer Forest, above Ludlow. The left of the two main summits visible is High Vinnalls, which rises to a height of 370 metres/1214 feet.

Nearing the railway lines, the wooded ridge on the right of the road is Tinkers Hill.

Continue past the dwelling (left) to reach a gate leading to a crossing over the railway lines (Manchester – Shrewsbury – Hereford – South Wales). Cross them, with care, and pass through another gate into a narrow field. Go straight ahead across this – under 10 yards – to reach a kissing gate situated to the left of a metal farm gate. Pass through this to emerge onto the busy A49 road. Cross the road, with care – more of a challenge than the railway crossing! **6**

Over the road, bear half-right up a metalled track. After only about 30 yards, and just before reaching a cattle grid, leave the track, half-left, to enter a field via a metal farm gate

Entering the field, the tower of St Laurence's church at Ludlow appears ahead in the distance.

From the gate bear very slightly left across the large field, aiming for a metal farm gate which will be seen in the far boundary – just to the left of houses beyond that boundary (Saltmoor) – and keeping to the right of overhead power lines/poles. Nearing the far boundary pass under the power lines to reach and pass through the aforementioned gate.

From the gate, go straight ahead along a dirt track which passes between two dwellings, hedgerows on either side of it. Beyond the dwellings it becomes more grassy underfoot. On reaching a metal farm gate pass through it to remain on the track, the Teme now alongside on the left.

Entering a field, the track becomes less distinct underfoot. Ignore a path going left to the riverbank but instead follow the right-hand boundary hedge through the field. Nearing the far corner of the field another track joins, sharp left. Follow the now obvious track ahead through a metal farm gate (may be open) and across a stream, under trees and in what can be a very muddy area after wet weather.

Follow the track ahead from the stream, which runs alongside on the right, for about 50 yards to reach a Y-junction. Here take the left track, which rises to pass through a metal farm gate and into another field.

Through the gate, follow a wire fence (right) ahead and then drop down, right, to follow the right-hand boundary hedge up the field – on a sunken grassy track.

As the gentle climb up the field progresses look left for a view of St. Laurence's church and Ludlow.

Where the field narrows to a section less than 10 yards across remain alongside the boundary hedge on the right. Reaching the end of the narrow section pass through a metal farm gate into the next field. Here again follow the right-hand boundary fence initially – ignoring two gateways through it (right), the second of which was gateless at the time of writing.

Divert through the second (gateless) gateway and walk a few paces left to find an ancient stone trough in use as a livestock water trough. It looks very old indeed, but did it start life as something grander?

Follow the right-hand boundary through the large field. Where that boundary bends right maintain direction, heading for a large house beyond the far boundary. Pass through a metal farm gate, just in front of this house (Steventon House), to emerge onto a quiet road. Turn left along this, effectively straight ahead from the gate – signposted to Ludlow. ❼

Passing alongside Steventon House (right) ignore a metalled track going left but continue ahead along the road. On reaching an 'avenue' section on the road – between rows of large trees – ignore a footpath going right over a stile (and running between wire fences towards railway lines, right), but remain on the road which begins to bend left and soon passes Steventon Cottage (left).

Passing the far end of the cottage garden look left to see part of the Elan Valley Aqueduct 'bridge' over the river. Again looking left, over on the distant hillside a small redbrick structure is a 'well house' for the aqueduct. These occur throughout the length of the aqueduct, usually at the junction of pipeline and tunnel sections, and contain stop gates and overflow channels – in case of bursts.

Remain on the road, past Steventon Cottage. On reaching a junction ignore a road going right but continue straight ahead – signposted 'Ludlow 1'. About 50 yards beyond the junction leave the road, turning left down a flight of stone steps – indicated by a footpath sign – which lead to the River Teme. These may be very slippery in wet weather. On reaching the river turn right along its bank. ❽

Look left, downstream, here to see the Elan Valley Aqueduct's Steventon Bridge crossing the River Teme.

Follow the riverside path until it emerges onto a road – via a stile situated to the left of a wooden gate. Cross the road and turn left along it, passing Temeside Mill (left).

A large cream-painted building, in stone and brick and with cast iron window frames, Temeside Mill dates from the nineteenth century. Known as the New Mill until the 1880's, corn milling ceased here at the turn of the century but in

Steventon Cottage and the Elan Valley Aqueduct

Steventon Cottage (at SO523737) is a walkman's cottage for the Elan Valley Aqueduct. A water company employee responsible for overseeing a section of the aqueduct would have lived here, and the building contains meters to monitor the water flow in the pipelines below.

The four pipes of the Elan Valley Aqueduct run for 73 miles from the Elan Valley dams, in mid-Wales, to Birmingham and have carried the water supply for that city since construction of the project between 1892 and 1904.

En route, it crosses the River Teme on three occasions. Steventon Bridge – beyond the cottage – is the last crossing, the other two being Graham's Cottage Bridge and Downton Bridge, both near Leintwardine. The latter is seen towards the end of Stage 5 of this walk.

A 128 mile, 10 day walk based on and along the course of the Aqueduct is the subject of my book, *The Elan Valley Way*, published by Meridian Books.

1921 the premises reopened as the Temeside Case Mill where cases for cutlery and jewellery were made. This enterprise only lasted a decade and since then the building has variously turned out false teeth and wood-burning stoves. It is still commercially active, at the time of writing being used by a company selling hardware for plumbing, heating, kitchens and bathrooms.

Follow the road to reach a T-junction, an old toll house on its right corner. Turn left here, crossing the road (Temeside) to gain the pavement.

The toll house is an early nineteenth century building. The blank window above the door probably contained the toll board.

Follow Temeside to another T-junction. Here, again turn left, to walk along a road beside the river. Ludford Bridge soon appears half-left ahead.

Ludford Bridge

Ludford Bridge, over the River Teme, is a fifteenth century structure although its foundations may be much older. There was formerly a chapel on it – St. Catherine's – which in 1406 was occupied by a hermit, Thomas Shelve of Leintwardine.

An older crossing of the Teme existed on the through route which pre-dated Ludlow, at the bottom of what is now Old Street.

On reaching a road junction, at the bridge, turn right to walk up Lower Broad Street to Broad Gate, where this stage of the walk ends.

Broad Gate is the only survivor of seven gates through Ludlow's town walls. It originally possessed a portcullis. The original medieval gate is largely hidden by sixteenth, seventeenth and eighteenth century domestic architecture but can be better appreciated from underneath, with the groove for the portcullis visible. The cellars of the adjacent Wheatsheaf public house contain the remains of the supports for the drawbridge which formerly spanned the defensive town ditch outside the gate.

The Wheatsheaf public house, to the right of Broad Gate, was built between 1664 and 1668 in the old town ditch and on the site of a building destroyed at the time of the siege of Ludlow, 1646, during the Civil War.

Ludlow

Whilst neighbouring Ludford is mentioned in *Domesday Book* (1086) Ludlow is not and it is not until 1138 that it is first recorded as a place name. The name itself is derived from 'Ludelaue' meaning a hill or mound beside loud waters, i.e. rapids.

Ludlow is very much a medieval planned town, begun under the de Lacy family – supporters of William the Conqueror who were given land hereabouts and began building the castle in about 1086. The town's obvious grid plan incorporates an earlier through route along the present Corve Street and Old Street. It seems likely that the original crossing of the River Teme was at the bottom of Old Street. The only other distortion of the grid plan is where the existing castle was enlarged into it, at its north west corner.

Between 1233 and 1304 the town was walled. The walls were one mile around with 7 gateways through them. Only one of these, Broad Gate, still stands although many sections of the wall remain, such as that in St. John's Road which runs right off Lower Broad Street by Broad Gate.

By 1377 the population of the town was 1700, making it the thirty-third largest settlement in England.

In the fourteenth century one third of the properties in the town were owned by the Palmers' Guild, a quasi-religious organisation formed in the thirteenth century and claiming links with the crusaders. The Guild invested in property and used its profits to help its less fortunate members and the town in general through the provision of almshouses and schools. It was dissolved in 1551, a late casualty of the Dissolution of the monasteries and religious orders started under Henry VIII.

Also in the early fourteenth century Ludlow Castle passed to the powerful family of Marcher Earls, the Mortimers, and thence to the House of York on the cessation of the direct Mortimer male line in 1425. In 1459, during the War of the Roses, the town was sacked after the rout of the Yorkists by Henry VI at the 'battle' of Ludford Bridge.

The town was at the zenith of its power and influence between 1534 and 1689 when it was the main seat of the Council of the Marches. Wales and the border counties were effectively ruled from the town during this period. Much building and rebuilding took place during these years – the Feathers Hotel is an example.

During the Civil War the town was besieged by Parliamentarian forces, in 1646, and many buildings outside of the town walls sustained damage. Ironically the siege seems to have seen only sporadic fighting and many of the houses destroyed at this time were in fact demolished by the Royalist defenders to deny the enemy cover. The siege itself lasted thirty-three days before the town was surrendered.

The Council of the Marches was suspended during the Civil War and was finally dissolved in 1689, the town then losing much of its former importance although it remained something of a fashionable social and cultural centre until the middle of the nineteenth century.

For a time the town was an important centre for the manufacture of gloves, the industry reaching its peak around 1700 but in decline by the early years of the nineteenth century. The major effects of the Industrial Revolution largely bypassed the town.

A railway from Shrewsbury reached Ludlow in 1852 – the Shrewsbury & Hereford Railway.

For such a small town Ludlow is rich with interesting buildings – in fact over 500 of the town's buildings are listed as being of historical interest, a higher proportion to population than any other town in the country except Bradford-on-Avon.

A walking guide such as this could not hope to do full justice to all the town has to offer but to briefly cover the highlights, there are:

(1) Ludlow Castle.

The original castle here pre-dates the town and was built between 1086 and 1094 by Roger de Lacy, a supporter of William the Conqueror. The castle was constructed of stone from the start – quite unusual as most were wooden initially – and it is likely that the earliest part of the town grew up between it and the river around the area now called Dinham (see note at Stage 5).

The castle has been much extended over the years, especially after it passed into the hands of the powerful Mortimer family, through marriage, in 1316. When the direct male Mortimer line died out in 1425 the castle passed, via the female line and marriage, to the House of York and thence to the Crown after the Yorkist Edward IV's victory at Mortimer's Cross (1461), about eight miles to the south-west of Ludlow – a decisive moment in the Wars of the Roses. It then became a royal palace.

The two sons of Edward IV – better known as 'the Princes in the Tower' stayed here for a time and it was at Ludlow Castle that Arthur, the elder son of Henry VII honeymooned with his bride Catherine of Aragon in 1501. Tragically Arthur was dead within five months – at just fifteen years of age – and his wife went on to marry his brother, later Henry VIII. Arthur's heart is buried in St. Laurence's Church while his body was taken for burial in Worcester Cathedral (Stage 1). Mary Tudor, Henry VIII's daughter by Catherine of Aragon, who spent several winters at the castle, was its last royal resident.

After 1534 the castle became the main seat of the Council of the Marches – the town effectively becoming the administrative and legislative centre for Wales and the English border counties. It was a Royalist stronghold during the Civil War and was besieged by a Parliamentarian force under Colonel Birch in 1646 and surrendered after thirty-three days. The Council of the Marches was dissolved in 1689 and after that the castle became disused and soon fell into disrepair. As a 'romantic ruin', in the eighteenth century, it began to attract visitors and walks were laid out around it from 1772. In 1811 it was purchased by the Earl of Powis whose descendants own it to this day.

Significant buildings within the castle grounds include:

(a) The Great Tower Gatehouse Keep – the original Norman gatehouse before the outer bailey, walls and gatehouse were built.

(b) The Chapel of St. Peter – built by Roger Mortimer in the early fourteenth century to celebrate and give thanks for his escape, in 1324, from the Tower of London where he had been imprisoned by Edward II on the grounds of treason.

(c) The Judges Lodgings – built, probably by Sir Henry Sidney before 1581, to house the many judges and court officials needed when the Council of the Marches was in session.

(d) The Chapel of St. Mary Magdalene – possibly founded under Hugh de Lacy and dating from the early years of the twelfth century, the chapel has an unusual round nave – a design which seems to have originated with the return from the Crusades of knights who had seen the church of the Holy Sepulchre in Jerusalem.

(e) The North Range – started in the thirteenth century and completed after Roger Mortimer had taken possession of the castle in 1308, this range of domestic buildings includes the Great Hall of the castle.

(f) The Garderobe Tower – built onto the outside of the Norman curtain wall of the castle in the early fourteenth century, by Roger Mortimer. It provided extra accommodation for the Mortimers, who entertained lavishly, and contained eight chambers each with its own garderobe (toilet).

(2) The Butter Cross.

Built 1742 to 1744 to replace the medieval High Cross. The architect was William Baker. The ground floor serves as a covered market; the upper has been a school and a museum in its time. The building is surmounted by a wooden cupola which contains a bell, thought to have come from the old chapel of St. Leonard in nearby Corve Street.

(3) The Chapel of St. Thomas.

The oldest building in Ludlow outside of the castle walls, built about 1190 and dedicated to St. Thomas a Becket, murdered in Canterbury Cathedral in 1170. The chapel is now incorporated into a later building, topped by an eighteenth century dovecote. It is situated just off Dinham – the road leading from the castle down to Dinham Bridge. Its single celled interior can be viewed through a large metal grille.

(4) The Feathers Hotel.

Probably the best known of all of Ludlow's timber-framed buildings. Situated at the top of Corve Street, this was a 1619 rebuild of an existing town house for Rees Jones, a Welsh attorney in the courts of the Council of the Marches, whose initials can still be seen on the surviving original door lock plate. The building became a pub in 1670. The balcony on the front of it was added in the nineteenth century for electioneering use.

(5) The Bull Hotel.

The oldest pub in Ludlow, having been carrying out that function for 500 years. Its frontage in Corve Street gives no clue as to the true age of the building as this was rebuilt after a fire in 1795. However, pass through to its inner yard to see its true character. The earliest record of it is as Peter the Proctor's House, in 1343, but it is thought to date back to 1199 in part. A priest hole and indoor well have been discovered within.

(6) The Tolsey.

Situated in the Bull Ring and probably of fifteenth century origin, the Tolsey was where the market courts were held. These dispensed instant justice and were known as the Court of Pie Powder – after the French 'Pieds Poudre' literally meaning the 'Dust off the Feet', ie. justice was dished out before one had time to shake the dust off one's feet. The detached nature of the building suggests that it is the successor to earlier temporary market stalls.

(7) The Reader's House.

In 1551 Ludlow Corporation appointed a Reader to carry out some of the duties of the Church. In the eighteenth century the Reader lived in this house, situated behind the church.

The building is a mid sixteenth century rebuild of a medieval stone house, to which a splendid Jacobean porch was added in 1616.

(8) St. Laurence's Church.

Dominates the whole town and is the largest parish church in Shropshire at 132 feet in height and 203 feet long. It dates from 1199 with much fifteenth century rebuilding in the Perpendicular style.

Apparently, some 83 different stonemason marks have been identified carved on the pinkish sandstone of the church.

Full of interest inside the undoubted highlights are the fifteenth century carved wooden misericords. Dating from around 1440 these are amongst the finest of their kind in the country.

The building also contains St. John's Chapel – the chapel of the Palmers' Guild, with its Golden Window containing a representation of St. Catherine and her wheel and Palmers' Window telling the legend of how that organisation got its charter from Edward the Confessor.

Across the church is the Lady Chapel which contains a restored fourteenth century Jesse Window. This chapel was formerly used to house the town fire engine and the wooden pegs for the fire buckets and a blocked access doorway remain.

The West window of the church depicts the Lords of Ludlow Castle ending – at bottom right – with Prince Arthur whose heart is buried somewhere in the building. He died in Ludlow Castle, aged just 15, in 1502 while staying there with his bride of five months, Catherine of Aragon.

The entrance porch to the church is hexagonal in shape – one of only three such constructions in the country, the others being at Chipping Norton and at St. Mary's, Redcliffe, in Bristol. It is of mid fourteenth century origin.

St Laurence was a third century deacon in Rome who was roasted to death on a grid iron over a fire.

A more detailed 'Town Trail' for Ludlow is included in my book, The Riversides Way, published by Meridian Books.

Stage 5

Ludlow to Leintwardine

Mileage: 11½ Miles
(From Ludlow: 3 miles to Bromfield; 5¼ miles to Bringewood Forge Bridge;
8 miles to Burrington)
O.S.Maps: 1:50000 (Landranger): 137 (Ludlow)
          1:25000 (Explorer): 203 (Ludlow)

*The route leaves Ludlow over Ludford Bridge and skirts the edge of
Whitcliffe Common, above the town, before dropping down riverside
to reach Dinham Bridge, beneath the castle walls. Low level fieldpaths
and a private road through the grounds of Oakly Park lead to
Bromfield.*

*Crossing the river for the second time on the stage, the route uses
more fieldpaths to reach Bringewood Forge Bridge and Downton
Gorge. A riverside path and then a track take it below the privately
owned Downton Castle, and to a third river crossing, before more
tracks and paths climb Hunstay Hill – with superb views back to the
castle. From here the route drops down into Burrington to visit the
church, with its well known collection of cast iron grave slabs.*

*Fieldpaths and a quiet road section – including a final river crossing
– lead to the outskirts of the small settlement of Downton on the Rock
from where the last climb of the stage – with further wonderful views
behind – leads back to the Teme and a riverside approach to
Leintwardine.*

Starting at Broad Gate, walk down Lower Broad Street and across Ludford
Bridge, over the Teme. Over the river, go straight ahead up the B4361
road but, just beyond the Charlton Arms and 'Cliff Villas' (both on the
right) take the first turning off it, right – signposted 'Burrington 5¼, Wigmore
7½'.

*For notes on Ludford Bridge see at Stage 4. The River Teme here originally
formed the boundary between Shropshire and Herefordshire, with Ludford,
across the bridge, being in the latter county. The county boundary has now been
moved some distance along the B4361 to the south and Ludford has joined
Ludlow in Shropshire. The route of the walk similarly remains in that county for
the time being.*

*Ludford is a much older settlement than its neighbour, Ludlow, and is
mentioned in Domesday Book, 1086, where it appears as 'Ludeford' – 'the ford
across the loud waters'.*

*Crossing Ludford Bridge, the tower of Ludford church – St. Giles – is visible,
just to the left ahead. To visit the church turn left off the B4361 opposite the
Charlton Arms public house into a quiet lane and then bear right through
ornate metal gates to walk up the churchyard path which bends to the right, a
row of old almshouses down to the left.*

On the corner of the first turning on the right after the bridge – that taken by the walk – are 'Cliff Villas', a wonderfully eccentric pair of dwellings with mock-Tudor windows and a black-and-white upper storey. They date from 1841 and were erected by Edmund Lechmere Charlton, squire of Ludford and the man reputed to have fought the last duel held in England.

Walk along the pavement, on the right-hand side of the road, to leave it up a flight of stone steps ahead. From the top of the steps follow an obvious stepped path straight ahead, climbing along the edge of Whitcliffe Common – the Teme far below on the right.

Where gaps in tree cover allow, there are superb views to be had across Ludlow – right – with both castle and St. Laurence's church prominent. The

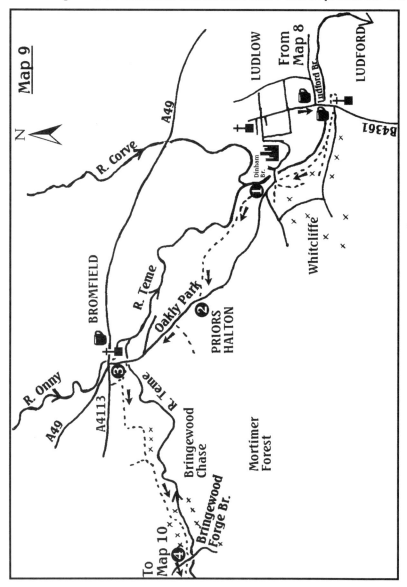

noise of the weirs on the river below remind one of the origin of the the town's name – from 'Ludelaue', meaning 'the mound/hill beside the loud waters'.

At a Y-junction go right, on a path which descends towards the Teme, down rocky steps – a large weir across the river below.

Nearing the riverbank look over the right shoulder, behind – along the weir – for a distant view of Titterstone Clee Hill, through the trees.

Whitcliffe Common

The common was acquired by the Burgesses of Ludlow in 1241, its 'common' status allowing the grazing of livestock, gathering of hay and firewood, and the quarrying of building stone. It is now owned by the Plymouth Estates and managed, for the public benefit, by The Friends of Whitcliffe Common – successors to the former Whitcliffe Commoners Association. At 42 acres the common is only one third of its previous size – reduced in extent by minor encroachments over the years and by the sale of 78 acres in 1793, to pay for paving and lighting in Ludlow.

Ludford Church

There has been a church on this site since at least the twelfth century – a Norman window from that period survives in the west wall of the nave – but until the dissolution of the monasteries under Henry VIII Ludford was only a chapelry, subservient to the Benedictine Priory at Bromfield, passed later on this stage of the walk.

The nave of the church is twelfth century (but was heavily restored in 1866), the chancel dates from about 1300, and the tower is fourteenth century in origin. The large chapel on the north side of the church (the Foxe Aisle) was added by William Foxe in the sixteenth century and contains brasses of him and his wife, Jane. These depict Foxe, who died in 1554, in armour somewhat old-fashioned even for this date.

The chapel contains other tombs of both the Foxe and Charlton families. The tomb of Sir Job Charlton, in its south-west corner, is particularly impressive – with the recumbent effigy of the baronet dressed in his judicial robes. He died in 1697.

Sixteenth century brass of William Foxe in Ludford Church

Follow the obvious riverside path to approach Dinham Bridge. On reaching the bridge ignore paths going up sharp left and left (up steps) but instead pass through a gap in the parapet wall ahead, cross the road (NOT the bridge) and turn left along it – riverside.

Dinham Bridge was built in 1823 and replaced an eighteenth century bridge which itself had replaced a timber bridge built on stone piers, the latter probably being reused in the eighteenth century structure. The old piers can still be seen just downstream of the current bridge when the river is low. The previous bridge and castle are the subject of a well-known Turner painting of about 1790.

The part of Ludlow known as Dinham takes its name from Joce de Dinan who was granted land here in 1130 when the de Lacy family – founders of both castle and settlement at Ludlow – temporarily fell out of favour with the Crown. He also held Ludlow Castle for a time during the troubled reign of King Stephen, 1135-1154.

Walk along the road – another large weir in the river alongside and the towering walls of Ludlow Castle opposite. It passes a row of almshouses, left.

The almshouses are known as Clive Cottages. They were built sometime around 1811 by the Earl of Powis and restored in the 1850's in memory of his nephew, Robert Henry Clive of Oakly Park – see note below.

Ludford House

Ludford House, to the west of the church, was originally built in the late sixteenth century by William Foxe, although the house has had a long and complicated architectural history since then. Foxe was a member of a successful legal family and had twice represented the borough of Ludlow in Parliament. After the dissolution of the monasteries under Henry VIII he purchased St. John's Hospital, just across the river in Ludlow, where he then lived, as Lord of the Manor of Ludford. It is thought that he originally built the mansion in Ludford for his son Edmund who was unfortunately to die before him.

The Foxe family did very well out of the dissolution of the monasteries for it was another son, Charles, who was to purchase the Priory at Bromfield – see note under Bromfield below.

It was William Foxe who first built almshouses on the site below Ludford church although the buildings now seen on the site were erected by a later resident of Ludford House, Sir Job Charlton, in 1672. They have since been known as Sir Job Charlton's Hospital.

The Manor of Ludford passed from the Foxe family to the Charlton family in 1637, sold for £500 to meet debts. It was not to change hands again until 1920. Job Charlton, who lived at Ludford from 1637 until his death in 1697 was one of the most distinguished judges of his day. He was Speaker of the House of Commons for a time. The importance of the Charltons locally is celebrated in the name of the public house which overlooks Ludford Bridge – the Charlton Arms.

The sixteenth century service range of Ludford House is visible from the route of the walk – look half-left ahead along the B4361, after crossing Ludford Bridge, to see its four large chimneystacks. These may be a legacy from a previous building on the site, the leper Hospital of St. Giles.

At a Y-junction, just beyond the almshouses, go right – along a quiet, narrow road which is indicated as being a No Through Road and signposted to Priors Halton. Passing the Cliff Park caravan/chalet park (left) ignore a dirt track going right but remain on the road. Less than 40 yards beyond this, and just before reaching the entrance to the Cliffe Hotel – ahead, left – leave the road, right, through a wooden kissing gate (to the left of a metal farm gate) into the corner of a field – SO505747. ❶

Go straight ahead from the gate across the field to reach a point, at its far side, where the land drops away to the river below. Here bear left to walk along the top of the slope down to the river – with initially trees and then, later, a hedge boundary on the right.

Crossing the field from the road there are good views, right, of both the castle and the tower of St. Laurence's church at Ludlow.

The River Corve

The streams which become the Corve rise on the eastern side of Wenlock Edge, just south of Much Wenlock, the river then flowing south-west, south and south-east – through Corvedale – before a final loop south-west, just to the north of Ludlow, brings it to its confluence with the Teme. An attractive little river, it passes through no major settlements en route. It takes its name from the Old English word 'corf' meaning 'a cutting'.

Walking along the field edge, above the Teme, depending on tree cover it may be possible to see the confluence with the River Corve, opposite.

On reaching the far side of the field drop down into a dip to cross a stile and then a makeshift footbridge over a side stream – a fallen tree which has been provided with a wooden handrail. Beyond this cross another stile to enter the next field. Turn right from the stile to climb out of the dip, following the right-hand boundary through the field – a wire fence in front of a hedge boundary with trees.

The low, wooded hills over to the left are the north-western ridge of Mortimer Forest – often referred to as Bringewood Chase.

Approaching the far side of the field look behind for an unexpected, good view of Ludlow Castle.

Reaching the far side of the field locate and cross a stile through the boundary ahead – situated some yards to the left of the field corner.

Crossing the next, very long field, the small farming settlement of Priors Halton appears, half-left, ahead.

Continue to follow the right-hand boundary through the next – very long – field. Breasting the final rise along it, and about 150 yards before the field corner ahead, look out for a footpath marker post at the field edge. Here bear left across the field – again over a slight rise – heading towards some barns at Priors Halton.

Over the rise in the field, maintain direction to locate another marker post and drop down into a dip, at the field boundary ahead. Here cross a footbridge over a small stream and then a stile into the next field.

Bear half-right up the field – well to the right of a lone tree in it and passing just to the left of one of a number of poles carrying overhead wires – towards its far right corner. On reaching the far corner cross a stile in the boundary on the right – situated to the left of a metal farm gate – into the adjacent field. Here bear half-left, to maintain direction.

Crossing the field look behind for a final view of St. Laurence's church at Ludlow.

On reaching a hedgerow corner – on the left – bear left around it to walk along a short section of track, between hedges, and emerge onto a quiet road. The small farming settlement of Priors Halton is just along the road to the left here. ❷

Turn right along the road.

Look right, after just a few yards on the road, for a superb distant view of Titterstone Clee Hill, with Cleehill village visible on its slopes (right) on a clear day.

The road descends gradually, passing an isolated dwelling on the right. Entering a wooded section it dips to cross a stream and then begins to climb gently to reach a metal farm gate across it.

Walk around the gate to continue along what is now a Private Road through the formal grounds of Oakly Park. Follow the road through these, ignoring all turnings off it. Oakly Park House itself lies some distance to the right but is just visible briefly as the walk progresses.

Oakly Park became the seat of the Herbert family after they had abandoned the old Bromfield Priory site – see note below – damaged by a fire in 1638. The estate later passed to the Clives and the Windsor-Clives and is now the property of the Earls of Plymouth. Both the Herberts and the Clives were very active in the politics of Ludlow, representing the borough in Parliament on many occasions during the seventeenth and eighteenth centuries.

The present house dates from the early eighteenth century but was much altered in 1800 and again in 1820. It is a large brick structure with prominent Tuscan columns.

The road eventually descends to pass a gatehouse (right) where the drive to Oakly Park House joins, sharp right. Pass through metal gates to leave the grounds of Oakly Park and walk ahead down the road to cross Bromfield Bridge over the Teme.

Over the river, leave the road, left, crossing a stile – situated at the end of the left parapet of the bridge – to drop down into a field. Follow a riverside path through this – the Teme on the left. (If visiting Bromfield or its church continue ahead along the road from the bridge.) ❸

The River Onny

The River Onny is formed by two streams – the West Onny and the East Onny – which unite near the small settlement of Eaton, just to the south-west of the Long Mynd. The streams which become the West Onny rise to the west of the Stiperstones, between that ridge and Corndon Hill. The tributary streams of the East Onny rise between the Stiperstones ridge and the Long Mynd itself. From Eaton, the river flows south-east – past Craven Arms, Stokesay and Onibury – to its confluence with the Teme.

The name 'Onny' is derived from Old English words meaning 'single river' and refers to it being an amalgamation of the two fairly equal-sized head-streams.

Bromfield

Bromfield takes its name from the large amounts of broom which once grew hereabouts, literally meaning 'the Field of Broom'. The settlement grew up just upstream of the confluence of the Rivers Teme and Onny.

The church of St. Mary the Virgin, Bromfield, stands between the two rivers. An earlier church on the site, possibly dating from about AD900, is mentioned in *Domesday Book* (1086). A Norman church, parts of which survive in the present building, was built here early in the twelfth century and in about 1135 a Benedictine Priory was founded.

The Priory buildings were adjacent to the south wall of the nave of the church. It is thought that an original central tower of the Norman church either collapsed or was dismantled at some point and was replaced by a new tower, at the north-west corner of the church, in the early thirteenth century.

The priory was dissolved in the reign of Henry VIII, probably in 1538.

After lying empty for some 20 years or so the old Priory buildings were bought by Charles Foxe who converted them into a house – the chancel becoming a dining room with a bedroom above it. The nave of the church remained in public use as a place of worship.

In 1638 a fire destroyed the house, although the church was saved. The chancel had also survived and was given back to the church in 1658 by Richard Herbert – the Herberts had acquired the property via marriage into the Foxe family. It was at this time that the plastered rounded ceiling of the chancel was painted with cherubs floating among clouds – completed in 1672 by Thomas Francis at a cost of seven guineas. Even after some 300 years this remains spectacular but is best described as 'naive' art and may not be to everyone's taste.

The masonry of the nave survives from the original Norman church, as do some arches from the original central tower. The present tower

Gatehouse of the old priory, Bromfield

and the north aisle are thirteenth century in origin. The font is fourteenth century.

The nave possesses an oak roof dating from 1577 and which was only revealed when the church was restored in 1890, having previously been concealed under plaster.

Outside to the west is the fourteenth century gatehouse to the Priory – of stone with a later timber framed upper floor. It has recently been restored by English Heritage and the Landmark Trust.

Against the south wall of the church are the ruins of Foxe's House – currently unsafe.

Sad to say but at the time of writing the church itself is suffering from serious structural problems and is full of scaffolding and rarely used. In 1997 a routine inspection revealed that one end of a roof beam had been eaten away by rot and that death-watch beetles were active within. The roof was found to have dropped by seven inches in one place!

A tablet on the north wall of the nave of the church commemorates Doctor Henry Hill Hickman. Born at nearby Lady Halton in 1800, the seventh of thirteen children of a tenant farmer, Hickman pioneered the application of anaesthetics by inhalation (nitrous oxide) during surgery. Unable to raise any interest in his work in England he was slightly more successful at the court of Charles X in France, although the French Academy of Science eventually proved just as sceptical of his procedures as their English counterparts. Disillusioned, Hickman returned home to England, where he ran a surgery at Tenbury Wells – see note at Stage 3. He died at the early age of 30 and is buried at Bromfield. The tablet commemorates the centenary of his death (1930).

Note the attractive old building – undergoing restoration work at the time of writing – to the right just before crossing Bromfield Bridge. It was formerly a corn mill.

The River beyond the church is the Onny, which joins the Teme just downstream. Beyond that is the A49 road which may be reached by continuing along the road past the church. The Clive Arms restaurant/public house, a small village shop, telephone box and bus stop are a little way along the busy road.

 Buses on the 738/740 Ludlow – Leintwardine – Knighton routes stop outside the Clive Arms (Cook House), Bromfield, on the A49. Also buses on the 745 Ludlow – Clun and 435 Ludlow – Shrewsbury routes.

Follow the riverside path to reach a stile, to the left of a metal farm gate. Cross this into the next field. Here again follow the riverside path.

This field is marked on Explorer Map 203 as 'Crawl Meadow'. Locally, several of its neighbours are known by the same name and this refers to an old legend. Apparently, the daughter of a local landowner fell in love with a landless knight. Her father, not surprisingly, was not over keen on the relationship and threatened her that if she chose to marry the man then her marriage dowry would only be as much land as she could crawl around between sunset and sunrise. She persisted with her plans and, dressed in leather in order to protect herself, managed to crawl a distance of four miles.

On reaching a field boundary ahead – formed by a side stream which joins the Teme here – bear right along it, climbing away from the riverbank into the field. Follow the boundary (left) to a point where there is a gateway through it – a track commencing along the boundary ahead here. Do NOT follow this track but instead turn left to pass through the gateway into the next field – SO476766.

From the gateway bear right to reach the corner of the field and then left, to walk along its long right-hand boundary. Follow this the length of the field – a large pond (Lower Pool) on the other side of it in the latter stages.

On eventually reaching the far corner of the field cross two stiles into the next and immediately turn left to walk up their common boundary. On reaching the corner, at the top of the field, turn right to walk the length of its boundary (left) with woodland beyond (Stocking Nursery).

This field and the previous one are of enormous size and length. The walk through them exceeds one mile even without the climb up their common boundary. One can only hope that the crawling maiden of the Bromfield legend did not have to pass this way!

On reaching the far corner of the long field – where the woodland on the left also ends – cross two stiles to enter the next field. Walk straight ahead down this field from the stiles, aiming to pass just to the right of an isolated large oak tree and heading towards the remains of a metal wind pump which will be seen below. Go straight across a grassy track, en route.

Passing the oak tree maintain direction towards the wind pump to reach a gateway with a largely redundant stile on its right. Pass through this – (the field boundary fence here is so incomplete as to be almost non-existent) – and then aim to pass just to the right of the aforementioned wind pump.

Follow an indistinct path ahead from the wind pump, walking along the top of a final slope down to the river, on the left, and passing below large patches of gorse bushes and a large oak tree – both on the right. Beyond these aim to maintain height while crossing the remainder of the field, passing above more patches of gorse (left) and bearing slightly around to the left. At the far side of the field locate and cross a stile.

Crossing the stile, the route leaves Shropshire to re-enter Herefordshire.

From the stile go straight ahead, down a small dip and across a short clearing, to enter woodland opposite through a gateway (gate off its hinges at the time of writing). A path bears left under the trees to reach the riverbank. Follow the obvious wide riverside path through woodland to reach Bringewood Forge Bridge – SO454749 – passing the ruins of an old mill *en route*. **❹**

A delightful section of woodland walking along the fast flowing Teme, which here boils over a series of rapids.

The graceful arch of Bringewood Forge Bridge was erected in 1772 as part of Richard Payne Knight's landscaping of Downton Estate – see note below. It was designed by the Shrewsbury architect Thomas Farnolls Pritchard, also responsible for the Iron Bridge at Coalbrookdale, who is supposed to have based it on his plans for that more famous structure. There is a semicircular weir immediately upstream of the bridge. The ruined mill passed en route to the bridge recalls the ironmaking industry which once thrived along the river hereabouts.

On reaching the bridge, cross the road (NOT the bridge) to continue along a riverside path ahead.

The spire of Downton church (St. Giles) appears ahead in the distance. The building stands in a field, at the end of a long vista from Downton Castle and was built to replace an earlier church – also dedicated to St. Giles – which stood about half a mile further south-west, at Downton on the Rock, and was abandoned in 1861. The architect of the new church was Samuel Pountney Smith. The building and its situation will be better seen and appreciated later on this stage of the walk, as the route climbs over Hunstay Hill.

The riverside path soon widens to track width and reaches a metal gate. Pass through this and continue ahead on the track/path, which becomes grassy underfoot and runs along a low embankment above a riverside meadow (left), now some little distance from the river itself. On reaching the end of this very slightly elevated section continue straight ahead through the meadow – where at one point (at the time of writing) a passage has been cut for the path through a fallen tree.

The path approaches the riverbank but then bears slightly to the right, away from it again, passing under the branches of a large oak tree and reaching another metal gate – crossing a culverted side stream as it does so.

Pass through the gate – a dwelling immediately ahead – and onto a track. Turn right, up the track, passing the aforementioned dwelling (left). About 25 yards beyond the house – with a corrugated metal garage on the right of the track – turn left, through a small wooden gate to the left of a farm gate, onto another track. Within 20 yards leave this over a stile, right.

From the stile bear very slightly left up a grassy slope, a steeper section of which then leads up to a stony/dirt track. Turn left along this.

Follow the obvious track, passing below Downton Castle (right).

Passing the castle, remain on the track which begins to descend slightly to approach Castle Bridge. Nearing the bridge, the track reaches a gate with a stile alongside on its right. Over the stile, follow the track around to the left – past a derelict cottage (right) – to cross Castle Bridge. **5**

Iron founding at Bringewood

Iron founding started at Bringewood in about 1600, using locally produced charcoal and iron ore and limestone from the Clee Hills, brought in by packhorse. In 1690 Job Walker purchased the lease of the works, having previously operated it for the Earls of Essex and Craven, and Francis Walker purchased Downton Estate in 1716. The Walkers sold out, in1727, to the Knight family who also owned furnaces at Wolverley and Madeley.

Several members of both Walker and Knight families are buried in Burrington churchyard – visited later on this stage of the walk – where they lie under cast iron grave slabs manufactured here.

Iron production reached its peak locally in the first half of the eighteenth century after which the area was overtaken by technological advances at developing Coalbrookdale. Ironfounding ceased at Bringewood in the latter years of the century and there is little evidence on the ground now to recall its former significance.

At the peak of its production there were no fewer than fourteen water wheels in action along a mile of river here – the highest concentration of water power in England at that time.

There are good views from Castle Bridge both right, up Downton Gorge, and back to the castle.

Across the river climb straight ahead up a stony track which soon bends left and then sharp right.

This is the start of the climb over Bringewood Chase, and specifically Hunstay Hill. The route climbs from a height of about 95 metres/312 feet at Castle Bridge to about 227 metres/745 feet at its highest point on the ridge.

The stony track climbs to a wooden farm gate (may be open) with a stile to its right. Cross this and continue up the track which bends left. About 80 yards after the gate, as indicated by a Public Footpath signpost, leave the track – half-right – to continue climbing across a hillside field.

Castle Bridge

Downton Castle

Downton Castle was built by Richard Payne Knight between 1772 and 1778. A member of the ironfounding dynasty, he was something of a scholar, anthropologist and archaeologist but also, more importantly, a leading light of the Picturesque Movement which denounced the formal landscaping of the likes of Capability Brown in favour of a wilder and more natural approach. At Downton, one might argue, Nature had done most of the hard work for him as regards the castle grounds.

The River Teme, its waters trapped at the end of the last Ice Age, has cut a spectacular gorge just upstream of the castle. Knight added walks, caves, tunnels and fine bridges across the river.

Unfortunately, there is no Public Right of Way through Downton Gorge itself, although English Nature – who have a reserve there – will occasionally take visitors through it. The gorge is home to both otter and polecat and is also well-known for the fossil fish found there.

Superb views to be had while climbing here. Look back over the left shoulder for the first sighting of Titterstone Clee Hill for some time. As the climb progresses look right to see the church of St. Giles, Downton – its setting, in the parkland of the Downton Castle Estate, now better appreciated.

Half-right ahead the rounded hill with the trees along the top of it is Tatteridge Hill (224 metres/735 feet). The route runs alongside the swathe of

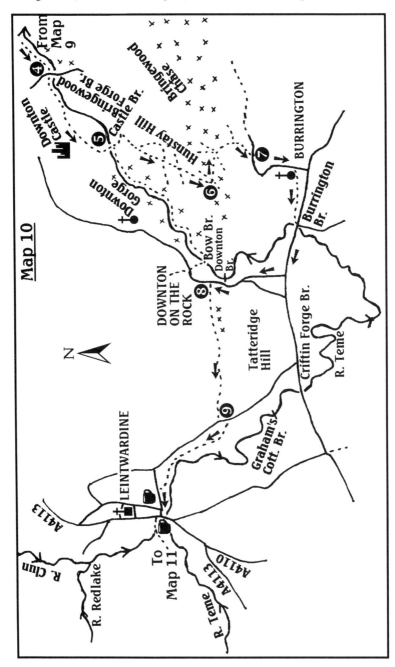

woodland which can be seen just to its right later on this stage. Later on the climb the twin summits of Brown Clee Hill come into view behind, over to the left of Titterstone Clee Hill.

Down to the right the course of Downton Gorge can be clearly seen, while Downton Castle finally reappears from behind the trees.

Maintain direction up the field to eventually approach the track recently vacated – which runs above and to the left. On reaching a wire fence, which borders the track, walk alongside it to reach a stile over it – situated almost in the top corner of the field. Cross this to regain the track, turning right along it.

Almost immediately the stony track passes through a metal farm gate (may be open). Just after this ignore a track going up sharp left through a metal farm gate but remain on the main track which bends slightly to the right to enter a wooded section. About 65 yards after passing through the gate – part of the way round the right bend and with a slight left bend visible on the track ahead – leave the track, half-left, up a steep narrow path. A footpath marker post should point the way – SO442736.

The path climbs steeply – through bracken in season – to reach a stile into a field. Crossing the stile head half-right steeply up the field, passing just to the right of the first large oak tree encountered and climbing towards a group of another six oaks, above. Pass to the right of these to near the top of the field, heading for another single large oak tree – well to the right of the aforementioned group of six – where the path meets a grassy track.

An absolutely stunning view back to Downton Castle and its grounds to be had here. Turning onto the track, the settlement of Downton on the Rock is visible across the valley, half-right.

Turn right along the track. Almost immediately, at a Y-junction, go left onto a grassy track which rises and passes under more oak trees to reach a metal farm gate. Pass through this into a field, the track underfoot becoming stonier and beginning to bend to the left. About 25 yards after the gate, at the apex of this bend, leave the track, right.

Leaving the track, look straight ahead. A small concrete structure reveals the fact that the original, lower, grassy track marks the course of the Elan Valley Aqueduct hereabouts.

Walk straight ahead across the large hill-top field to locate a stile at its far boundary, woodland beyond – SO439732. **❻**

Wonderful views open up while crossing this field. Downton Castle, Titterstone Clee Hill and Brown Clee Hill are initially still visible behind. Half-left ahead the long wooded hill now in view is Gatley Long Coppice – at the eastern edge of the Vale of Wigmore – with the windmill at Leinthall Starkes likely to be visible on its slopes. Running left from that are the hills which make up the opposite ridge of Mortimer Forest, with the high point of High Vinnalls. To the right of Gatley Long Coppice the view may extend between the hills around Aymestrey as far as the northern escarpment of the Black Mountains, while continuing right – almost straight ahead – are the hills around Aymestrey Gorge, and along the River Lugg, and – slightly right ahead – the Wigmore Rolls. Looking right the high hills up the Teme valley towards Knighton – Bucknell Hill, Bucknell Wood and Stow Hill should be visible. The route climbs the latter on Stage 6.

Cross the stile and bear half-left down a narrow path at the edge of the woodland. On reaching a wider grassy path, after just a few yards, turn left along it for just a couple of paces and then half-right off it and down through the trees – almost a staggered 'crossroads' of paths, in fact.

The path descends steadily through the woodland to reach a five-way junction. Here ignore a path going right and two more going left but continue straight ahead to drop down into a dip and reach a stile. Cross this and follow the path straight ahead to emerge into a field, through bracken in season.

Continue almost straight ahead across the field – a distance of about 60 yards – to walk up a stony/dirt track which climbs half-right and then bends around to the left. As the track straightens after this bend leave it, right, to pass through a gateway into a field.

From the gateway bear very slightly left, passing just to the left an isolated oak tree and heading towards the far left-hand corner of the field – woodland beyond. On reaching the field corner drop down a slope to reach a stile over a fence. Cross this and go straight ahead, through a small clearing to reach a stream.

Cross the stream via a footbridge, situated just to the right of a ford of sorts. From the end of the footbridge go right, initially alongside the stream for a few yards but then out into a field. Maintain direction across this, aiming for a small wooden gate situated just to the right of a pole carrying overhead wires.

Passing through the gate continue straight ahead up a path, confined between trees and bushes as it climbs, to reach a stile. Cross this to emerge onto a concrete track – SO443726. ❼

Turn right along the track which soon makes a sharp bend to the left.

At the apex of the sharp left bend look ahead, if the hedgerow allows, for a good view across the valley with Burrington church in the foreground and the wooded hill of Gatley Long Coppice in the distance. Leinthall Starkes windmill should again be visible, on the lower slopes of the latter.

The descent steepens and the track soon reaches the village of Burrington. The half-timbered Burrington Farm, on the right, is the first building passed.

While walking the road through Burrington look right to see Tatteridge Hill, shaped like an upturned boat and with the line of trees across its top.

On reaching the settlement proceed straight ahead down the road. After a little less than 400 yards take a footpath which goes off right, alongside a house called Church Bank and opposite the School House, and leads – initially up a short track – to the gate of Burrington churchyard. Enter the churchyard and follow the gravelled path around to the left-hand side of the church, through a short avenue of yew trees.

The gravelled path finishes at the church porch. Here go straight on to a stile in the churchyard boundary ahead. Cross this and proceed along a narrow path between a fence on the right and bushes on the left. The path opens out into a rough paddock area, the boundary fence remaining on the right. Follow the fence to reach another stile giving access to a field. Head straight across this to cross another stile into the next field. Again go straight across this field, a pond on the left, to another stile. Cross this to enter a field which has a watery depression (stream) along its left boundary. Walk along the edge of this and then bear left to the far left-hand corner of the field to cross a stile by a metal farm gate. This leads onto a road at a junction, another road joining opposite (SO436721).

Turn right along the road, which immediately crosses the River Teme via Burrington Bridge, and remain on it as it starts to climb.

Crossing Burrington Bridge, Tatteridge Hill is directly ahead. A concrete structure which may be seen high on its slopes is a valve chamber for the Elan Valley Aqueduct.

At a road junction turn right, signposted for Downton.

This section along the road to Downton is the only one on the entire eight stage walk where the route is actually heading 'downstream' along the Teme valley. The river may be glimpsed through the trees, down to the right.

The quiet, narrow road climbs gently and bends towards Tatteridge Hill. At a junction, where another road comes in from the left, go straight on. The road begins to descend gently and starts a long bend to the right.

At SO427728 a small Severn Trent building, on the left-hand side of the road, is passed – with access gates to a path leading up to the valve chamber on Tatteridge Hill. Opposite, on the right of the road, is a wooden stile. Look over this for a view of the Elan Valley Aqueduct's Downton Bridge crossing of the Teme. The river cannot be seen but the line of the Aqueduct up the slope beyond it – towards Hunstay Hill – is unmistakable.

Burrington Church

Burrington Church – St. George's – was largely rebuilt in 1864 and has a timber spire. Little is known of the earlier building on the site but a rough drawing of 1842 suggests it was a much lower structure than its replacement. The current building is the work of two architects – Samuel Pountney Smith and G. F. Bodley. Pountney Smith worked on the nave, Bodley the chancel. This unusual job-sharing arrangement was the result of a disagreement between the local landowner, Mr. A. Broughton-Knight of Downton Castle, who was meeting the cost of the nave and the Vicar (Philip Hale) who was responsible for the chancel. Fortunately that difference of opinion has not affected the finished product, the church being very simple in style and decoration – and in no way as overstated as some Victorian architecture.

Outside, at the east end of the church lie a series of cast-iron grave slabs (covers) dating from the early seventeenth century. These would have originally been inside the old church – the chancel of which was longer than the present building – and if not unique are certainly the finest collection in the country. There are eight slabs, all cast at the Bringewood forge location visited earlier, and they commemorate members of the local ironfounding families, such as the Walkers and the Knights – see note on Bringewood, above.

The settlement of Burrington dates back beyond Domesday Book (1086) when it was known as Boritune, to Saxon times. Its name means 'farmstead by a fortified place'. At the time of the Norman Conquest the manor was held by the Herefordshire nobleman known as Edric the Wild, the source of many legends and an opponent of William the Conqueror during the English uprising of 1069.

Finishing its long bend to the right, the road bears left and begins to climb. Passing through a short cutting, it reaches the first houses of Downton on the Rock. About 60 yards after passing Bow Cottage (right) leave the road, left, over a stile into a field – SO428732. ❽

Go straight ahead from the stile up the field to reach another stile in its top boundary. Cross this into the next field.

Climbing the field to the stile, look behind for a view over to Hunstay Hill and the route climbed earlier on the stage. Gatley Long Coppice and Leinthall Starkes windmill are directly left during the climb.

Again go straight ahead from the stile up this field – heading for a point in it where the left-hand boundary, which has woodland beyond it, bulges out into it. (The woodland is the swathe sighted earlier on the stage, from Hunstay Hill.)

The twin summits of Brown Clee Hill appear behind as the climb continues, the spire of Downton church also visible – in the foreground, to the left of them. Nearing the boundary with the woodland look over the left shoulder for a possible distant sighting of Burrington church.

On reaching a point alongside the 'bulge' in the left-hand boundary, by a Public Footpath marker post, continue straight ahead up the field – aiming to keep the boundary with the woodland between 35 and 40 yards distant, on the left, throughout the ensuing climb.

Approaching the top boundary of the field bear very slightly to the right to reach a gap in the hedge which is situated just to the left of a single large ash tree – about 75 yards in from the top left-hand corner of the field. Another Public Footpath signpost points the way.

Reaching the gap, look behind for the best views to date. Both summits of Brown Clee Hill, the spire of Downton church, Titterstone Clee Hill, Hunstay Hill and the earlier route of the walk, and High Vinnalls should all be visible.

Passing through the gap, and across a dirt track, go straight ahead through the next field to reach a double metal farm gate through its far boundary, a footpath signpost to its right.

Crossing the field look left. The low hill with the line of trees across it is Tatteridge Hill again, here seen from a very different viewpoint than earlier and appearing almost insignificant.

Reaching the farm gate, spectacular views open up ahead. Slightly to the right, in the middle distance, the round wooded hill is Coxall Knoll – see note at Stage 6. Beyond that are the high hills running up the Teme valley, such as Stow Hill. Looking to the left of Coxall Knoll, Brampton Bryan Park, Pedwardine Wood and the field-covered, rounded mass of Harley's Mountain (386 metres/1266 feet) will be seen. Continuing around to the left there are the wooded Wigmore Rolls and the Vale of Wigmore itself, stretching down to the hills around Aymestrey. Behind the Wigmore Rolls the long tree-covered mass of Shobdon Hill Wood may be seen.

Passing through the gate, ignore the obvious dirt track beyond – which runs right to farm outbuildings – but instead go straight ahead to cross a stile into a field. Here bear slightly to the right ahead to locate and cross a stile over the right-hand boundary fence.

Crossing the stile, Leintwardine makes its first appearance ahead, the large tower of the church of St. Mary Magdalene very prominent.

Go straight ahead from the stile to reach a stony track. Bear half-left across this to cross a stile into another field, a dwelling down to the left. Go half-left from the stile across the field to reach another stile in the opposite boundary – beyond which the land drops away steeply. Cross the stile and immediately turn left, along a narrow path – the steep drop on the right – passing alongside the aforementioned dwelling (left).

Cross a stile – just beyond the house – and continue to follow the narrow but obvious path, a wire fence on its left. The path descends gradually.

Ahead and below, the River Teme will be seen meandering in its wide valley. Nice views of Leintwardine over to the right.

I descended this section of path, one afternoon in late October, picking my way between hordes of pheasants – many of them an exotic deep blue colour – and rabbits.

Continue down the path, following the fence on the left – beyond which a metalled track soon appears. When a metalled track appears slightly to the right, ahead and below, bear slightly right – away from the fence on the left – to drop down and pass through a metal farm gate and emerge onto it.

Go straight ahead from the gate and then half-left down an arm of the track to reach a quiet road (NOT the arm of the track which goes left from the gate and climbs) – SO414729. Turn left along the road.

After about 180 yards on the road – alongside the last of a series of poles which carry overhead wires along its right-hand side – leave it, right, through a wooden kissing gate to drop down into a field – SO414728. **⑨**

From the kissing gate head half-right across the field, aiming between a very large oak tree (right) and the banks of an abandoned river channel (left), and following the line of the foot of the original slope down from the kissing gate.

Approaching the far boundary of the field bear slightly left towards a line of willow trees, which mark the course of another old river channel, to reach another kissing gate to the right of a metal farm gate in the far left-hand corner of the field. Passing through this follow roughly the same direction – initially along the foot of the slope in the field and then keeping the boundary fence to the left about 20 yards distant as the foot of the slope veers away right.

Crossing this field, the tower of Leintwardine church reappears ahead. Beyond the abandoned channel, on the left, the main river is now much nearer.

Maintaining the same general direction, approach the boundary on the left and walk along it – the river now just beyond. Passing a redundant stile continue to follow the fence, a small farm settlement (Trippleton) and the recently vacated road across the field to the right.

Continue to follow the fence as it bows out in a long sweeping bend to the left – caused by it following the banks of yet another abandoned river channel. At the end of the long bend walk past another redundant stile, continuing to follow the fence with the main river alongside again.

On reaching another fence, ahead (SO407736), turn right to walk along this, heading towards an enclosed area which houses a small sewage/recycling plant.

Reaching a kissing gate through the fence (left) pass through it and go straight ahead to cross a slight depression (ditch) in the ground – where it appears part of a hedge boundary has been removed – and enter the adjacent field. Here turn right to follow the boundary hedge (right) along. On reaching the aforementioned recycling plant that hedge boundary is replaced by a high fence. Continue to follow it past a redundant kissing gate.

The footpath emerges through a small wooden gate (to the right of a wooden farm gate) onto a quiet road (Rosemary Lane). Turn left along it into Leintwardine, past the fire station, on the left, and the Sun Inn and a fish and chip shop (the Fiddler's Elbow), both on the right. Ignore a road on the right (Watling Street), and on reaching a T-junction cross over the road to the Lion Hotel, where this stage of the walk ends.

Leintwardine

The large north Herefordshire village of Leintwardine represents that most unusual of settlements, a Saxon village built on the exact site of a Roman garrison town. The Saxons were a superstitious people and generally regarded it as unlucky to build over previous remains. In this instance however the importance of the site, on high ground above the confluence of the Teme and Clun, appears to have outweighed their fears.

The Roman fort and settlement here – known as Bravonium or Branogenium – was established around AD160 at the point where the Roman road of Watling Street crossed the Teme. The settlement was rectangular in layout and surrounded by a wall and ditch. Watling Street ran to the immediate east of the wall. The present main street, High Street, runs north-south through the middle of the site.

The name 'Leintwardine' is of Saxon origin and means the 'enclosure on the River Lent'. 'Lent' was an alternative name formerly used for the River Clun – of Celtic origin, meaning 'torrent' or 'stream'.

The Saxon king Edward the Confessor owned the 'Hundred' of Leintwardine (Lenteurde) which extended into more modern Shropshire, Herefordshire and Radnorshire and contained 49 manors at that time.

By the time of Domesday Book (1086) the manor of Leintwardine was under the control of the powerful Mortimers of Wigmore Castle, one of some 130 manors given to Ranulph (Ralph) de Mortimer by William the Conqueror in return for his support.

Seen from a distance the village is dominated by the buff sandstone tower of its church, dedicated to St. Mary Magdalene, which seems to glow almost golden on sunny days.

The church stands just inside the original eastern wall of the Roman settlement. Built on Saxon and Norman foundations the current building is of mainly thirteenth and fourteenth century origin with 1865 rebuilding. The oldest visible part is a blocked doorway in the west wall of the nave which is twelfth century. The church is mentioned in Domesday Book.

The tower of the church is thirteenth century in origin and was built as much for defence as any other reason – with walls up to six feet thick. It is 76 feet in height and there is a spiral staircase of 103 steps to the top.

A chamber at the second stage of the tower was once home to Thomas Shelve, a hermit. who had previously resided in the small chapel on Ludford Bridge.

The top storey of the tower contains the eight bells of the church. The tenor bell bears the inscription 'I to the church the living call. I to the grave do summon all'.

Inside the entrance porch to the church is a peculiar iron grille which looks as if it might have been used as some form of punishment but in fact is to prevent anyone from standing under the weights of the church clock and meeting with an accident.

The old clock of the church may be seen preserved inside. Made of wrought iron and brass and with two crude stone weights it worked only one hand on a slate dial which is now hidden under the stucco and later dial on the tower outside. It is one of the oldest of such mechanisms in the country, dating back to at least the early sixteenth century.

Also in the church is an octagonal fourteenth century font on a more modern base.

Standing at the steps leading from the nave to the chancel look at the base of the arches left and right to see carved heads of King Edward III and a lady, possibly his wife Philippa. In 1328 Roger de Mortimer set aside the income from some of his lands to pay for nine chaplains to say mass daily, in the church, for the souls of himself, his wife Countess Joan, his mistress Isabella (known as the She Wolf of France because of her numerous political intrigues – such as with Roger against her own husband Edward II), Isabella's son Edward III, and his wife Philippa.

The unusually great difference in floor levels between the nave and chancel is down to the church being built upon the old Roman embankment. Roman bricks and tiles have been discovered below the floor of the building.

In 1181 Hugh de Mortimer had given the church to the abbey he had founded at Wigmore. At the time of the Dissolution of the monasteries and abbeys under Henry VIII (1538), the carved wooden misericords, choir stalls and benches of the Abbey, dating from the fifteenth century, were brought to the church where they can still be seen. The misericords are very similar to the better known examples in St. Laurence's Church in Ludlow but have suffered far more damage.

Outside, in the churchyard, is the grave of General Sir Banestre Tarleton. The son of a Liverpool draper, Tarleton purchased a commission in the Kings Dragoon Guards and fought in the American War of Independence, rising to the rank of Lieutenant Colonel and earning such a reputation in the eyes of his American foes that he became known as 'Bloody Tarleton'. His role in the war was portrayed, in a very unsympathetic light, in the Hollywood film *The Patriot* which starred Mel Gibson.

Returning to England as a hero after the war, Tarleton became a close friend of the Prince of Wales eventually taking on a mistress – the actress Mary Robinson – of whom the Prince had grown weary and living with her for five years. In 1798 he was promoted to Major General and married the daughter of the Earl of Alcester, Susan Priscilla. The couple left London and moved to Leintwardine, living at Leintwardine House. Although distant from the capital Tarleton remained friends with the Prince of Wales and would sometimes send him gifts of salmon which he had caught in the River Teme.

Tarleton died in 1833. There is an imposing monument to him in the Mortimer Chapel of the church – a marble tablet surmounted by laurel wreath, helmet, breastplate and sword and with an eloquent eulogy – erected by his wife.

Modern Leintwardine has a fish & chip shop (The Fiddler's Elbow – passed in Rosemary Lane on the way into the village), a Post Office cum Store, a Petrol Station with Shop, a general store (on Watling Street), a Butcher, and a very small HSBC Bank branch with limited opening hours – two days per week as of the time of writing. There is a public phone box 100 yards or so up the High Street from the Lion Hotel, outside the bank.

The village has three public houses. There is the Lion Hotel by the bridge over the Teme (recalling the lion on the Mortimer coat of arms), and at the far north of the village is the Cottager's Comfort – known as 'the Poker' or 'the Poker and Hole' by some of the village's older residents. Finally, along Rosemary Lane – and passed as our route enters the village – is the Sun Inn, a real old-fashioned alehouse with no frills or pretensions.

Coracles may sometimes be seen on the Teme hereabouts and the village still boasts a coracle maker, based in Watling Street.

Leintwardine to Knighton

Mileage: 10 Miles
(From Leintwardine: 3½ miles to Bucknell; 8 miles to Stowe Church)
O.S.Maps: 1:50000 (Landranger): 137 (Ludlow)
          1:25000 (Explorer): 203 (Ludlow); 201 (Knighton & Presteigne)

The route leaves Leintwardine, crossing the River Clun and heading towards the hill fort of Coxall Knoll – on a mixture of fieldpaths and tracks. Rounding the hill fort it approaches Bucknell alongside the River Redlake – again on fieldpaths. It remains riverside through the settlement, passing the church, before turning west towards Bucknell Wood.

Skirting the wood, on a fine forest track, it reaches a quiet road section which takes it to the beginning of its only climb of the stage – over the large mass of Stow Hill. The hilltop is reached via tracks, paths and finally open grassland, with superb views across the Teme valley and beyond.

Descending from the summit via a rocky valley, beneath Holloway Rocks, a fine stony track leads to the little church at Stowe – in a beautiful setting high in a fold of the hills. From here tracks and fieldpaths take the route down towards Knighton – approached through Kinsley Wood. The only crossing of the Teme on this stage of the walk takes the route into Wales for the first time as it enters the town.

Starting outside the Lion Hotel, facing the road, turn left up High Street. After a few yards turn left into Mill Lane – between the Post Office and the Petrol Station. Follow the lane and where it swings right, into the grounds of Seedley House, go straight ahead and onto an unmetalled track.

Passing a house called 'Troutbeck' (left) look left – across and beyond its garden – to see the confluence of the River Clun with the Teme.

Following the track, pass through a metal farm gate, the River Clun now on the left. On reaching another metal farm gate, leading into a field, do not pass through it but instead turn left to reach two bridges, side by side, over the Clun (SO400741).

The River Clun

The Clun rises in the hills near the settlement of Anchor, and the Kerry Ridgeway, and flows south-east and then east through Newcastle, Clun, Clunton and Clunbury. Skirting Aston on Clun it turns south, past Clungunford, to reach its confluence with the Teme.

A very attractive river, the small settlements it passes through, and which take its name – (an old Celtic river name, 'colun' or 'colauno', which simply translates as 'water') are still very much among 'the quietest places under the sun'!

A former alternative name for the river was the Lent – another Celtic river name meaning 'torrent' or 'stream'. As such it gave its name to Leintwardine.

Cross the river, via the footbridge (left) and go straight ahead across the field so entered to reach a stream at its far side. Cross this, via another footbridge, into the next field. Here turn right to cross a depression – possibly containing water – and to walk alongside another depression (on the left of the footpath) which again may contain water after wet weather. Follow this across the field – half-right from the point where the field was entered over the footbridge – to a stile in the far boundary.

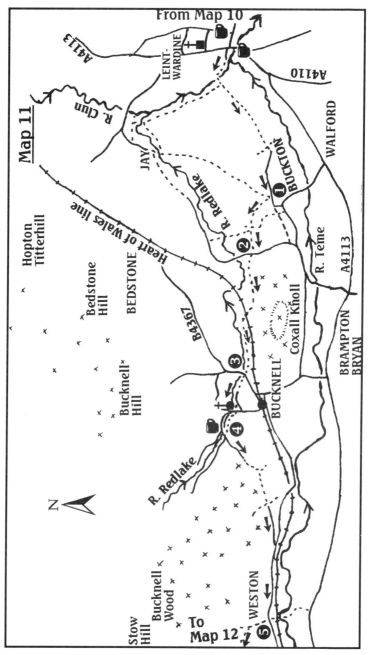

The hills over to the left are the Wigmore Rolls.

Cross the stile and two others which follow immediately. Head straight across the field now entered to a stile in its far boundary. This is situated just to the right of a group of wooden buildings which will be seen ahead. Cross this stile to enter an orchard area and maintain direction through this, the wooden buildings on the left, to cross a further stile onto a dirt track.

Turn left along this and then immediately (within five yards) right, through a metal farm gate (may be open) and along another dirt track. In about 40 yards this reaches a T-junction with another track – this time with a metalled surface. Turn right to walk along this.

Walking along the track look ahead to see the round, wooded hill of Coxall Knoll. The hills to the right of it are those behind Bucknell, such as Bucknell Hill and Hopton Titterhill. The hills to its left are those above Brampton Bryan.

Coxall Knoll has an Iron Age hill fort at its summit. It has often been claimed to be the site of the last stand of the ancient British leader Caractacus against the Roman legions under Scapula in AD51 but this is now considered unlikely for no other reason than the fort here is not of any significant size. Coxall Knoll is also known locally as Onion Hill – apparently a reference to the scent of the large number of ramsons which grow on its slopes.

The small settlement just ahead to the left is Buckton.

The track makes a sweeping bend to the left to head directly towards Coxall Knoll. On reaching a junction, where another track joins from the right – at SO386735 – leave the track, half-right, over a stile and into a field. **①**

Go straight ahead from the stile – roughly mid-way between the two track options just ignored – to a gap though the boundary opposite, situated just to the right of a pole carrying overhead wires. Pass through the gap into the corner of the adjacent field. Here bear very slightly to the right of the original heading to reach and cross a stile in the far boundary of the field, situated between two trees there – an oak (right) and an ash (left).

Head very slightly to the left up the next field – aiming towards the right-hand corner of a group of trees therein. Pass just to the left of this corner – between the trees (which surround a pond) and a low red-brick structure. Here bear half-left to cross the remainder of the field, aiming to reduce the distance to a boundary fence at the top of the field (on the right), and finally walking alongside this to reach the far corner.

The trees around the pond (left) are home to a small heronry.

At the corner of the field cross a four bar wooden fence, in the facing boundary, to emerge onto a grassy track. Go straight across this and over a stile into another field. Here there are two footpath options. Ignore a path going right but instead go half-right from the stile, across the field – aiming for a hedge corner and two large trees in the boundary opposite.

Crossing the field, look right for a distant view of the eastern edge of the Long Mynd and its outliers, such as Caer Caradoc Hill (459 metres/1506 feet), either side of Church Stretton (not visible).

Passing the aforementioned hedge corner (left) and the two trees – an ash and an oak – maintain direction, following a hedge boundary (on the left) to reach a stile through the boundary hedge ahead. Cross this into the next field and here follow the left-hand boundary hedge.

Look right from the stile. Below the wooded slopes of Hopton Titterhill will be seen the handsome large building of Bedstone College and, just to its right, the spire of Bedstone church. Walking along the field boundary, the wooded hill directly ahead in the distance is Bucknell Wood, with Stow Hill beyond it.

Follow the boundary the length of the long field, finally dropping down to pass through a metal farm gate (may be open) onto a quiet road. Turn right along this for about 60 yards and then leave it, left, over a stile into a field – SO373741. ❷

From the stile bear slightly right across the large field to reach its far right-hand corner. Here cross a stile over the facing boundary into the next field.

The river just beyond the boundary on the right is the Redlake, which now accompanies the walk to Bucknell and through the village itself. A tributary of the River Clun, it supposedly takes its name from the aftermath of a nearby battle when its waters ran red with blood. Some maintain that this battle was the last stand of Caractacus against the advancing Roman legions – at Caer Caradoc hill fort a little further up the valley.

The Redlake rises in the hills to the west of Clun and flows, generally east or south-eastwards, to join the Clun near Jay Bridge – not very far north of the place (seen earlier) where the latter river itself joins the River Teme. Its upper valley – part of which is seen early on Stage 7 – is particularly beautiful and unspoilt, and well worth exploring.

Bear half-left across the field, towards a stile in a distant corner – just below the wooded lower slopes of Coxall Knoll (left). (Navigation Note: Initially aim to walk parallel to, and about 30 yards distant from, a boundary fence on the right.)

Nearing the stile, the first houses of Bucknell appear in the distance, slightly to the right ahead.

Cross the stile into the next field. Here initially follow the left-hand boundary – that with the woodland on the slopes of Coxall Knoll. After about 180 yards turn half-right across the field, passing to the left of the fourth of a series of poles carrying overhead wires which run through it and heading towards a crossing over a railway line at its far (right) side, (Heart of Wales line).

On reaching the railway cross a stile, the rails and another stile to enter a field at its far side. Bear left to follow a slight depression through the field and reach a small wooden gate through its boundary. Pass through this into the next field.

Passing through the gate the route leaves Herefordshire to re-enter Shropshire.

Go straight ahead from the gate through the large field, trees on the right and the River Redlake beyond. Keep the trees just to the right, the path bending very slightly to the right as progress is made. Nearing the end of the field, walk alongside the river and then a wall (both on the right) to reach a wooden kissing gate, situated to the right of a low barn and a wooden farm gate. Pass through the kissing gate and walk straight ahead from it to reach a road – the B4367 – and Bucknell. ❸

The Sitwell Arms public house was just across the road here but closed in April 2002. It is rumoured to be reopening as a B&B/Tea Room. Bucknell railway station is about 300 yards left along the road. There is a small newsagent/general store just beyond the level crossing adjacent to the station. A garage, just across the bridge over the Redlake – right – also has a small shop on its premises.

Bucknell Station is on the Heart of Wales Railway line, part of the national rail network, with direct trains to Knighton, Llandrindod Wells and Swansea, in the one direction, and to Craven Arms and Shrewsbury, in the other (Wales & Borders Trains).

Buses on the 738/740 Ludlow – Leintwardine – Knighton routes also stop hereabouts.

The Heart of Wales Railway Line

The Heart of Wales Line is a fairly recently coined name for the 120 mile route from Shrewsbury through Craven Arms, where it leaves the main line between Manchester and South Wales, and on via Knighton and Llandrindod Wells to Llanelli and Swansea.

Formerly also known as the Central Wales Line the through route between Craven Arms and Swansea was constructed piecemeal over thirty years and by six different railway companies, the last link in the chain being the Llanwrtyd Wells to Llandovery section which was completed in 1868 by the Central Wales Extension Railway.

By the time the through route was opened all of the six original companies had passed under the control of either the London & North Western Railway or the Great Western Railway so the route operated very much as a joint concern. At the time of Nationalisation in 1948 the line became part of the Western Region of British Railways.

The line was threatened with closure several times in the 1960s and that decade marked its downgrading from an important cross-country route to a light passenger-only route of more local importance. One of the reasons it has survived is that for many of the communities it serves there is no viable public transport alternative. It was once calculated that to travel from Shrewsbury to Swansea using connecting bus services along the route of the line would take in excess of a week and that even then not all of the small settlements served by train would be visited!

Whatever the full secret of its survival it remains a 'gem' of a railway line with its unstaffed stations, request stops, ungated crossings, tunnels and viaducts – and above all miles and miles of glorious scenery. The 120 mile complete journey from Shrewsbury to Swansea takes around four hours.

The highest point on the line is Llangunllo, between Knighton and Dolau, at 980 feet.

Services on the line are now operated by Wales & Borders Trains. There is an active Heart of Wales Line Travellers Association. The line is extensively used by walkers at weekends and there are programmes of organised walks running to/from several of the stations on the line, the brochures for which can be obtained at larger railway stations.

The banks of the River Redlake through Bucknell are home to a large number of ducks – always ready to share a lunch break! These birds must obviously occasionally stray onto the B4367 road – a fact which accounts for a couple of unusual road signs hereabouts.

Bear very slightly right across the road and walk ahead along a tarmac path which runs alongside the River Redlake – the river on the right.

An old wooden sign on the door of the half-timbered 'Old School House' at first sight appeared to read 'Beware of the Dog' but closer inspection revealed the words to be 'Beware of the Rod'. It had, unfortunately, disappeared as of April 2002 but hopefully will be restored in the near future.

Passing a half-timbered dwelling (right) – 'The Old School House' – continue straight ahead, now on a quiet road. Remain on this until it bends left and then leave it, walking straight ahead to enter Bucknell churchyard through a lychgate. (A path leaves the road half-right at the same point to skirt round to the right of, and outside of, the churchyard but should NOT be taken.)

Though the lychgate, walk straight ahead up a path which passes to the left of the church to reach its entrance porch. Continue straight ahead past this, the path bearing right to round the far corner of the building and emerge onto a road

Leaving the churchyard, bear very slightly right across the road and up three steps opposite to pass through a kissing gate into a field – a wooden, clinker built barn/shed alongside on the left.

Bucknell

Bucknell is mentioned in *Domesday Book* (1086) as 'Buckenhalle'. The name comes from 'Bucca', a Mercian (Saxon) personal name, and 'Hale', meaning a waterside pasture, nook or corner. At the time of Domesday Book the settlement was a divided manor, part held by William Pantuff for Roger de Montgomery and part by Ralph de Mortimer – founder of the powerful Wigmore dynasty. Before the Norman Conquest it had belonged to the Saxon, Aluii.

The rough square of the original village had a motte and bailey fortification at its centre, of which traces of the motte remain.

The village originally lay on the border of Shropshire and Herefordshire but this was realigned in its present form in 1554.

Bucknell Church

Dedicated to St. Mary, a church has stood on this site since the twelfth century and the masonry of the nave dates from this period. The chancel is fourteenth century in origin. A major restoration took place in the 1870s, at a cost of £2000, and the north aisle dates from this time.

The font – early Norman or late Saxon in origin – is crudely carved with an interlaced cord pattern, Celtic in influence, and a small representation of the head of either a lion or a man. (The lion was a medieval symbol of resurrection.)

The fine timber roof of the nave features eight carved heads on its beam ends, their date of carving unknown.

Outside the building, by the porch is a Weeping Pear Tree (a type of willow). It is known locally as the 'Devil's Pear Tree'.

There is a small sub post-office, which doubles as a tourist information centre of sorts, just along the road to the right.

In the field, initially follow the right-hand boundary. Where this bends away to the right bear slightly right to reach a stile in the facing hedge of a field corner, ahead. Cross this into the next field and here again initially follow the right-hand boundary. When this bends away right maintain direction across the field ahead – following what appears to be the course of an old field boundary.

At the far side of the field – with dwellings on the right – cross a stile into another field and follow its right-hand boundary to reach a stile, situated to the left of a metal farm gate. Cross this to emerge onto a road. ❹

Not many yards along the road, right, is the Baron of Beef public house.

Turn left along the road for about 30 yards and then, as it bends right, leave it, left (effectively straight ahead), along a metalled track – SO350739. Follow this as it climbs slightly towards Bucknell Wood.

The climb steepens and the track passes through a gateway (gate may be open) and loses its metalled surface, becoming stony underfoot.

During the steady climb, beyond the gateway, look behind for a nice distant view of Bucknell church through the trees.

About 220 yards beyond the gate, still climbing, the track reaches a junction – the main track bending left. Here go right, passing through a gateway – gateless at the time of writing – on a stony/dirt track. Ignore a path going off and up into the trees on the right, about 10 yards after the gateway, but continue on the track – a wire fence boundary on the left, with a hedgerow of bushes and a field beyond, and woodland on the right.

Remain on the obvious track along the edge of the wood. At a slightly staggered 'crossroads' of tracks go straight ahead, a slight descent beginning and a metalled surface recommencing underfoot as the track runs through denser woodland.

The descent steepens and the track finally drops down to reach a quiet road, a dwelling up to the right. Turn right along the road which immediately bends right and, passing another dwelling (Cubbage), then left, crossing a stream as it does so. Rising from this it begins to meander along, the Heart of Wales Railway line soon joining it – alongside on the left.

Stow Hill looms half-right ahead. The route will shortly climb to a height of about 430 metres/1411 feet on it – just below its summit – from its current height, on the road, of about 160 metres/525 feet.

Over a slight rise, a more pronounced left bend in the road leads to another stream crossing. Beyond this it bends right, with a dwelling on its left. Just before reaching this house, by a post-box (left), leave the road, right, onto a stony/dirt track – the entrance drive to the farm settlement of Weston – at SO329734. ❺

Walk up the track, keeping the farm outbuildings to the left. Against the end of the first group of buildings is a recently (2002) restored waterwheel. Just beyond this, at a Y-junction, take the track on the left which rises and immediately passes through a metal farm gate – the farmhouse on the left and an outbuilding on the right just beyond this.

Restored waterwheel at Weston Farm

The waterwheel before restoration

The track climbs through a second metal farm gate. Beyond this, at another Y-junction go left, the track bending left – a wire boundary fence on its left. At a point where a slightly sunken grassy track crosses it leave the stony/dirt track, half-left, to follow the grassy track along the wire boundary fence (left) past (BUT NOT THROUGH) farm gates at two field corners.

Look left to see the bare Llan-wen Hill with the Powys Observatory building (Spaceguard Centre) at its 417 metre/1368 foot summit, across the Teme valley.

At the second of the farm gates/field corners turn right to climb alongside the boundary (left) and rejoin the main stony/dirt track just before a metal farm gate on it. Pass through the gate and climb up the obvious track ahead.

The track climbs steeply from the gate, a wire fence alongside it on the right. At the end of an initial straight section it bends left.

As the track bends left look over to the left to see a distant flat-topped hill mass bearing a mast. This is Black Mixen, at 650 metres/2133 feet not quite the highest point in Radnor Forest. It is about 15 miles distant.

Beyond the bend the climb, while still steady, eases somewhat.

Look left across the Teme valley to see an avenue of large trees which marks the course of the drive up to Stanage Park House from the A4113 road.

As the climb continues there are good views of the Teme in the valley below. Walking here in the sunshine one squally late October afternoon the sudden appearance of a train on the Heart of Wales Line, along the foot of the slope below, seemed almost unreal – and almost like God was playing with his toy train set!

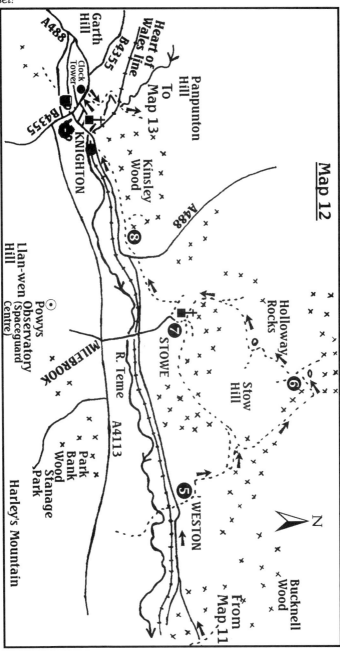

Where the fence on the right bends away, uphill, from the track – at SO324737 – leave the track, right, to cross a metal farm gate. Over the gate, follow a sunken path which climbs steadily and bears slightly left, following a fence (left) and just within woodland. After about 135 yards, at an indistinct Y-junction of paths where the fence bears slightly left again, go right to climb away from the fence and through the woodland. After a further 120 yards the path reaches a T-junction with a track – a wooden fence a few yards along this to the left. Turn right along the track, through woodland.

(Note: If unable to cross the gate at SO324737 then remain on the stony track to pass through two metal farm gates. Immediately after passing through the second of these – at SO321736 – and with a conifer plantation just ahead on the left (Jutland Plantation), turn very sharply right – through almost 180 degrees – onto a grassy/dirt track which continues the steady climb. Remain on this to enter woodland where the main route, as described above, joins from the right.)

Continuing through the woodland – of mainly oak trees – the track bends left. Remain on it as, the left bend becoming more pronounced, the climb steepens. Becoming stony underfoot, the track reaches the top of the wood where it passes through a gateway.

Through the gateway, with a choice of tracks ahead take the one on the right. A sunken, grassy track, it climbs alongside a wire boundary fence (right) with an extension of the woodland beyond. Nearing the corner of this woodland, where another track joins sharp left, continue straight ahead to pass through a metal farm gate in a fence (may be open). Continue – up an indistinct grassy track, heading for another gateway through a fence which will be seen ahead.

Passing through the gateway (metal farm gate likely to be open) go straight ahead towards another gateway further up the hillside – still with an indistinct grassy track underfoot, and with a plantation of conifers over to the left.

A superb panoramic view continues to improve behind. It includes, (right to left), Black Mixen, Llan-wen Hill and Powys Observatory (Spaceguard Centre), Stanage Park, Harley's Mountain and Shobdon Hill Wood beyond, Brampton Bryan Park and Pedwardine Wood, the Vale of Wigmore and the hills beyond it, (such as Yatton Hill, Croft Ambrey and Gatley Long Coppice), Coxall Knoll, Mortimer Forest, and Titterstone Clee Hill.

Passing through the gateway bear half-left, towards the conifer plantation – a gentle climb across open hillside with no obvious path underfoot. The right of way passes through the plantation (as shown on Explorer Map 201), but tree growth had rendered it impassable at the time of writing. Instead aim for the boundary fence of a section of the plantation which protrudes out, right, from the main body and walk along this to its far (top) corner where there is a gateway.

The summit of Stow Hill (432 metres/1417 feet) – marked by a triangulation point – is just to the right, along the fence, here.

Pass through the gateway and turn left, to follow the fence along the far side of the protruding section and reach a corner with the main body of trees, and then right, to follow the boundary of this along. On reaching the far corner of the plantation turn left to walk alongside its far boundary (left).

On reaching the far corner of the plantation look slightly right ahead for a view over to the Long Mynd and its outliers, Caer Caradoc and the Lawley. To the right of this – half-right ahead – the twin summits of Brown Clee Hill are visible. Unfortunately, at the time of writing, views left ahead at this point are obscured by another plantation. Situated immediately beyond this – but again hidden by its trees – is another Caer Caradoc, a prominent hill of some 399 metres/1309 feet with fortifications at its summit which dominates the Redlake valley.

Walk alongside the boundary of the conifer plantation (left) – another, larger, plantation over to the right – to reach a metal farm gate, a pond just beyond it on the right (SO315746). ❻

From the gate, Black Mixen is almost directly ahead and Powys Observatory (Spaceguard Centre), on Llan-wen Hill, left.

Pass through the gate and go STRAIGHT AHEAD for about 55 yards – to a point just beyond the pond (right) – and then turn left to walk along a narrow worn path, heading roughly towards the Powys Observatory (Spaceguard Centre) building (across the Teme valley on Llan-wen Hill) and parallel with the boundary of the conifer plantation (left).

Just before the left turn onto the narrow path, beyond the gate and pond, almost the whole of Knighton suddenly appears ahead and below in the distance.

A short diversion at this point brings superb views down into the Redlake valley and of the hill fort of Caer Caradoc.

Rather than turning left along the narrow path instead turn right along it, heading for a conifer plantation. On reaching the boundary fence to that plantation do not cross the stile into it but instead turn right and walk to a metal farm gate. Pass through this and onto a wide track which initially has the aforementioned conifer plantation on its immediate left. Passing the corner of the plantation continue for about another 200 yards along the track, looking left for views of Caer Caradoc and the Redlake valley. Half-left are distant views of the Long Mynd and its outliers while straight ahead are Titterstone Clee Hill and, just left of it, the twin summits of Brown Clee Hill. Retrace steps to rejoin the main route.

After about 80 yards on the path – just after a slight dip – leave it, right, to walk down what is initially an indistinct grassy track. Follow this as it bends left towards an obvious 'V' in the land ahead, becoming 'sunken' and more distinct underfoot as it does so.

The track drops steeply down through a steep-sided 'V'-shaped valley, becoming stony underfoot. Emerging from the valley, beneath rocky outcrops (Holloway Rocks), the track bends first left – passing a quarry (left) – and then right to a metal farm gate, a stile on its right.

Cross the stile and walk down the obvious track ahead. It bends right and passes a pond – in a hollow on the right. Ignore a track going off, left, through a metal gate just before reaching this. Passing the pond the stony track bends left to head more steeply downhill, towards woodland below.

The track descends alongside a boundary with the woodland (left) to reach a metal farm gate, a stile alongside to its right – a steep, stony path joining sharp right just beforehand.

Cross the stile. Ignore a grassy path/track going down through the trees to the right but remain on the obvious stony track which bends left to descend below, and along the edge of, the woodland. Remain on it as continues to bend (mostly to the left) and descend and eventually reaches Stowe Church (right).

The track runs above the wall of the churchyard. Reaching the far corner of this – at a 'crossroads' of tracks – go right to reach its lychgate entrance. **❼**

Beyond the lychgate the track descends steeply, bending left then right – past a parking area (left) – and gaining a metalled surface to become a quiet road. Follow this down a steep hill to a sharp left bend, the entrance to the drive of the Old Vicarage just to the right – SO311736. Here leave the road, right, for a stony track.

The track immediately passes through a gateway, descending slightly as it does so, initially bending left and then right. It crosses a small stream, in a culvert, and starts to climb gently, crossing a cattle grid (a farm gate alongside on the right) and the stream once more. Remain on the track until reaching some cottages, on the right, and then turn very sharply left – through almost 180 degrees – to ford the stream and climb up to the top left-hand corner of the field beyond. Here cross the fence (left) to reach a stony track at the top of the adjacent field.

(Note: At the time of writing there was no stile over the fence at the top corner of the field but the barbed wire could just about be stepped over. The blockage has been reported to Shropshire County Council for appropriate action. Until this is resolved an alternative route would be to proceed as above until the cattle grid is reached but then instead of crossing it turn left off the track and up through a metal farm gate to climb up the right-hand boundary of the field so entered. On reaching the top of the field the stony track is met and the route as above rejoined.)

Stowe Church

Stowe Church is a beautiful little stone building with a small wooden tower. It stands in a fold of the hills at a height of 225 metres/738 feet, below Stow Hill, and has magnificent views of the Teme Valley below. Powys Observatory (Spaceguard Centre), on its hilltop site, is directly opposite across the valley.

The village here was formerly of greater importance than its size today would suggest as it stood on the meeting place of one of the main Drovers' Roads from Wales into England and the old main road from Knighton to Bucknell. There is some evidence of deserted dwellings just below the church.

The church, with its dedication to St. Michael and All Angels, is medieval in origin but the churchyard in which it stands is of an oval shape which suggests a sacred site of much earlier date. This is borne out by the fact that the settlement takes its name from the Old English 'stow' meaning 'assembly place' or 'holy place'.

Some restoration took place in the 1870s and the fine stained glass windows date from this time. Inside, the timber roof is most impressive and indicative of the age of the building. On the wall just inside the door is a list of incumbents as far back as 1308.

Cross the stony track and pass through a metal farm gate, opposite, into a field (SO309735).

Look behind here for a good view of Stowe Church and vicarage, with the mass of Stow Hill above. Passing through the gate, Knighton appears again – ahead to the right. The large wooded hill to its right is Kinsley Wood.

On entering the field bear left to reach its left-hand boundary and follow this down it, heading directly towards Knighton. Pass through a metal farm gate to enter another field and again follow the left-hand boundary. Continue to do so through a further field, which is again entered via a gate. On passing through yet another metal farm gate to enter the next field follow the right-hand boundary.

Entering the field, look over the right shoulder to see Holloway Rocks and the 'V'-shaped valley descended earlier.

A road and the railway line appear below – about 150 yards away on the left – as the steady descent continues. Follow the right-hand boundary of the field down to its far corner where a metal farm gate leads onto a road – the A488.

Go slightly left across the road to cross a stile into a field. Bear half-left to cross a sturdy footbridge over a small stream. Continue in roughly the same direction gradually approaching the left-hand boundary of the field and road beyond. Keep that boundary about 20 yards distant as the latter stages of the field are crossed. Cross a stile – situated about 25 yards in from the far left-hand corner of the field – and climb a short flight of wooden steps beyond to enter Kinsley Wood. **❽**

The steps emerge onto a broad forest track, on a sharp bend. Turn right up this but as a sharp right bend commences take a narrower track which goes down to the left off the main track. It descends for about 45 yards to a junction. Here go right, on a track which runs through the woodland – a road (A488) down to its left. After a while the track begins to lose height rapidly in preparation for joining the road.

Stowe Church

Knighton Church

With the exception of its tower, the current church of St. Edward dates mainly from the late nineteenth century. There was previously an eleventh century church on the site, itself replacing an older building, but this was largely demolished in 1756 and all that now remains of it is the lower tower. The new church of 1756 has itself been replaced by the current Victorian building although the top of the tower is a survivor from it. The Victorian building was built in two stages – the nave in 1876 and the chancel twenty years later.

The dedication refers to Edward the Confessor, King of England, who died in 1066. If it seems unusual for a Welsh church to be dedicated to an English king/saint then it must be remembered that until the establishment of the Church in Wales, in the 1920s, Knighton was in the diocese of Hereford.

Inside, the chancel walls have some unusual murals by an unknown Italian artist and there are fine stained glass windows throughout the building. Outside, an anchor leaning against the south wall recalls Commander Henry

J. Bray, a former organist.

Interestingly, some medieval documents describe the church as being merely a chapel of ease for the more important church at Stowe – visited earlier – more evidence of the former greater size and importance of that village and the obvious reversal in the fortunes of it and Knighton since.

Anchor outside Knighton Church

On reaching the road turn right along it, the Heart of Wales Railway line (and Knighton Station) alongside on the left. Turn left to cross a bridge over the railway.

Crossing the railway the route leaves Shropshire (England) to enter Powys (Wales) for the first time.

The road crosses the River Teme and bears right to enter Knighton. Take the first turning off it on the right – Church Road.

Walk up the road, ignoring a turning right (Mill Green), to reach Knighton church – St Edward's.

Just past the church gates (right), turn left into Church Street. Walk the length of this – ignoring a turning left (Wylcwm Street) – to reach West Street at a T-junction. Turn left for a few yards to reach Knighton's clock tower where this stage of the walk ends.

The clock tower, Knighton

Knighton

Knighton literally means 'the town/settlement of the knights'. However its Welsh name, Tref-y-clawdd, is more significant meaning 'The Town on the Dyke' which emphasises the importance of its position astride that fortification built under King Offa of Mercia around AD780. The crossing point on the River Teme here must have also contributed to the early growth of the settlement while in more recent times the arrival of the railway, in the 1860's, brought a degree of prosperity. Latterly the town has seen a growth in tourism due in no small part to its central position on the Offa's Dyke National Trail. The Offa's Dyke Centre is situated in an imaginative, purpose-built, modern building in the town (passed on Stage 7 of the walk).

The town was given the name of Tref-y-clawdd in about AD840 by the Welsh king Rhodri Mawr (Roderick the Great). It is in *Domesday Book* (1086) that it is called Chenistetone

– the town of the retainers or armed freemen (later knights). After that it was variously referred to as Chnicheton, Kenithtun or Knyteton – by Saxon, Welshman or Norman.

The middle of the town – Broad Street – is marked by a fine clock tower of 1872, quite a common feature in Welsh towns.

Off Broad Street by the clock tower is High Street, also known as the Narrows, which dates from Tudor times but today contains buildings mainly from the seventeenth century.

. Near the top of High Street, in a private garden, are the scant remains of Knighton Castle. Probably founded in the eleventh century it was partially destroyed, in 1215, by Llywelyn ap Iorwerth. By 1230 it was under the control of the Mortimers and in 1262 was destroyed by Llywelyn ap Gruffyd. Restored by the Mortimers it was finally destroyed by Owain Glyn Dŵr in 1402.

Set back from the street where the Narrows joins Broad Street is the Old House. Its seventeenth century half-timbered front hides a medieval Cruck built structure – formerly an open hall. Smoke-blackened roof timbers herein indicate the earlier existence of an open fire on a central hearth with no chimney but just a smoke hole in the roof above.

Parts of the Knighton Hotel, on Broad Street, are also older than it might seem at first sight – the building containing a fine timber-framed medieval hall.

Also on Broad Street, the George and Dragon public house bears the date 1637. When the eighteenth century church was taken down, in 1876, the oak from its box pews was reused as panelling in the lounge bar here. A good excuse to visit the pub!

Stage 7

Knighton to Felindre

Mileage: 13 Miles
(From Knighton: 5½ miles to Llanfair Waterdine; 10 miles to
Bettws-y-Crwyn)
O.S.Maps: 1:50000 (Landranger): 137 (Ludlow); 136 (Newtown,
Llanidloes)
1:25000 (Explorer): 201 (Knighton & Presteigne); 214
(Llanidloes & Newtown)

*The first 2½ miles of the stage are spent in the company of Offa's Dyke
Path. The route climbs north out of Knighton via Panpunton Hill and
then runs north-west above the Teme valley as far as Cwm-sanaham
Hill.*

*Leaving the waymarked National Trail the route runs above the
upper Redlake valley, via tracks and fieldpaths, before descending to a
quiet road section. Heading west, via Selley Cross, this leads to a
bridleway which continues westwards to the small settlement of
Llanfair Waterdine, beside the river. The successful 1953 Everest
expedition is celebrated here.*

*Quiet roads and tracks climb north-westwards to the farm at Cwm.
From here an almost straight road section – quiet and with superb
views – continues the climb to the lonely little church at
Bettws-y-Crwyn – the highest in Shropshire. More quiet roads lead to
the start of the final descent of the stage into the Teme valley, which is
via a track, fieldpaths and another road. The latter crosses the river to
enter the small settlement of Felindre, the stage destination.*

Starting at the clock tower walk along the right-hand side of West Street –
ignoring all side streets – to reach the Offa's Dyke Centre. Turn right
through the gateway of the centre and then drop left to round and walk
alongside the left of the building.

*The purpose built Offa's Dyke Centre was formally opened on 3rd May
1999. It was designed to resemble a Welsh castle in part and includes a Tourist
Information Centre as well as Offa and Dyke related displays.*

*Either from the road, just to the right of the building, or from the recreation
area at its rear look across to Kinsley Wood to see the large letters 'ER' formed
by the planting of a different species of tree within a dark green coniferous
stand. This was done to commemorate the coronation of Queen Elizabeth II
and these trees will not be felled until after her death. The effect is best
appreciated in the spring or autumn and can also be viewed from a large rear
window in the Centre itself.*

Continue straight ahead from the rear of the building, along the left edge of a
small recreation area – a children's playground over to the right. On reaching
the far side of the grassy area continue straight ahead down steps and towards
two gaps in a tree boundary ahead. Pass through the left of these to descend

more steps to a path along the banks of the Teme. Turn left along the riverside path, the Teme on the right, soon passing through a kissing gate into a field.

Passing through the gate the route leaves Powys (Wales) to re-enter Shropshire (England).

With a gravel surface underfoot, the path continues along the riverbank through the field. Passing through a second kissing gate it runs along the outside of a field boundary, still alongside the river. Beyond a third kissing gate, the gravel underfoot ceases and the riverside path again runs through a field.

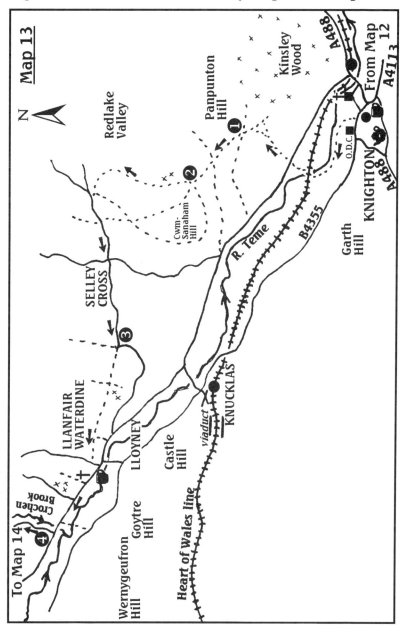

The prominent hill to the left bearing a mast is Garth Hill, which rises to a height of 346 metres/1135 feet.

Continue to follow the riverside path which bears right and soon approaches a bridge carrying the Heart of Wales Railway line across the river.

The prominent hill straight ahead is Panpunton Hill which rises to 375 metres/1230 feet and up which the route will soon climb.

Pass through a small metal gate and up some steps to cross a footbridge (alongside the railway bridge) over the river. From the steps at the far side of the footbridge turn left to cross the railway line and then pass through a second small metal gate into a field. Here continue to follow the riverside path until a point where a hedge boundary, right, finishes. Then bear half-right to walk towards a barn to the left of which is a metal farm gate and a stile. Cross the stile to emerge onto a quiet road.

Cross the road and pass through a small wooden gate opposite – situated to the left of two metal farm gates. Climb straight ahead up Panpunton Hill on an obvious path, initially stony and with woodland on the right.

Emerging onto more open hillside the steep climb continues, the path underfoot now wide and grassy. Ignore a path going right into the woods – indicated by a signpost.

Still climbing, at an insignificant Y-junction go right. On reaching a 'crossroads' of paths – with a stile over a fence ahead – go left, as indicated by the National Trail 'acorn' on a signpost and with the aforementioned fence on the right. When the path reaches a stony track – with a metal farm gate to the right – go straight across this and underneath a large ash tree to continue to follow the wire boundary fence – (about 10 yards distant on the right; woodland beyond it) – up the hill. **❶**

Where the boundary fence bends away right the narrow path parts company with it. Follow the obvious path ahead to almost reach another wire fence. Now follow a narrow path parallel to and about 10 yards distant from the fence (right).

There now commences a superb high level walk above the Teme valley with good views to the left throughout and the earthwork of Offa's Dyke immediately on the right – varying in size and impressiveness.

Continuing to follow the path, parallel to the fence, pass through a small wooden gate.

A small stone cairn/memorial, just beyond the gate, recalls Roy Waters, a former Chairman of the Offa's Dyke Society. The views from this point are superb on a good day. Behind, Powys Observatory (Spaceguard Centre) may be seen on top of Llan-wen Hill. Most of Knighton is visible, with the

Offa's Dyke

Offa's Dyke takes its name from Offa II of Mercia, the first Saxon leader to bear the title 'King of the English'. He ruled between AD757 and AD796.

The dyke was constructed sometime after AD780 to mark and fortify the western boundary of his kingdom and was probably the result of an agreement between Offa and the Welsh, or Cymr. There appear to have been jointly administered laws governing trade and movement across the dyke and the recovery of stolen livestock. It was therefore almost as much a trade boundary as a defensive structure.

wooded Ffridd Hill behind. Garth Hill is prominent straight across the valley to the left while Black Mixen, in Radnor Forest, may be visible behind and above it – some eight miles distant. The view up the Teme valley extends past Knucklas – with its majestic thirteen arch railway viaduct, alongside, and the prominent rounded Castle Hill above the settlement – to take in Goytre Hill and Wernygeufron Hill, and the higher Beacon Hill and Pool Hill beyond. Down in the valley itself the river will be seen describing large loops. A bench alongside the memorial tempts the walker to stay awhile!

Passing through a second small wooden gate continue to follow the path, parallel to the fence.

Pass through another small wooden gate – the third encountered – situated to the right of a metal farm gate. Continue to follow the fence (right) along towards a point where it bends away half-right. Here pass through a fourth small wooden gate, again situated to the right of a metal farm gate and with a small group of fir trees just beyond (half-right).

Through the gate, follow the bank of the Dyke (right) along. Passing some barns (left) and a redundant stile (right), continue to follow the path ahead. On reaching a small wooden gate, situated to the right of a metal farm gate, pass through it to emerge onto a stony track. Go straight across this and climb the path ahead, a wire fence immediately alongside on the right.

The prominent hill straight ahead is Cwm-sanaham Hill which rises to a height of 406 metres/1332 feet.

Continuing to follow the fence, the path rounds a plantation of fir trees (right), a steep drop commencing on the left as it descends slightly to circle a cwm, crossing a stile in the dip midway.

From the stile, midway around the cwm, look left for a good view of Knucklas, its railway viaduct and the prominent Castle Hill, above and to its right.

Climbing out of the cwm but then descending gently, the path reaches a stony track (SO274755) where the route parts company with the waymarked National Trail. ❷

Turn right up the stony track, immediately passing through a metal farm gate. Emerging from an initial sunken section into a field follow the less

---

Knucklas

The name 'Knucklas' is an anglicised version of the Welsh name for the settlement, which is Cnwc-las, meaning 'Green Mound' – presumably referring to the castle/hill fort site.

The scant ruins on the green hilltop site are thought to belong to a castle built here sometime between 1220 and 1230 by Hugh Mortimer and destroyed in 1262 by Llywelyn ap Gruffyd and again, in 1402, by

Owain Glyn Dŵr. This structure seems to have been built on the site of an earlier hill fort or castle which has Arthurian connections.

Legend has it that the original castle here was the birthplace of King Arthur's queen, Guinevere. It is said that Arthur married Guinevere (Gwynhwyfar) at Cnwc-las and that the couple lived in the castle, founding the Round Table and mounting campaigns against the

Saxon invaders. These claims are based on ancient Welsh legends – as told in the ballads and stories of the Mabinogion – which predate the Arthurian tales of Chretien de Troyes and Geoffrey of Monmouth. Given this, it would seem that Knucklas has as least as strong a claim to being considered as the site of Camelot as do Tintagel or Winchester.

Another story – connected with the site – is that stone from the ruins of the later castle was used in the construction of the railway viaduct alongside (Heart of Wales Line).

The thirteen arch viaduct was built in 1863 for the London & North-Western Railway. Designed by H. Lotte, a German, it is 190 yards long and rises to a maximum height of 75 feet above the valley of the Ffrwdwen Brook, a tributary of the River Teme. At either end of the structure are crenellated half-round corbelled turrets – which seem quite fitting given both its location and also the supposed source of some of its building stone. Another story concerning the viaduct is that of a fox which was being pursued by hounds across it and which leapt from it to its death.

substantial but still obvious track ahead. Ignore another track going right, towards a barn. On reaching a metal farm gate – at the far end of a small group of pine trees – do not pass through it but instead bear half-left to follow a fence (right). At the next field corner pass through a metal farm gate and continue to follow the right boundary fence through the next field.

Walking through this and the next two fields, look right for superb views on clear days. Right to left, in the middle distance, are Stow Hill (almost directly right, and bearing dark conifer plantations at its summit. It was climbed on Stage 6 of the walk), the slightly lower rounded hill of Caer Caradoc (hill fort at its summit), with Brineddin Wood opposite it across the Redlake valley, and the long, dark Black Hill (more to the half-right, and again with conifers on it). Peeping out from behind these – depending on the viewpoint – in the far distance may be seen Titterstone Clee Hill, the twin summits of Brown Clee Hill, and (again more half-right) the Long Mynd and its outlier – another Caer Caradoc.

Reaching the far right-hand corner of the field pass through another metal farm gate to again follow the right-hand boundary through the field ahead – a small plantation of deciduous trees beyond the fence.

Reaching the far right-hand corner of the field again pass through a metal farm gate and follow the right-hand boundary ahead, bearing right with it. At the far right-hand corner of the field again pass through a metal farm gate, the track underfoot becoming stony and more substantial again.

Look directly right from the gate to see Caer Caradoc – the bare, rounded hill which bears a hill fort at its summit and rises to a height of 399 metres/1309 feet. To the left of, and opposite, this the wooded slopes on the other side of the Redlake valley are Brineddin Wood. Framed between the two, in the far distance, is Bucknell Hill. The hills ahead, at the gate, are – left to right – Llanfair Hill (432 metres/1417 feet), Cefn Hepreas (412 metres/1352 feet), and Rock Hill (436 metres/1430 feet).

The obvious, stony track begins a steady descent through the next field – alongside the right-hand boundary. Pass through another metal farm gate and remain on the track which continues its descent, now bearing around to the left.

Eventually reaching another metal farm gate pass through this to emerge onto a quiet road.

Turn left along the road. It descends to a point where a stile on the left and then another – a few yards further on – on the right mark the crossing of Offa's Dyke Path. Ignore both these turnings but remain on the road which then climbs.

On reaching a crossroads (Selley Cross) go straight ahead – not signposted, but with an 'Unsuitable for Motor Vehicles' sign a few yards along it. The road climbs from the crossroads and then begins to descend, bending left.

Nearing the top of the climb from the crossroads, the large bare hill straight ahead in the distance is Goytre Hill which rises to a height of 372 metres/1220 feet.

Remain on the road, the surface of which now deteriorates somewhat as it descends. After a short level section it crosses a stream, in a culvert, and begins to climb again. At a point where the road bends 90 degrees left, with a stony track going right – SO254762 – go straight ahead through a small metal gate to enter a field. ❸

Here follow the right-hand boundary, climbing slightly but avoiding the highest part of the field which lies over to the left. An old sunken path runs along the right-hand boundary but this may be so overgrown as to necessitate walking alongside rather than along it.

Nearing the far right corner of the field pass through another small metal gate – similar to the one through which the field was entered – and continue straight ahead along the sunken path, which again may be quite overgrown in season. There is a hedge boundary on the left and a bank on the right.

Passing through another small metal gate walk straight ahead, through a short field section – a wire fence immediately on the right – to cross a dirt track and pass through another small metal gate, woodland ahead. Bear half-right to descend to the right of the trees and then continue to follow the grassy, slightly sunken path towards the corner of an adjacent field (broken tree/hedge boundary) ahead, keeping a row of trees on the immediate right.

From this point onwards the sunken path may carry a small stream so on reaching the corner of the field climb out of the depression to walk along its left-hand side.

Notice a memorial stone – similar to an old milestone – which is situated on the opposite bank of the depression, above the stream. It bears the inscription 'P.V.S. 1951 – 1999'. It commemorates a Shropshire County Council workman who, sadly, died at work on clearing the bridleway in the latter year.

The settlement visible down in the valley, half-left, is Lloyney, across the Teme.

On reaching a fence ahead, turn right to cross the stream/depression and then immediately left to follow it along the left side of the next field. At the far left-hand corner of the field drop down into the depression and bear right to follow it along, a boundary fence on the immediate left. Ignore a stile which crosses the boundary at this point (SO246763).

Looking over the stile Lloyney is again visible, slightly to the left, with the prominent Goytre Hill beyond.

Follow the fence, left, to reach another small metal gate. Pass through this onto a sunken stony/dirt track which descends, bending left, to reach a small stream. Cross this via a wooden footbridge – the track itself crossing by way of a ford alongside on the right. Follow the track which rises slightly, through a metal farm gate, to emerge onto a quiet road. Turn left along this. The road continues the slight climb and reaches another road at a T-junction, by the entrance drive to The Vedw, right. Turn right along the road.

A very limited bus service, 774 – Tuesdays and Thursdays only – links Lloyney with Knighton, in the one direction, Felindre and Newtown in the other. Another limited service – once daily, Monday to Saturday – links Lloyney to Knighton. Lloyney lies just across the river from Llanfair Waterdine, on the B4355 – left instead of right at the T-junction by the drive to The Vedw and then right at the next junction – about a quarter of a mile distant in total.

Walk along the road into Llanfair Waterdine, passing Everest Hall and the Waterdine inn/restaurant (both on the left).

Goytre Hill is prominent to the left, across the river, during this section along the road.

Llanfair Waterdine

The name Llanfair Waterdine – it appears as 'Watredene' in Domesday Book (1086) and 'Thlanveyr' in a record of 1284 – comes from the Welsh 'Llanfair' meaning the church of St. Mary and the old English 'Denu' meaning water or wet valley. The name thus means 'the church of St. Mary in the watery or wet valley' or 'above the water'.

Llanfair Waterdine's village hall was renamed Everest Hall in celebration of the first successful expedition to climb that mountain in 1953 which was led by the late Lord Hunt, who lived in the village.

The Waterdine, formerly the Red Lion Inn, is an old drover inn – a Welsh long house built sometime between 1540 and 1600 – which is now run more as a restaurant. At the time of writing it was open lunchtimes and evenings Tuesday to Sunday inclusive. It also offers limited accommodation (01547 528214).

Llanfair Waterdine Church

The church of St. Mary, Llanfair Waterdine, dates from between 1852 and 1854 when an old twelfth century church here, thought to date from about 1140, was demolished and rebuilt at the cost of £1000. The only features of the old building to survive what the Rev. H. Cranage, writing in 1900, described as 'one of the most wicked cases of vandalism I have ever come across' were the carved altar rail and the font bowl.

The rail is made of oak from the rood screen of the old building, beautifully carved with foliage and hunting scenes. An inscription, on the lifting barrier at its centre, defied attempts at interpretation for many years but is now believed to be in old Welsh and to read 'Sir Matthew and Meyrick Pitchgar of Clun set it up for £10 together'. It is thought to date from about 1500. Sir Matthew Pitchgar was rector of Clun (Llanfair

Waterdine church was a chapel of ease to the church at Clun until 1593) between 1485 and 1520; Meyrick was his brother.

The old stone font bowl, beneath the pulpit, is thought to be Saxon in origin. The font presently in use dates only from 1916.

The pew ends bear the name of local farm settlements – a common feature in these parts – and were strictly used by members of those farming households, often being mentioned in sale details for the farms.

Near the east end of the church hangs the banner of Lord Hunt. It depicts a Himalayan bear, with a view of Mount Everest from Darjeeling in the background.

Outside, near the door stands a small sundial, dating from 1812, while the churchyard also contains, within iron railings, the grave of a gypsy man who died in a tent fire while camping on Offa's Dyke. The bottom portion of the tombstone is inscribed in the Romany language, an unusual feature.

In 1869 and again in 1870 a racehorse called 'the Colonel', owned and trained by John Davies of Cwmsannum, won the Grand National. In the latter year the horse was led into the church for a special service.

On reaching the Waterdine inn leave the road, right, to enter the churchyard through metal gates. Walk along the left-hand side of the church to leave the churchyard, via a gate, and rejoin the road. Ignore a public footpath which departs, right, just beyond the church but continue along the quiet road, the Teme just a field away on the left.

At a road junction go straight ahead – signposted 'Mellin-y-Grogue ½,   Bettws-y-Crwyn 4'.

Wernygeufron Hill (395 metres/1296 feet) is directly to the left, across the river.

Passing the farmhouse at Mellin-y-Grogue, right, ignore a track going sharp left – and signed as a Public Footpath – but remain on the road which soon crosses a sizeable stream (Crochen Brook) via a bridge.

Old Welsh carving on the altar rail, Llanfair Waterdine church

Lord Hunt's banner in Llanfair Waterdine Church

Beyond Crochen Brook the road begins to climb and reaches another junction. Here go right (SO231771). **④**

The quiet road climbs from the junction, Crochen Brook down to the right in a deepening valley. On reaching a T-junction go left and then, in just over 20 yards, at a Y-junction (where the road bends sharp left) go right (SO229777), onto a metalled track signed as being 'Unsuitable for Motor Vehicles'. The long, steady climb up the road comes to an end. **⑤**

After an initial slight dip the metalled track meanders along, slightly undulating – a considerable drop on its right-hand side down to a stream.

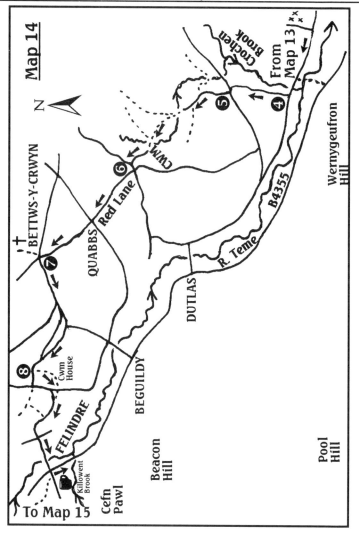

Ignore a footpath which departs, right, over a stile to drop down into this area. The metalled track begins to climb and reaches a Y-junction, with a track going left. Ignore this but remain on the metalled track (right) (SO227781).

Passing New House (dated 1797) the track reaches a metal farm gate – a cattle grid to the left – where it loses its metalled surface. Pass through the gate and continue straight ahead on what is now a stony track. It descends, bending right, to cross a stream in the valley bottom via a low culvert, a footbridge alongside on the right.

Climbing from the stream, within 50 yards – at a Y-junction of tracks, under a large oak tree – ignore a grassy track (signed as a Bridleway) going off and up, half-right, but continue ahead along the stony track which now shows traces of metalling again. It climbs gently.

Ignore another track joining from the right but remain on the, by now, partly metalled track ahead, soon passing a large pond down to the left. Ignore a track going right, down to the pond, at a Y-junction.

Now on a level, the track continues past a quarry area, right, and two more ponds, down to the left. Passing the second of these ponds it reaches a metal farm gate and again loses its metalled surface, becoming stony.

Pass through the gate and go straight ahead along the track, ignoring a footpath which goes right through another metal farm gate. The track reaches its second crossing of the stream – again via a low culvert with a footbridge alongside. Across the stream, walk ahead up the track to approach the isolated farm of Cwm.

Go through a metal farm gate (may be open) into the farm yard and pass to the left of the farm house, outbuildings to the left, and straight ahead through another farm gate, beyond which the track takes on a metalled surface to become a quiet road.

Walk up the road. On reaching a T-junction go left and at a crossroads, within 20 yards, right. ❻

The two bare rounded hills visible straight ahead at the crossroads are Beacon Hill (547 metres/1795 feet) and Pool Hill (516 metres/1693 feet).

The quiet road (Red Lane) climbs from the crossroads. Ignore a footpath going right over a stile early on it.

Nearing the top of the initial climb on the road, on a clear day, look behind for superb views back down the Teme valley to Knighton. Powys Observatory (Spaceguard Centre) should be visible on its hilltop site. Also, look over the left shoulder for a distant view of Black Mixen, with its mast.

Beacon Hill now dominates the view across the Teme to the left.

Reaching the top of its long initial climb from the crossroads the road dips slightly before beginning to climb again. A long straight section of road follows. Reaching the top of the second climb the road begins to undulate gradually downwards, still straight.

Passing an isolated barn on the right the road at last bends, to the right, and climbs slightly. On reaching a crossroads go straight ahead – signposted 'Bettws-y-Crwyn ¾'. The road undulates along. Ignore a track going right.

On reaching a five-way junction – with roads going left, ahead and sharp right and a stony track, going half-right – turn left (signposted 'Llanllwyd 1, Mountflirt 1¾, Anchor 3') to continue the walk. However go half-right along the wide, stony track to visit the lonely little church of St. Mary, Bettws-y-Crwyn. ❼

There is a telephone box a few yards along the road which goes sharp right at the junction.

In the churchyard, walk to the east end of the church for superb views across into the upper Clun valley.

Having turned left at the five-way junction follow the road which meanders and eventually climbs to a Y-junction. Here go left and then, at a second junction (after about 30 yards), left again – signposted 'Llanllwyd ½'.

A large (about 2 inches long) devil's coach-horse (beetle) was encountered on the road surface hereabouts one October afternoon. Despite the great disparity in our respective sizes it challenged me – in typical 'scorpion-like' fashion – to move out of its way!

The quiet, minor road descends from the junction, initially between wire fences and rowan trees. At a junction, ignore a road which goes left, (signposted to Beguildy).

The road climbs to a T-junction. Here go left onto another quiet road which initially climbs but soon bends right to drop down into what is shown on Explorer Map 214 as Cwmhouse Dingle. Here it crosses a stream and bends sharply to the left, beginning to climb again.

About 100 yards after the stream crossing, and just before an outbuilding on the left, leave the road – left – through a farm gate which bears a sign, 'Cwm House Farm 250 yards down the track' (SO184823). ❽

Through the gate, follow an obvious stony track ahead down the field so entered. Passing through a metal farm gate continue ahead on the track to reach Cwm House. Here turn right to cross a stile (to the right of a metal farm gate) into an enclosure. Go straight ahead through this – crossing a boggy area – to pass through another metal farm gate into a field. Here go half-right to locate a farm gate in its far boundary – located underneath and immediately to the right of an ash tree.

Passing through the gate – and crossing a small stream which runs down the boundary just beyond it – go straight ahead through the next field to its far boundary. Here locate another farm gate – very much the worse for wear at the

---

Bettws-y-Crwyn

The church of St. Mary, Bettws-y-Crwyn, is the highest and probably the most remotely situated in Shropshire – standing at a height of 382 metres/1253 feet.

The chancel, porch and all of the windows date from 1860 but the nave is probably thirteenth century in origin. Its fine roof timbers date from the fifteenth century and the building contains a wooden rood screen of about the same period. A chapel here is mentioned in the records of Wenlock Priory for 1276.

There are simplified poppy-heads on the ends of the pews, which also bear the names of local farms.

The font inside the church is modern. Its predecessor, probably discarded at the time of the 1860 restoration work, was rediscovered in use as a drinking trough and returned to the churchyard where – at the time of writing – it was planted with flowers.

An old stone mounting block stands by the churchyard gates.

In the churchyard is the unmarked grave of a pedlar – one William Cantlin – who died in the hills hereabouts (just off the route of the Kerry Ridgeway) in 1691, after being set upon by robbers. The surrounding parishes argued over who should be responsible for his burial and Bettws-y-Crwyn finally agreed to inter him here. A stone was erected on the spot his body was found inscribed 'W.C. decsd here, buried 1691 at Betvs'. This was supplemented, in about 1850, by a carved stone cross.

Bettws-y-Crwyn means 'chapel of the fleeces' ('bed-hus' is Old English for 'oratory' or 'bede house'; 'crwynwr' is Welsh for a 'skinner') – the settlement being situated near to one of the main drove roads from Wales into England, and in the midst of sheep country.

time of writing – and pass through it into the next field, again crossing a small stream just beyond.

In the new field follow an incomplete boundary hedge, ridge and ditch on the left – also a line of poles carrying overhead wires. Nearing the far side of the field bear half-right to reach a metal farm gate through the boundary. Pass through this onto a quiet road. Go straight across the road and through another metal farm gate into a field opposite.

Entering the field, bear slightly left across it to locate a metal farm gate in the far boundary.

Crossing the field, the hillside opposite – across the Teme valley – is Cefn Pawl, which rises to a height of 447 metres/1467 feet. To the right of it, a road between the two, is Coety Bank (418 metres/1371 feet).

Felindre appears for the first time, down in the Teme valley, straight ahead.

Pass through the gate onto a road and turn left down it. It descends steeply, bending to the right and then meandering. Ignore a track going off it, left. After a very steep section the road bends left and reaches a crossroads. Go straight ahead here. The road soon reaches a bridge over the River Teme.

A few yards before the bridge the route leaves Shropshire (England) to re-enter Powys (Wales) in which it remains for the rest of the walk to Newtown.

Across the river, continue to follow the road to reach a crossroads. Here turn left – along the B4355 – to enter Felindre, crossing the road when it is safe to do so. The stage ends at the Wharf Inn, on the right of the road in the small settlement.

Felindre

Felindre takes its name from the Welsh for 'mill town' and was formerly a prosperous settlement engaged in the wool trade. The field behind the Wharf Inn is known as 'Rack Meadow' and is where the fleeces were dried.

The Wharf Inn here is the highest on the Teme but, at the time of writing, only opened on Monday, Tuesday, Wednesday, Friday and Saturday evenings. Despite a claim to the contrary on its name board it does NOT offer accommodation. In fact the only accommodation I am aware of in the village are two B&Bs – Trevland (Mrs. Edwards, 01547 510211), and the Brandy House Farm (Mr. & Mrs. Brock, 01547 510282) – although enquiries with Knighton Tourist Information at the Offa's Dyke Centre may prove otherwise.

Next door to the Wharf is a small sub Post Office/shop which opens Mondays to Saturday mornings and Tuesday and Friday afternoons. There is a telephone box outside. Opposite is a bus stop/shelter.

Along the B4355 beyond the Wharf is a bridge over the substantial Killowent (Cill Owen) Brook – with a delightful cottage, ('Swn Yr Afon' – the Sound of the River), alongside the confluence of that stream and the Teme. Beyond that, on the left of the road, are two chapels – the first of which is no longer in use. One of the aforementioned B&Bs – Trevland – is on the left of the road beyond these while the Brandy House Farm lies up to the right, just off the road, a little further on.

Stage 8

Felindre to the Source of the River Teme
and the Newtown link

Mileage: 12 Miles (From Felindre: 6¾ miles to the Source of the River
Teme)
O.S.Maps: 1:50000 (Landranger): 136 (Newtown, Llanidloes)
             1:25000 (Explorer): 214 (Llanidloes & Newtown)

*The route climbs north-west out of Felindre on a hillside above the
Teme valley, via a track, before descending to cross the river for a final
time. Another track climbs to a quiet road which leads to the farm
settlement of Medwaledd. From here more tracks lead first to a fording
of a stream – Nant Medwaledd – and then up and across open
moorland to reach the ancient Kerry Ridgeway.*

*After almost two miles on the ancient track, with superb views, a
short diversion off it leads to the source of the Teme – in a quarry on
the slopes of Bryn Coch.*

*Returning to the Kerry Ridgeway the route descends northwards,
via tracks and roads, to reach the farm at Lower Wig – the infant River
Mule nearby. A road section then climbs over the final ridge before
Newtown, which is reached via paths and tracks. The 8 stage, 93 mile
walk ends at Newtown railway station.*

Starting at the Wharf Inn, facing the road, turn left and walk along the
B4355 as far as a crossroads. Here turn left along a road, signposted
'Llanbister'. After about 70 yards, and just after passing a farm outbuilding
on the right, leave the road – right – through a metal farm gate. A Public
Footpath signpost points the way.

Walk straight ahead from the gate, further outbuildings on the right, to pass
through a second metal farm gate (may be open), and then a third – the
farmhouse immediately on the right. Bear right, around the house, and pass
through another farm gate into a field.

In the field, follow the obvious stony track ahead from the gate – a fence
initially alongside on the right but the track then bending left and climbing. Still
climbing the field, the track bends right towards a small quarry area at the top.
Approaching this, at an indistinct Y-junction bear left – up the clearer track –
towards a metal farm gate situated in the top boundary of the field (the leftmost
of two gates here), some yards to the left of the small quarry.

Passing through the gate, in the next field go straight ahead along a slightly
sunken track, a wire boundary fence about 35 yards away on the right. Head
towards a metal farm gate across the field – the sunken grassy track becoming
less distinct underfoot as progress is made – and pass through this. Again follow
the slightly sunken track ahead from the gate – a gentle climb – with a short row
of trees, including hawthorns, on the immediate right. Again the track becomes
less distinct as progress is made but it remains slightly sunken, with low banks
on either side, as it passes just to the left of several small isolated trees.

Eventually only the low bank on the right of the track remains to mark its course until, on reaching the near corner of an adjacent field on the right, an incomplete boundary of mainly hawthorn trees begins on the right again. Follow these along.

Nearing the far right-hand corner of the field the grassy track runs along a fence, on the right, with a coniferous plantation beyond. At the corner of the field cross a stile, to the right of a metal farm gate, and continue straight ahead up a sunken grassy track between trees which runs along the right-hand field boundary. This may be so overgrown as to necessitate walking alongside and to its left. A steady climb begins.

Where the fence on the right ends continue straight ahead, now on a fairly obvious grassy track, running just to the left of some isolated trees. Beginning to descend slightly the track reaches the near corner of an adjacent field on the right, where an incomplete tree boundary runs downhill to the right (SO155816). Here leave the track, right, to walk downhill – to the immediate right of this boundary, an obvious track underfoot. ❶

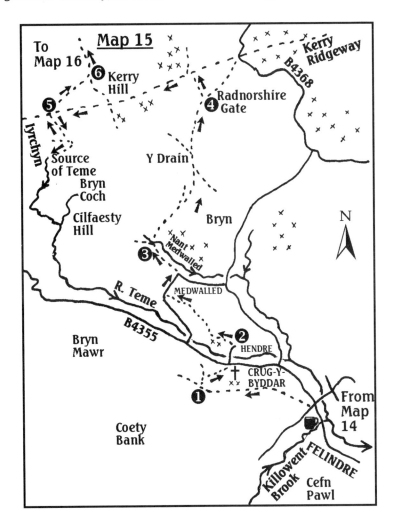

Where the incomplete tree boundary, left, ends and as the track bends left leave it to head half-right downhill – aiming roughly towards a farm settlement (Hendre) which will be seen in the valley bottom. Locate a metal gate in the field boundary on the right and pass through this, maintaining direction down the next field, a steep descent.

Passing through a gap in an incomplete tree boundary on the far (right) side of the field maintain direction to locate a metal farm gate in the bottom boundary. Pass through this into another field and again maintain direction, heading for a farm gate in the bottom boundary – a few yards in from the bottom right-hand corner of the field. Pass through the gate onto a road – the B4355 again.

Go straight across the road and walk up a metalled farm track opposite – the drive to the aforementioned farm of Hendre – which immediately crosses the Teme via a bridge.

This is the last crossing of the Teme on the walk.

A short (250 yards) diversion along the B4355 to the right here brings one to the church of St. Peter, Crug-y-byddar – the first on the Teme. A plain and simple, typically Welsh, church of 1858, it possesses a churchyard which is a botanist's dream – full of wildflowers all year round.

Walk up the farm drive, passing through two metal farm gates – a livestock impounding area between them. Both gates may be open. Pass between the farmhouse, right, and its outbuildings, left. Following the left wall of the house pass through another farm gate and climb straight ahead up a track with a concrete surface, passing through a further farm gate (may be open).

Before reaching the top of the concrete track leave it, left, for a stony track which runs alongside a wire fence, left, and below open hillside, right – SO156823. ❷

The track climbs steadily, its first few hundred yards home to many old and broken farming implements, vehicles and parts thereof (right). Woodland (Tyn-y-pant Wood) begins beyond and below the fence on the left as the climb continues.

When the woodland on the left thins out there are good views to be had over in this direction, up the Teme valley. The prominent hill is Bryn Mawr (485 metres/1591 feet).

As the woodland on the left thins out, at a Y-junction go left – on the major track – the climb now ceasing. Pass through a metal farm gate (may be open) and continue to follow the track ahead. At an indistinct Y-junction bear right, again on the more distinct track – and with an incomplete boundary of mainly hazel trees on the immediate left.

We walked along this section, one fine but breezy October morning, to the sounds of buzzards above and all around us. When these birds put in an appearance they were unmercifully mobbed by crows.

The track passes to the left of a stand of pine trees and bends slightly to the right, beginning to climb very slightly again – still with a row of trees and a wire fence on the left of it. It is now grassy and stony underfoot. Becoming level again it makes for a plantation of fir trees, which will be seen ahead, and – just before reaching these – passes through another metal farm gate.

Beyond the gate, the track bears left and passes to the left of the aforementioned fir trees – now stonier again underfoot. A small rise – with a small raised, banked area bearing conifers alongside on the right – is followed by a dip as it passes a large ash tree (left).

About 100 yards after the ash tree – or 275 yards after the gate – at a gateway, (metal farm gate), leave the track straight ahead over a facing gate on its left to enter the corner of a field. The gate leading into the field was very much the worse for wear at the time of writing, to the extent that it needed to be climbed over – SO148833.

In the field, follow the right-hand boundary fence – the track just vacated on the other side of this. Continue to follow the fence, descending through the field towards a large plantation of fir trees, ahead, an indistinct track now underfoot.

Follow the grassy track, along the fence, to reach a metal farm gate and pass through this into another field. Here continue to follow the right boundary – fir trees beyond this. On reaching another farm gate pass through it to emerge onto a quiet road.

Turn right along the road, immediately passing through another metal farm gate. Ignore a dirt track departing on the left but remain on the road which descends steadily.

The road descends to cross a stream, in a culvert – the outbuildings of the farm settlement of Medwalled soon appearing ahead. On reaching the farm the road passes through a metal farm gate with a cattle grid alongside and runs between outbuildings and through a second farm gate to a T-junction of sorts – SO149839. Here, where the road bends right to pass the farmhouse, go left onto a stony track.

After a few yards the track passes through a metal farm gate, in the shade of an ash tree, and becomes 'sunken' between high, tree-lined banks. This section can be very muddy after wet weather and, in fact, carries a small stream in its latter stages.

Follow the obvious sunken track. It climbs slightly to reach a more open, but still sunken, section – coniferous woodland over to the right concealing the course of a stream (Nant Medwalled).

Eventually the track descends gently to reach a metal farm gate, through a fence ahead, with a ford across Nant Medwalled beyond. The track actually bears left along the fence here but leave it (at what is effectively a Y-junction of sorts), passing through the gate and fording the stream ahead – SO148847. ❸

Across the stream, follow the obvious track ahead. It begins to climb, woodland to its immediate right, and soon passes into more open country (moorland).

Continue to follow the obvious track as it climbs alongside trees on the left – mainly willows.

The track climbs between the uplands of Bryn (457 metres/1499 feet), right, and Y Drain (462 metres/1516 feet), left. The route itself reaches a height of about 420 metres/1378 feet hereabouts.

At a Y-junction bear right – although the two arms of the track remain fairly close together. The track bends gradually to the left as it climbs – large plantations of coniferous woodland in the distance, both to the right and half-right.

The grassy track now undulates along between heather and bracken, in season. Where another grassy track joins from the right continue straight ahead – the area near the junction slightly boggy. Soon after this ignore a grassy track going half-left off the main track.

A gentle descent begins, towards a small group of fir trees. On reaching these the track bends right and passes through a metal farm gate – named on Explorer Map 214 as Radnorshire Gate. **④**

This was the border between the old counties of Radnorshire, to the south, and Montgomeryshire. Both are now included in Powys.

Beyond the gate the track becomes less distinct. Continue to follow it for about 50 yards – a gentle rise – and then leave it, left, through another gate (may be open) (SO146857).

Through the gate, walk straight ahead – a boggy depression on the right – uphill towards the near right-hand corner of a distant plantation of conifers, the distance to a fence on the left becoming less as progress is made. There is no obvious path underfoot here.

As the climb progresses look behind, on a good day, for views as far as the hills of Radnor Forest. The flat topped hill mass of Black Mixen – with its mast – on the far horizon, is over 20 miles distant. The bare rounded hill just to the left of that, in the middle distance is Beacon Hill, previously seen on Stage 7.

Approaching the conifer plantation walk alongside the aforementioned boundary fence (left) to reach a stony track – the Kerry Ridgeway (Cefnffordd Ceri). Turn left along this.

Approaching the top of the climb to the Kerry Ridgeway look half-right, on a good day, for a sighting of the town of Welshpool – the slopes of Yr Allt beyond the town and the distinctive knobbly heights of Breidden Hill and Moel y Golfa to its right. The River Severn flows between the town and the latter two hills.

Walk along the wide track, passing through a metal farm gate and ignoring a bridleway going off to the right – through a small wooden gate – after just a few yards. The stony track passes to the left of the aforementioned coniferous plantation and through a second metal farm gate.

The Kerry Ridgeway

The origins of the Kerry Ridgeway are lost in the mists of time. What is certain, however is that this is the oldest route in Wales – probably dating from the Stone Age. It follows a high sandstone ridge between the Severn valley and the Teme and never descends below 1000 feet above sea level. The resulting views from it, on clear days, are phenomenal and can extend up to 70 miles. The route was last used regularly and commercially by nineteenth century drovers. The walk uses it for some 1¾ miles, rising to a height of 500 metres/1640 feet.

Look half-right ahead to see a prominent gap through which the River Severn flows, between Caersws and Newtown – near the settlement of Aberhafesp.

The track passes through a third metal farm gate.

Look half-right to see a hill bearing two large masts, and one smaller one. This is Moel Iart, which rises to a height of some 457 metres/1499 feet where the two main masts stand.

Almost directly ahead a wind farm comes into view – Llandinam

Wind-farm, at the time of writing the largest in Britain.

The track passes through a fourth farm gate, a coniferous plantation one field distant on the left. It next passes an area of recently cleared (at the time of writing) conifers which appears to have been replanted with deciduous trees – on the immediate left.

Passing through a fifth metal farm gate, a livestock impounding area to its left, the track rounds a small pond, also on the left.

The flat, bare summit half-left ahead is Bryn Coch (518 metres/1700 feet) on the slopes of which the Teme rises. The hill is effectively a continuation of Cilfaesty Hill (528 metres/1732 feet) just to the south.

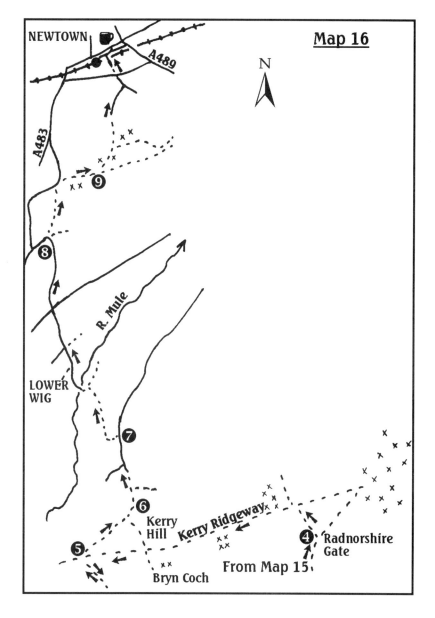

The track passes through a sixth farm gate, a small plantation of conifers far over to the left, and soon crosses a small stream in a culvert. A bridleway crosses the route just before this but is hardly noticeable on the ground. Remain on the main track.

Just after the stream crossing, at a Y-junction of sorts, ignore a stony track which bears right and rises to pass through a farm gate ahead but instead continue straight ahead on the Ridgeway – the track now less distinct underfoot – keeping a wire fence on the right.

On reaching another farm gate – the seventh encountered on the Ridgeway – pass through it. Beyond the gate the track underfoot almost disappears but continue to follow the wire boundary fence on the right, keeping it about 25 yards distant. Part way through this field the fence bends away, as the track passes a pond on the right, but soon returns alongside.

At a point alongside a metal farm gate which leads through the fence on the right, and about 40 yards before an eighth gate on the Ridgeway – at SO119852 – a right of way (bridleway) departs for the Source of the River Teme. **❺**

On reaching the gate through the boundary fence on the right stop and then turn 90 degrees left (i.e. back to gate). From this position walk slightly left across open grassland – there is initially no obvious path hereabouts. Continue straight ahead in this direction to eventually drop down onto a grassy track. Turn left along this.

Just before joining the grassy track look half-right to see the infant River Teme flowing past an isolated farmstead, Iyrchyn.

The grassy track almost immediately makes a sharp, horseshoe bend around to the right – a quarry area just up to its left – and reaches a low, grassy mound ahead.

The Source of the Teme

The infant Teme begins its 75 mile journey to the River Severn amidst old quarry workings and immediately flows past an isolated farmstead, bearing the same name as the quarry – Iyrchyn. For more than a mile it wanders through moorland on the lower slopes of Cilfaesty Hill, gathering small streams from other hillside springs before entering its upper valley, about two miles upstream of where the route of the walk last crossed it. This upper valley of the Teme is known as Cwm Gwyn, 'the White Valley', supposedly after the early mists which occur hereabouts.

Walk straight ahead over the mound to reach a wire fence and then turn right, along this, for a few yards – a steep drop. One of the springs regarded as the source of the river lies a few yards to the right of a left bend in the fence, at SO121847.

The Newtown Link

Retracing the route, return to the point where the Kerry Ridgeway was vacated. **❺**

Here pass through a farm gate in the boundary fence which was previously on the right of the Ridgeway but is now ahead as the latter is rejoined – SO119852. (Note: The route does NOT use the Ridgeway; it merely returns to cross it.) Through the gate, turn half-right onto an obvious stony/grassy track which begins to descend steadily and passes through a field boundary, via a metal farm gate (may be open).

The route here is heading directly towards Welshpool and the distinctive hills beyond the town.

Descending, virtually straight, the track passes through another boundary fence – again via a farm gate which may be open.

There are superb views to be had during the initial stages of the descent on the track. All the features previously recorded as being visible from the section along the Kerry Ridgeway should still be in view. In addition far over to the right the distinctive, almost pyramidal hill is Corndon Hill (513 metres/1683 feet) with the jagged spine of Stiperstones (536 metres/1759 feet) behind. Those with keen eyesight may be able to spot the slender monument on Town Hill, above and to the west of Montgomery. It lies between Welshpool and Corndon Hill, on the line of vision, and is nearer than the latter.

On a really clear day higher mountains, up to 70 miles distant, may be visible on the far horizon over to the left. These may include Cadair Idris, Aran Fawddwy and the Berwyn Mountains.

The track makes a long bend to the right, a wire fence alongside on its left, and reaches a T-junction, with some sheep pens just along the track to the right – SO125857. Here bear left, the track immediately passing through a metal farm gate. **❻**

At the time of writing an old horseshoe was in use as a retaining bracket for the sliding bolt of this gate.

The stony track initially runs between two wire fences. Ignore another track which eventually leaves it, right, through a metal farm gate but remain on the main track which bends left and, shortly afterwards, itself passes through a farm gate (may be open). After a slight rise the track eases right and descends again, eventually taking on a metalled surface to become a quiet road.

Within 10 yards of the metalled surface commencing, at a junction, ignore another minor road going left but continue straight ahead. (At the time of writing the road left had a sign for Ceulanau Pottery at the junction.)

The quiet road descends and bends slightly to the right. It passes a small quarry area – in a field, beyond a farm gate on the right. About 120 yards beyond this leave the road, sharp left, dropping down through a metal farm gate onto a sunken stony track, which descends between high banks and hedgerows – SO125871. **❼**

The track descends, bending to the right. Its rate of descent lessening, it passes through a metal farm gate. Through a further farm gate, the descent becomes steeper again before the track finally levels out to approach another gate – the isolated farm of Lower Wig just beyond this, on the left.

Pass through the gate and go left at a T-junction just beyond it. The track bears right, past the black and white Lower Wig farmhouse (left), to cross the infant River Mule, (Afon Miwl), via a bridge. It gains a metalled surface. Continue ahead past the outbuildings of the farm and through a farm gate, (may be open), on what is now a quiet, narrow road.

The road climbs gently at first but soon, at a right bend, a steep climb commences on it. At the top of the initial very steep climb ignore a track leaving the road sharp left – the entrance drive to Upper Wig farm.

Remain on the road which continues to climb.

Look behind for views back to the Kerry Hills. The course of the track recently descended to Lower Wig farm is clearly visible.

At a junction ignore a road going left and a footpath which goes right, through a farm gate, at the same point but continue straight ahead up the road. The rate of climb lessens and the road passes the entrance drive to Cefn-Vastre, right. It then dips and passes another farm settlement – Pantgwyn – also on the right.

> ## The River Mule
>
> The River Mule, (Afon Miwl) rises on the north side of the ridge of the Kerry Hills, within one mile of the Teme's own source. It flows north-east, through Kerry, and then north-west and finally north to join the River Severn at Abermule, about four miles to the north-east of Newtown – a total length of about six miles.
>
> I am unable to discover a completely satisfactory explanation as to the origin of the river's name. The best I can offer is that it is derived from the Welsh word 'moel' meaning 'bare' and which is usually applied to hills. It may therefore originally have been known as 'the river which rises in the bare hills'. Alternatively it may derive from a personal name, perhaps belonging to an early landowner hereabouts, or be a lost Celtic river name.

Rising again, the road reaches a crossroads. Go straight ahead here.

Just before the crossroads, look behind to see almost the entire route down from the Kerry Ridgeway. The road here is at a height of about 350 metres/1148 feet – on the last ridge before Newtown.

The road descends from the crossroads but then rises very slightly, passing the drive to Little Blackhill, right.

Reaching the top of the rise, Newtown appears slightly to the left ahead, down in the Severn valley.

Reaching the top of its climb the road immediately begins a steep descent towards Newtown. It reaches a sharp bend to the left, where a stony track leaves it, right – SO112894. Here follow the left bend on the road for about 10 yards beyond the point where the track departs and then leave the road, right, to pass through a metal farm gate into a field. (Navigation Note: The farm gate used is NOT the one which is visible ahead as the road approaches the bend but a second gate, a few yards to the left.) ❽

There is a nice view of Newtown from the top of the field.

In the field, follow the right-hand boundary down – a steep descent – to reach a metal farm gate through it, near the bottom. Pass through this and turn immediately left to follow the boundary down the next field, alongside a stream which runs in a small depression here.

On reaching the bottom boundary of the field locate a stile – situated about 25 yards in from the left-hand corner – and cross this into another field. Here follow the right-hand boundary down to the bottom – dwellings beyond – a final steep descent leading to a stile situated in the corner there. Cross the stile and go straight ahead down a path which runs to the right of a row of fir trees – the garden boundary of one of the aforementioned dwellings – to emerge onto a road. Turn right along this.

(Note: Some construction/landscaping work was in progress to the right of the final path onto the road as of April 2002. It is to be hoped that this does not interfere with the right of way hereabouts.)

After about 35 yards on the road leave it, right, initially turning onto a short drive leading to a garage but then, before reaching this, bearing left up a grassy track and through a metal farm gate – SO110898.

Beyond the gate the track narrows to path width and climbs. Reaching the top of its initial rise it passes through another farm gate. Remain on it, fording a small stream in a dip after which the path rises to pass through another farm gate, fording another very minor stream en route. Through this gate the path reaches what can be a very boggy area – with a number of small springs above the path hereabouts. A short diversion up to the right around this may be advisable.

Continuing along the path ignore a track which goes up sharp right (and actually crosses the path to enter a field via a metal farm gate, left), but walk across this and pass through a green metal farm gate in the boundary ahead – dropping down a slight dip to reach this.

Through the gate, cross a small stream (and possibly a resulting boggy area), and go straight ahead – now under trees, and with a wire boundary fence on the immediate left. Cross a further side stream/boggy area – a water trough for livestock on the right of the path here. Another side stream/boggy area follows almost immediately, beyond which the path rises into a field ahead. Crossing this boggy patch do NOT follow the path as it rises but instead look out for a metal farm gate on the left and go through this (or over it) into the corner of an adjacent field – SO115902. **⑨**

Entering the field, head half-right down it to locate a gap into woodland at its bottom boundary. The field can be quite boggy.

Having located the gap into the woods, walk down through the trees on an obvious stony track – which maintains the same direction as the descent through the field before. Emerging from the small area of woodland the track becomes sunken and more grassy underfoot and heads directly towards Newtown. Ignore another grassy track rising to the right off it but remain on the main track which continues its steady descent and passes along the left-hand boundary of another small area of woodland.

Beyond the woodland the track emerges to run between field hedges, the farm settlement of Upper Brimmon ahead. Approaching the farm the track passes through a metal farm gate and runs between the outbuildings. It bends right to pass the farmhouse, left, and takes on a metalled surface.

The now metalled track undulates downwards towards Newtown. Passing through another farm gate it bears slightly to the right, crossing a stream in a culvert. With a wire fence alongside on its left the track rises slightly towards two small blocks of flats and a bungalow, ahead, and – passing through a final farm gate (which may be open) – reaches a road. Turn left along this. After about 70 yards, where it reaches a busier road at a T-junction, go straight ahead – across the road – to walk along an alley opposite, a telephone box on the right at its entrance.

With bungalows on its right the alley becomes a quiet road. Continue to follow this, straight ahead.

The large red brick buildings directly ahead are the Royal Welsh Warehouse premises – see main note on Newtown.

The road descends steeply and bends left, a pavement beginning on its right-hand side. Follow it to reach a bridge over railway lines, right. Cross the bridge and remain on the road which bears right to approach the right of the two large Royal Welsh Warehouse buildings. At the road junction here go sharp left to reach Newtown railway station, where the 93 mile walk ends.

Newtown

Newtown is today the largest town in Powys. The settlement originated when, in 1279, Roger Mortimer (of the powerful Wigmore based dynasty, and later Marcher Earls) was granted the right to hold a weekly market in his manor of Cedewain hereabouts. The market town which grew up as a result became known as Newtown (Newentone) because it effectively replaced an earlier market at Dolforwyn, near Abermule.

It is possible, however, that there was some sort of settlement on the site of the current town before this as a chapel (Llanfair/St. Mary's) is mentioned in records of 1253. By 1291 this had become independent of its mother church of Llanllwchaiarn – now a small settlement about one mile downstream of Newtown on the Severn – and was known as Llanfair-yng-Nghedewain.

The oldest surviving building in the town is the medieval church (St. Mary's) – its tower of thirteenth century origin, surmounted by a timber bell-stage which was restored in 1939. The building stands near the Severn and was always prone to flooding. By the middle of the nineteenth century it was in a very poor condition and considered to be too small to serve its congregation and so was replaced, in 1847, by St. David's church – a yellow brick construction. St. Mary's was abandoned in 1856 but the tower and some walls of the building have been preserved. Outside the church is the grave of Robert Owen (1771-1858), the great social reformer and the inspiration behind the co-operative movement, who was both born and died in the town. A statue/monument to him is elsewhere in the town, as is a museum telling his story.

The replacement church, St. David's – visible, left, from the bridge over the railway as the route of the walk enters the town – was built between 1843 and 1847 at a cost of £4600. Its architect was Thomas Penson. Inside is a carved wooden screen dating from about 1500 and a fifteenth century font which were originally in St. Mary's but were moved here when that church was abandoned.

The other dominant buildings of the town are the premises of the Royal Welsh Warehouse (Pryce Jones) – the first mail order business in the world when it began in 1859. The building on the left – as the route approaches the station – dates from 1879. The redbrick structure bears a wealth of external decoration – from the statues and coat of arms above the door to the round plaques on the walls, celebrating the company's success at various international exhibitions. The building on the right bears the date 1895 and imposing Welsh dragons. Known as Agriculture House, it was built as a factory for the company.

Probably the most famous customer of the Royal Welsh Warehouse was Queen Victoria who was supplied with, among other things, Welsh flannel. At that time Newtown rivalled Welshpool as the centre of the flannel market, based on the wool of the local Kerry sheep.

In the nineteenth century, in a bid to encourage the development of the woollen trade and the town in general, it was linked, in turn, to both the canal system and the railway network. The railway remains – the current station dates from 1868 and was built for the then Cambrian Railway Company. The canal – the Montgomery Canal Western Extension, which opened in 1821 – was effectively closed in 1936 but only officially abandoned in 1944. Its basin was on the other side of the River Severn from the town centre and has, along with two miles of the navigation, long been drained and filled in/built on.

The grave of Robert Owen outside the abandoned St Mary's church, Newtown

Acknowledgements

This walk could not have been designed nor the book written without the help and kindness of many people and my thanks go out to all of them.

In particular my thanks to:

Rebe Brick (Offa's Dyke Centre) – for research into the 'P.V.S.' stone above Llanfair Waterdine.

Brian Draper – for sharing his vast knowledge regarding the River Teme.

Peter Groves (Meridian Books) – for his continuing friendship, advice and encouragement, and making possible the realisation of my dreams of authorship.

David Higham Associates Ltd on behalf of the estate of Francis Brett Young – for permission to use the Francis Brett Young quotation at the head of the 'River Teme' section of the book.

Alan Jones – for his help and company on the walk, transportation, continuing friendship, support and tolerance.

K T Publications – for permission to use the poem *On Walsgrove Hill* from the collection *Past Landscapes* by R. Tomas.

'Red' and Tom Morrow – for doing all of the test walking....and still not complaining!

Pearl Wright – my sister, for proof-reading the original manuscripts of this book and its two predecessors.

Worcester Evening News/Keith Blackham – for permission to use the photograph of the author on page 15.

Extract from The Gypsy by Ralph McTell © Onward Music Ltd. Used by permission.

Recommended Further Reading

C. Barber. *In Search of Owain Glyndŵr* (Blorenge Books,1998.)

K. Beddoes & W. H. Smith. *The Tenbury & Bewdley Railway* (Wild Swan Publications, 1995.)

T. Clift. *The Central Wales Line* (Ian Allan, 1982.)

B. Draper. *The River Teme, from its Source to the Severn* (Brian Draper)

G. Hodges. *Ludford Bridge and Mortimer's Cross* (Logaston Press, 1989.)

G. Hodges. *Owain Glyn Dŵr & the War of Independence in the Welsh Borders* (Logaston Press, 1995.)

J. Jeremiah. *The River Severn, A Pictorial History* (Phillimore, 1998.)

D. Lloyd. *Ludlow* (Chalford Publishing Co.,1995.)

D. Lloyd. *The Concise History of Ludlow* (Merlin Unwin Books,1999.)

R. Morriss & K. Hoverd. *The Buildings of Ludlow* (Alan Sutton, 1993.)

R. Morriss & K. Hoverd. *The Buildings of Worcester* (Alan Sutton, 1994.)

P.M. Ray *Ashford Carbonel – A Peculiar Parish. A Brief History* (P.M. Ray, 1998.)

M. Salter. *The Old Parish Churches of Herefordshire* (Folly Publications, 1998.)

M. Salter. *The Castles and Moated Mansions of Shropshire* (Folly Publications, 1988.)

M. Salter. *The Old Parish Churches of Shropshire* (Folly Publications, 1988.)

M. Salter. *The Castles of Mid Wales* (Folly Publications, 1991.)

M. Salter. *The Old Parish Churches of Mid Wales* (Folly Publications, 1991.)

M. Salter. *The Old Parish Churches of Worcestershire* (Folly Publications, 1995.)

M. Salter. *The Castles of Herefordshire and Worcestershire* (Folly Publications, 1989.)

W.H. Smith. *The Bromyard Branch* (Kidderminster Railway Museum, 1998.)

S. C. Stanford. *The Archaeology of The Welsh Marches* (S.C. Stanford, The Old Farm House, 1991.)

V. Thackeray. *Tales from the Welsh March* (Cressrelles Publishing, 1992.)

Various authors. *The Gale of Life – Two Thousand Years in South-West Shropshire* (South-West Shropshire Historical & Archaeological Society/Logaston Press, 2000.)

Also by David Milton...

The Elan Valley Way

A long distance path loosely based around the course followed by the Elan Valley aqueduct along which Birmingham's water supply has passed since 1905.

The Elan Valley Way starts on the western fringe of Birmingham at Frankley reservoir and ends at the Elan Valley in mid-Wales. It does not aim to slavishly follow the course of the aqueduct but visits many of the more obvious signs of the pipelines on the ground. Although it is never more than about three miles from the line of the aqueduct it takes 128½ miles to do the journey that the aqueduct does in 73½!

The walk, largely following footpaths and bridleways, and with many superb views, passes through some delightful walking areas in the counties of Worcestershire, Shropshire, Herefordshire and Powys. It has been split into ten stages based on the availability of accommodation and public transport and can therefore easily be followed either as a whole ten-day affair or in parts, as time and inclination permit. No section should present any problems for the reasonably fit and there are no prolonged steep ascents.

The book is illustrated with sketch maps and photographs, some of the latter dating from the time when the aqueduct was being constructed.

Price £7.95. ISBN 1 869922 39 5. 160 pages. Paperback 229mm × 145mm. 21 photographs. 21 maps.

The Riversides Way

This long distance walk follows a circular route through the beautiful and secretive countryside of the Welsh Marches to the south and west of Ludlow – almost entirely over footpaths, tracks and minor roads.

It takes its name from the Riverside Inn at Aymestrey – where the walk starts – and from the fact that it remains in the valleys of the rivers Lugg and Teme, and the surrounding hills, throughout its length.

The 72 mile walk is divided into eight stages, the longest of which is 13 miles and the shortest 6½ miles. No stage of the walk should present any great problem for the experienced, fairly fit walker.

The Riversides Way passes through spectacular border scenery and includes locations which are well off the main tourist routes and remain largely unspoilt as a result. It visits many sites of interest – castles, churches, mills, hill forts and numerous small settlements – some of historic significance.

The book also includes a Ludlow Town Trail, a 2½ mile walk around a small town rich in attractive buildings, over 500 of which are listed as being of historical interest.

Price £8.95. ISBN 1 869922 43 3. 160 pages. Paperback 229mm × 145mm. 14 photographs. 15 maps.

Also from Meridian...

Walks Through History in the Heart of England

by Roger Seedhouse

The Heart of England is rich in history, both ancient and more modern, and the twenty-four walks in this book will offer the enquiring walker many intriguing glimpses of a bygone age – with iron-age forts, battle sites, medieval castles and even a second world war camp. All of them start at, or pass through, places of historical interest that will add greatly to your appreciation of a day out in beautiful walking country.

ISBN 1-869922-41-7. 160 pages. 38 photos. 24 maps. Price £8.95

The Birmingham Greenway

by Fred Willits

A walk from the northern to the southern boundary of Birmingham passing through its many parks and open spaces, using footpaths, riversides and canal towpaths. A unique opportunity to discover what is often hidden to the road user and to learn much about the history and current activities of this bustling city.

ISBN 1 869922 40 9. Price £4.95. 64 pages. 33 photographs. 3 drawings. 10 strip maps.

Railway Inn Signs: Book 1, Derbyshire

by Bryan Veitch

There are some 1100 inns linked with railways in the UK, about sixty-two of which are located in Derbyshire. In this volume the author discusses the long association of inns with railways and the influence that the early railways and their modern counterparts have had on inn signs. Many are discussed in detail and the text and illustrations will provide a wealth of information for not only the railway enthusiast but for travellers, ramblers, all those interested in history – and, of course, in good ale!

ISBN 1 869922 42 5. Price £8.95. 88 pages. 32 colour and 13 black & white photographs.

Walks in South Warwickshire From Shakespeare Country to the Cotswolds

by John W Parnham and Barry R Wills

This collection of circular walks represent the authors' favourites within this lovely, varied region. The walks will take you along ancient trackways and paths, past standing stones, earthworks, country estates and grand houses. In the Arden countryside as well as finding connections to William Shakespeare you will discover hidden valleys and distinct wooded hilltops that offer wonderful views. Further south the walks will take you through delightful villages and into remote areas in the Cotswold Hills that rival in many ways the better known parts of this beautiful region.

ISBN 1 869922 38 7. Price £6.95. 112 pages. 36 sketches. 18 maps.

Walks To Wet Your Whistle

by Roger Seedhouse

Eighteen walks covering some of the most beautiful countryside in Shropshire and along its Staffordshire borders, each providing an opportunity to visit a pub in which the walker will feel welcome and comfortable. The main walks range in distance between 7 and 11½ miles but each has a shorter alternative of between 2¾ and 5¼ miles.

ISBN 1 869922 41 7. 112 pages. £6.95. 17 photographs. 18 maps.

More Walks to Wet your Whistle

by Roger Seedhouse

Following the author's highly successful first book he now presents a second collection of walks with a pub in Shropshire and along its Staffordshire borders.

ISBN 1 869922 36 0. £6.95. 112 pages. 24 photographs. 18 maps.

Walks Around the Malverns

by Roy Woodcock

The Malvern Hills and their surroundings provide magnificent opportunities for rambling, and in this book of twenty walks Roy Woodcock explores many of their superb features. The walks cover the entire range of hills and the neighbouring commons, together with some of the delightful countryside nearby. Distances range from two miles to eight miles, plus a leg stretcher of between ten and sixteen miles (depending on the starting point) that takes in the full length of the ridge and ascends all the Malvern peaks.

ISBN 1 869922 32 8. £6.95. 112 pages. 32 illustrations. 20 maps.

The Navigation Way: A Hundred Mile Towpath Walk

by Peter Groves and Trevor Antill

Starting from the centre of Birmingham and encompassing fourteen West Midlands canals the Navigation Way follows a meandering course through varied urban areas and delightful countryside until terminating at Chasewater. Now again revised to cover the many changes and improvements that have been made to the towpaths its twelve sections provide a series of walks ranging from 5¼ to 11 miles. The book also contains ten additional circular 'canal-link' walks in some of the attractive walking areas adjacent to the canals.

Third revised edition. ISBN 1 869922 35 2. £5.95. 112 pages. 34 photographs. 24 maps.

Country Walks in Warwickshire and Worcestershire

by Des Wright

Twenty circular walks that explore some of the two counties' most attractive areas. The walking is easy, mostly on the flat and with few climbs. Distances range from 2½ to 8½ miles although some can be combined to give longer walks.

ISBN 1 869922 33 6. £5.95. 96 pages. 16 photographs. 21 maps.

More Country Walks in Warwickshire and Worcestershire

by Des Wright

A second collection of circular walks in two fine counties from a popular author whose love of the countryside is abundantly evident in this book. As in his first collection the walking is not difficult with few climbs. Distances range from 4½ to 11½ miles, with most walks having a shorter option of between 1½ and 8 miles. All are readily accessible by car and by public transport.

ISBN 1 869922 37 9. £5.95. 112 pages. 22 photographs. 20 maps.

Waterside Walks in the Midlands

by Birmingham Ramblers: edited by Peter Groves

Twenty-two walks featuring brooks, streams, pools, rivers and canals. Some can be found a short distance from the centre of Britain's second city; others will take the reader further afield in the West Midlands and into the attractive counties of Warwickshire, Worcestershire, Shropshire, Staffordshire and Derbyshire.

ISBN 1 869922 09 3. £4.95. 112 pages. 28 photographs. 22 maps.

More Waterside Walks in the Midlands

by Birmingham Ramblers: edited by Peter Groves

Following on the success of their first book, *Waterside Walks in the Midlands*, members of the City of Birmingham Branch of the Ramblers' Association have now prepared another collection on a similar theme. As before, the walks feature brooks, streams, rivers, canals and pools - sometimes as a major aspect of a walk, sometimes as a feature to encounter as you ramble through some of the fine Midlands countryside. Distances range from 4½ miles to14 miles.

ISBN 1 869922 31 X. £5.95 112 pages. 21 photographs. 18 maps. Paperback. A5.

The Monarch's Way

by Trevor Antill

A new long distance walk that closely follows the route taken by Charles II after his defeat by Cromwell's forces at Worcester in 1651. Starting from Worcester it goes first north, then south through the Cotswolds and the Mendips to the coast, then along the South Downs to Shoreham where Charles escaped to France. Visiting many historic places, perhaps previously known to readers only through the history books, it also goes through some of the finest scenery in western and southern England.

Book 1: Worcester to Stratford-upon-Avon. 175 miles.
ISBN 1 869922 27 1. £5.95. 112 pages. 19 photographs, 19 maps.

Book 2: Stratford-upon-Avon to Charmouth. 210 miles.
ISBN 1 869922 28 X. £6.95. 136 pages. 21 photographs. 23 maps.

Book 3: Charmouth to Shoreham. 225 miles.
ISBN 1 869922 29 8. £6.95. 136 pages. 21 photographs. 25 maps.

Heart of England Hill Walks
by John Newson

The eighteen circular walks in this collection explore a variety of hills in the Heart of England – some well known, others that may be less familiar. The distances of the main walks vary from 10½ to 14½ miles. However, most include the option of a shorter walk and these range between 6 and 10 miles.

ISBN 1 869922 30 1. £5.95. 96 pages. 21 photographs. 18 maps.

Ridges and Valleys
Walks in the Midlands
by Trevor Antill

A selection of walks within the counties of Shropshire, Staffordshire and Worcestershire taking in some of the better known, and some lesser known hills; and most with one or two pleasant surprises.

ISBN 1 869922 15 8. £3.95. 96 pages. 12 photographs. 19 maps.

Ridges and Valleys II
More Walks in the Midlands
by Trevor Antill

Following the theme established in the first volume Trevor Antill describes eighteen further walks in the counties of Shropshire, Staffordshire and Worcestershire. Some of the areas explored are among the lesser known parts of the region.

ISBN 1 869922 20 4. £4.95. 112 pages. 21 photographs. 19 maps.

Ridges and Valleys III
A Third Collection of Walks in the Midlands
by Trevor Antill

Rolling hills, delightful woodlands, charming villages, attractive rivers and fine views are some of the features that readers of the previous two volumes have come to expect. They will not be disappointed with this new collection of eighteen more walks in the counties of Shropshire, Staffordshire and Worcestershire.

ISBN 1 869922 22 0. £4.95 112 pages. 11 photographs. 19 maps.

Favourite Walks in the West Midlands

by members of the Birmingham CHA Rambling Club,
Edited by Tom Birch and Mary Wall

A collection of twenty-two attractive walks from members of one of Birmingham's oldest walking clubs.

ISBN 1 869922 26 3. £4.95. 112 pages. 24 photographs. 23 maps.

Hidden Herefordshire

A Book of Country Walks
by Julie Meech

A churchyard awash with spring daffodils, a river bordered with ancient willows, a unique Norman church with comic, grotesque and erotic carvings, a fourteenth century dovecote with 666 nesting places, a Neolithic burial chamber, countless medieval timber-framed buildings, a chance to see the rare Red Kite – these are but a few of the delights encountered in this book of twenty circular walks.

ISBN 1 869922 16 6. £4.95. 112 pages. 21 photographs. 20 maps.

And the Road Below

by John Westley

The entrancing account of the first complete walk around the coastline of the British Isles, a distance of 9,469 miles, that earned for the author a place in the *Guinness Book of Records*. Undertaken in aid of multiple sclerosis this book shows how a relatively inexperienced walker could, with courage and an over-riding determination to succeed, overcome what seemed at times to be near-insurmountable problems. *The author has donated half his royalties from the sale of this book to the Multiple Sclerosis Society and this sum will be matched by an equal contribution from the publishers.*

ISBN 1 869922 25 5. £8.95. 208 pages. 11 photographs.

In the Footsteps of the Gunpowder Plotters

by Conall Boyle

When the Gunpowder Plotters failed to blow up Parliament they fled, visiting their houses in Warwickshire and Worcestershire. In this unique guide you can follow their trail – by car, by bicycle, or on foot – and discover many of their most secret places in the Midlands.

ISBN 1 869922 23 9. £4.95. 96 pages. 13 drawings. 19 maps.

Beyond the Bars

Ten Walks from York City Walls
by Ivan E Broadhead

Circular walks into the countryside and villages surrounding York, ranging in distance from two to seven miles and starting from the ten historic exits from the city walls.

ISBN 1 869922 05 0. £5.95. 192 pages. 84 photographs. 10 maps.

Waterside Walks in North Yorkshire

by Ivan E Broadhead

Twenty walks, featuring brooks, streams, canals, waterfalls, lakes, rivers and the sea, in one of Britains most beautiful counties.

ISBN 1 869922 07 7. £3.95. 96 pages. 32 photographs. 20 maps.

Survivors

Jewish Refugees in Birmingham, 1933-1945
by Zoë Josephs

The stories, sometimes harrowing, of some of the refugees who fled from Nazi Germany in the 30s and 40s. The book describes problems they encountered in wartime Britain, the generous support they received from members of the local communities, the hardships encountered by those who were interned as enemy aliens and, eventually, the successful lives that many achieved.

1988. ISBN 1 869922 02 6. £7.50. 224 pages. 86 illustrations.

Wanderers in Northamptonshire

Following in the steps of George Harrison, artist, writer and poet
by John and Vera Worledge

George Harrison (1876-1950) was a fine artist with a great love for the countryside who travelled Northamptonshire in the 1920s, 30s and 40s sketching and writing for local newspapers. The authors have combined some of George Harrison's original material with their own photographs and accounts to create a series of delightful cameos of a lovely county as it is today and as it was half a century and more ago.

ISBN 1 869922 18 2. £5.95. 112 pages. 53 photographs, 73 drawings.

Wanderers in Northamptonshire: The Second Journey

Following further in the steps of George Harrison
by John and Vera Worledge

In this second volume John and Vera Worledge complete their tour and combine more of George Harrison's original material with their own photographs and accounts of visits to this attractive county.

ISBN 1 869922 24 7. £5.95. 112 pages. 53 photographs, 73 drawings.

All Meridian titles are available from booksellers or, if in difficulty, direct from the publishers.

Please send your remittance, including the following amounts for postage and packing:

Order value up to £10.00 add £1.00; over £10.00 and up to £20.00 add £2.00; over £20.00 add £2.50.

Meridian Books
40 Hadzor Road Oldbury West Midlands B68 9LA
Tel: 0121-429 4397